The American Law Dictionary

THE AMERICAN LAW DICTIONARY

Peter G. Renstrom
Western Michigan University

ABC-CLIO

Santa Barbara, California
Oxford, England

Library of Congress Cataloging-in-Publication Data

Renstrom, Peter G., 1943–
    The American Law Dictionary / Peter G. Renstrom
    (Clio dictionaries in political science)
    Includes index.
    1. Law—United States—Dictionaries. I. Title. II. Series
KF156.R46   1990   348.73'03   90-24114

ISBN 0-87436-226-1 (alk. paper)

98 97 96 95 94 93 92   10 9 8 7 6 5 4 3 2

ABC-CLIO, Inc.
130 Cremona Drive, P.O. Box 1911
Santa Barbara, California 93116-1911

Clio Press Ltd.
55 St. Thomas' Street
Oxford, OX1 1JG, England

This book is printed on acid-free paper ∞ .
Manufactured in the United States of America

To Bobbi, Dan, and Joelle,
for their ever present
love, support, and encouragement

Clio Dictionaries in Political Science

SERIES STATEMENT

Language precision is the primary tool of every scientific discipline. That aphorism serves as the guideline for this series of political dictionaries. Although each book in the series relates to a specific topical or regional area in the discipline of political science, entries in the dictionaries also emphasize history, geography, economics, sociology, philosophy, and religion.

This dictionary series incorporates special features designed to help the reader overcome any language barriers that may impede a full understanding of the subject matter. For example, the concepts included in each volume were selected to complement the subject matter found in existing texts and other books. Most volumes utilize a subject-matter chapter arrangement that is useful for classroom and study purposes.

Entries in all volumes include an up-to-date definition plus a paragraph of *significance* in which the authors discuss and analyze the term's historical and current relevance. Most entries are also cross-referenced, providing the reader an opportunity to seek additional information related to the subject of inquiry. A comprehensive index, found in both hardcover and paperback editions, allows the reader to locate major entries and other concepts, events, and institutions discussed within these entries.

The political and social sciences suffer more than most disciplines from semantic confusion. This is attributable, *inter alia*, to the popularization of the language, and to the focus on many diverse foreign political and social systems. This dictionary series is dedicated to overcoming some of this confusion through careful writing of thorough, accurate definitions for the central concepts, institutions, and events that comprise the basic knowledge of each of the subject fields. New titles in the series will be issued periodically, including some in related social science disciplines.

—Jack C. Plano
Series Editor

CONTENTS

A NOTE ON HOW TO USE THIS BOOK

The American Law Dictionary focuses on concepts, terms, and phrases common to the American judicial system. The volume is organized so that entries can be located with ease. The entries are arranged alphabetically within subject matter chapters. Each entry has also been assigned its own number. If there is doubt about which chapter contains a term or concept, consult the general index. An entry number appearing in bold face in the index indicates there is a full entry for the term or concept. Items covered within the discussion of other terms will show entry numbers in regular type.

Readers can pursue a topic further by using the cross-references provided with most entries. The entry numbers shown at the end of the definition paragraph will lead the reader to discussions contained in the same chapter or other chapters.

The author has designed the book to offer the reader a variety of useful approaches to locating information. The book may be used as (1) a dictionary or reference guide to the language and concepts of the American legal system; (2) a study guide for students in law school or political science courses; (3) a handbook for use by those working in the legal system; (4) a supplement to a textbook or book of readings on the legal processes; (5) a source of review materials for the attorney, academic, or student of the law and legal processes; and (6) a social science aid for use in cognate fields such as business and commercial law, criminal justice, history, and public policy.

PREFACE

This volume is a part of a series founded on the idea that precise language is the primary tool of every discipline. This is particularly true in the field of the law. *The American Law Dictionary* was undertaken to bring such precision to the consideration of the legal process.

The objective of this volume is to explain the fundamental terms and concepts of the legal process. The writing involves an attempt to integrate many elements representing the multidimensional character of the subject. I hope to reach both a general audience as well as special interest audiences. A major objective is familiarizing those considering a career in law with some of the organizational and operational concepts in the field. It is also my intention to reach the legal community, especially those who may have become removed from courtroom practice over the years.

The terms and concepts selected for this volume were chosen with some care. They reflect my best judgment about how to represent the essentials of the American judicial system. A much larger number of terms and phrases could have been included. Indeed, most of the law dictionaries currently available contain many more terms than this volume. My selection of terms was substantially influenced by the reality that this volume was to become part of ABC-CLIO's series of political dictionaries. The volumes that precede mine have placed a premium on working extensively with a relatively limited number of terms. I wished to maintain that practice here. Furthermore, my perspective is the product of my training as a political scientist. I wished to work with those terms that best enabled me to explore those aspects of the American judicial process that highlight its political dimensions. Ultimately, my selections were guided by the question: Does discussion of this term further the reader's understanding of the American court process? By focusing the dictionary in this way, it is my view that a uniquely useful volume was made possible.

Preface

Although all dictionaries tend to resemble one another, *The American Law Dictionary* has several unique features. First, entries have been selected to reflect the way the subject matter is discussed by the leading textbooks in the field. The book has a subject matter chapter format in which key terms and concepts are separated for study and review purposes. This allows the dictionary to be used both in and out of class as a medium of teaching and learning. A second unique feature is the inclusion of a *significance* paragraph following the definitional discussion. I sought to provide additional background or historical perspective through this paragraph and to offer comments that underscore why the term or concept is particularly important. A third feature is the inclusion of cross-references that function as guides to additional information about a particular topic in the volume. Finally, the book contains a comprehensive index to facilitate the location of entries. This is particularly important for those entries that might reasonably be included in more than one chapter, or terms which might, for example, properly apply to the trial process, either criminal or civil.

The material for this volume has been drawn from many sources. It is difficult if not impossible to always identify the original sources of these terms and concepts that have become the foundation of the study of judicial processes and behavior. I wish to acknowledge the many scholars who have contributed to this volume through their valuable work in the field of judicial politics. I also wish to acknowledge the stimulation and encouragement given me by my colleagues in the Department of Political Science at Western Michigan University. I wish as well to thank the ABC-Clio staff for its help in the preparation of this volume. I wish to extend a special thanks to Professor Jack C. Plano, editor of the Clio Dictionaries in Political Science series and long a valued department colleague. Jack has given this manuscript many hours of his time and provided me with extraordinary counsel. It is very likely that *The American Law Dictionary* would not have been undertaken without Jack's involvement and encouragement. Finally, I wish to thank my wife Bobbi for her ongoing support and her many hours with red pen in hand. These people made this project possible. I, of course, accept full responsibility for errors of commission and omission. I invite comment on any aspect of this volume.

—Peter G. Renstrom
Western Michigan University

The American Law Dictionary

1. Law, Judicial Environment, and Judicial Function

The terms contained in this chapter were selected to illustrate some of the fundamental elements of the American legal system. These include such things as the characteristics of the legal system itself, law and its various forms and sources, jurisprudence, the judicial process and its functions, and the environment in which the judicial process operates.

There are several components of a legal system. One is an organized framework. An appreciation of the system's structure is a necessary condition for understanding what each of the pieces contributes as well as how the system as a whole functions. Second, the system is affected by cultural influences of several kinds, including the attitudes and expectations we have of the law. These, in turn, substantially shape legal philosophy or jurisprudence. The third element is the substantive legal rules. These rules and principles reflect the policy preferences of the legal system as applied by the judicial institutions within it. The fourth element of the legal system is the human factor. All other components are affected by the human beings who serve as judges, prosecutors, defense counsel, and in other capacities, and who interpret, guide, and operate the system.

The substance of a legal system can be found in law. Law is often simplistically perceived as a set of rules established and applied by officers of the government. While such a perception is not necessarily wrong, it is distorted. Law is not quite so comprehensively definitive or as mechanistically applied as we might imagine. While we know generally what the law requires, law contains ambiguity and is subject

3

to varied interpretations by those exercising authority within the system.

One of the reasons for this is that law has a number of sources. There is the law that comes from constitutions, both federal and state. Under provisions of the U.S. Constitution, federal constitutional law is paramount or supreme. Law also emanates from legislatures. This is called statutory law. In addition, law may originate with the executive in the form of executive orders or rules fashioned by administrative agencies. Finally, there is law produced by judges as decisions are rendered in cases before the courts. One of the reasons "the law" cannot be mechanistically applied is because the sources of law are both numerous and, often, contradictory.

Other influences affect the judicial system. One such influence is legal philosophy or jurisprudence. Conceptualizations about law and courts are governed by the particular jurisprudence to which one subscribes. Several different ways of looking at the law are represented in this chapter through the discussion of the principal schools of jurisprudence.

The legal culture also has a direct impact on the operation of the judicial system. The legal culture refers to the particular values about such things as how courts should work and what law should do. Commitment to such principles as the primacy of law or the adversary system are among the elements comprising the legal culture. The beliefs and expectations of the legal culture define the unique character of the judicial system. It is partially because of legal culture influences that judges are expected to behave in ways dissimilar to other public officials.

The judicial system is also influenced by the political culture. The political culture consists of those values and institutions upon which the political system is founded. Included are such things as the other branches of the government, political party identification, and public opinion. It is through the political culture that accountability is attached to the judicial system. The principles of democracy are linked to the courts through the political culture. Manifestations of the political culture are reflected in the various judicial selection techniques. Similarly, legislative definition of court jurisdiction is a direct product of the political culture.

A final theme of this chapter is the basic role of courts within the legal system. Several are particularly important. First, courts are institutions designed to resolve disputes. Under the auspices of courts, techniques of fact-finding may be undertaken through a judgment rendered on a question. Often courts resolve conflicts by presiding over settlements arrived at by the parties to the dispute. A second role is to provide redress for injury. In criminal cases, this may take the form of imposing sentence. The possibilities are more numerous for civil cases. Payment of money by one party to another may be involved or the awarding of child custody may occur, to mention only two. The assignment of remedies as a means of closing the dispute also sends messages to society at large about appropriate conduct and the consequences of failing to comply. Finally, courts establish public policy as an inevitable product of deciding cases. While substantive policy is established by each component of the judicial system, it is especially true of appellate courts because they focus exclusively on questions of legal principle rather than fact issues.

Adjudication   (1)
The judicial act of making a judgment in a legal action. Adjudication involves formal decision making processes as a court moves to a final judgment in a lawsuit. Adjudication requires, at minimum, notice to all parties that a decision is being sought, and an opportunity for all parties to present evidence or arguments on the matter(s) before the court. In adjudicating cases brought before them, judges may be required to make a number of decisions at the pretrial and trial stages. A variety of motions, each requiring a formal response, may be filed by the parties. Judges must also rule on questions raised during the examination of witnesses. Unless the parties agree to a settlement, the process of adjudication yields a decision on the merits. At the trial stage, a decision on the merits occurs when a judge or jury renders a decision or when the parties agree to settle the dispute in a particular way. *See also* JUDGE, 91; JUDICIAL FUNCTION, 16.

Significance   Adjudication is the judicial function most people relate to the functioning of the court system. This is especially true of adjudication in the form of trial court fact-finding. The act of adjudication goes to the core of the judicial function. It is also the judicial activity most often represented in film and television dramas and that citizens can directly observe if they visit courtrooms. In addition, adjudication is the activity that occupies the largest portion of judges' time. Adjudication occurs at the appellate level as well, although it occurs in a fashion quite different from the trial level. Adjudication at the appellate level in the federal system and in most state systems is a group process with at least three judges participating. The collective decision at the appellate level goes beyond fact considerations to issues of legal principle. As a consequence, appellate adjudication is more likely to have policy making dimensions not present at the trial stage.

Administrative Law (2)

The body of law that concerns the powers of and procedures to be used by administrative agencies. Administrative law also includes the law that creates such agencies and the provisions that define the extent to which agency decisions and practices may be reviewed by the courts. In addition, administrative law concerns the transfer of power from legislative bodies to administrative agencies. Finally, administrative law covers the nature of protections afforded those coming under the regulatory authority of administrative agencies. *See also* CONSTITUTIONAL LAW, 11; JUDICIAL REVIEW, 18; STATUTE, 35.

Significance Administrative law has become increasingly important because of the enormous expansion of administrative decision making in the United States. The increasing use of administrative agencies to regulate and prescribe social as well as economic policy has produced an extensive body of law governing the conduct of individuals and corporate entities. The basic problem of administrative law is to create a system of restraints that limits the possibility of arbitrary bureaucratic behavior while at the same time allowing agencies to pursue their policy objectives effectively.

Adversary System (3)

A set of processes intended to allow opposing parties in a dispute to present their arguments. Under the adversary system, formal notice is served on the party against whom an action has been filed to allow that party an opportunity to respond. The adversary system is typically self-initiated although the prosecuting attorney acts on behalf of the victim and the public in criminal matters. The burden of proof falls to the parties under the adversary system. Most often, the judge's role is to preside over the proceeding rather than function as an actual fact-finder. The outcome in an adversary proceeding is almost always all or nothing, and, unlike mediation or conciliation, is zero-sum in character. That means there is seldom a middle-ground outcome, and whatever the successful party wins is necessarily lost by the unsuccessful party. The outcome of such proceedings is authoritative; it is enforced upon the losing party. An adversary proceeding is different from an *ex parte* proceeding, where only one party appears. An adversary proceeding also differs from a summary proceeding, where no significant fact dispute exists and where the court may hasten and simplify the resolution of an issue. *See also* ADVISORY OPINION, 200; CASE OR CONTROVERSY, 6.

Significance   The assumption underlying the adversary system is that out of the legal and factual contest of the parties the truth will emerge. The adversary system forces a plaintiff and defendant in a legal action to contest each other with evidence gathered in support of their respective cases. The system is generally regarded as the most effective means of evaluating evidence. The adversary system also features a diffusion of power among its principal participants, such as judge, prosecutor, jury, and defense counsel. Each actor helps to produce a check and balance effect, thus safeguarding against arbitrary or abusive judgments.

Arbitration (4)

The submission of a dispute to an impartial third party selected by the disputants whose decision is binding on the parties. Arbitration is a legally authorized means of dispute resolution in most states and decisions reached through the process can be enforced by courts. The arbitrator in the process may either be an individual or a board of impartial persons (usually three). The parties agree in advance to comply with the arbitrator's decision which comes at the conclusion of a proceeding where both parties to a dispute have an opportunity to present their arguments. Arbitration is most often used in labor-management disputes, but it is an approach that lends itself to a wide variety of dispute situations. Some states require compulsory arbitration where disputes involving public utilities exist. Arbitration is also used in the international arena to resolve disputes between sovereign states. *See also* MEDIATION, 25.

Significance   Arbitration is a process for obtaining a judgment on a disputed matter without (or before) taking it to court. The outcome of arbitration is enforceable by courts, but it is secured in a less formal and less expensive manner. Use of arbitration expedites resolution of a dispute because the extensive docket backlog encountered with the court system is bypassed. Arbitration also relieves the courts of matters that would otherwise appear before trial courts. Thus, arbitration is an alternative method of dispute resolution endorsed and encouraged by the courts. Arbitration allows disputes to be resolved by recognized experts, which is especially important when disputes are of a highly technical nature. Professional arbitrators are generally known to those who utilize the process. Arbitrators are also available through such organizations as the American Arbitration Association.

Behavioral Jurisprudence (5)

A jurisprudential view that features theories of human decision making. Behavioral jurisprudence attempts to explain law as emanating from the individual values of the principal official participants in the legal process. Behavioral jurisprudence had its origin among those legal realists who sought to integrate the approaches of behavioral science with the study of law and legal processes. Although judicial behaviorists began to emerge a decade earlier, the work of C. Herman Pritchett in the 1940s is generally regarded as providing the foundation of behavioral jurisprudence. Using a quantitative methodology, Pritchett sought to explain court decisions in terms of judicial attitudes and values. Judicial behavioralism is thus an almost exclusively human-oriented approach to the examination of law. Unlike political jurisprudence, behaviorists devalue the study of legal norms as well as the political dimensions of the judicial processes. *See also* JURISPRUDENCE, 20; LEGAL REALISM, 23; POLITICAL JURISPRUDENCE, 27.

Significance Behavioral jurisprudence refocused the study of public law, particularly within the discipline of political science. Like political jurisprudence, the behavioral approach represented a substantial departure from the traditional study of constitutional law and legal norms. The lines of distinction between political jurisprudents and judicial behaviorists is more difficult to establish. Even the leading behaviorists have been unable to precisely delineate behavioral and political jurisprudence as they continue to work with many of the concepts associated with the latter. Nonetheless, it is clear that the behavioral approach expanded our knowledge of judicial processes through the use of research techniques derived from such disciplines as psychology and social psychology. Indeed, many of the findings produced through the behavioral approach are currently embraced by judicial scholars. At the same time, the general orientation of those conducting research in this area more closely resembles that of political than behavioral jurisprudence.

Case or Controversy (6)

A properly asserted legal claim made in a manner appropriate for judicial response. A case or controversy may be decided by federal courts under Article III of the U.S. Constitution. For a case to constitute a bona fide controversy sufficient to satisfy Article III requirements (1) it must involve parties who are truly contending or adverse, (2) there must exist a recognizable legal interest arising out of a legitimate fact situation, and (3) the issue must be capable of resolution through the use of judicial power. Similar if not identical threshold conditions exist in state law as an entry condition for state courts. A person bringing a claim or petitioning a court is known as a *party* or *litigant.* The initiating party to a legal action is also called a *plaintiff* or *petitioner.* The party against whom such action may be brought is a *defendant* or *respondent.* Cases are named for the parties involved. The designation *et al.* is used after the first named party in a suit where there are several plaintiffs or defendants. Cases designated *in re,* or "in the matter of," are proceedings that are not wholly adversarial, such as a juvenile case. The abbreviation *ex. rel.* may be made when a legal action is initiated by the state at the instigation of a party with a private interest in the result. *See also* ADVERSARY SYSTEM, 3; JUSTICIABLE ISSUE, 231; STANDING, 246.

Significance   A case or controversy is a justiciable case. In *Aetna Life Insurance Company v. Haworth* (300 U.S. 227: 1937), the Supreme Court described a justiciable case as one in which the controversy is "definite and concrete," touching the legal relations of parties having "adverse legal interests." Such a controversy must also be "real and substantial, admitting to specific relief through a decree of a conclusive character." A true case or controversy is opposite from a hypothetical or abstract question upon which a court might render an advisory opinion. Substantial restrictions exist on the capacity of courts—federal or state—to hear cases of a hypothetical or abstract nature. The Supreme Court also restrains itself when it reviews actions of the other branches. The basic ground rules were nicely articulated by Justice Louis Brandeis in *Ashwander v. TVA* (297 U.S. 288: 1936). The *"Ashwander* rules" urge the Court to make every effort to find statutes constitutional if at all possible. The rules also encourage the Court to focus on the narrowest possible grounds for decision and to avoid the broad constitutional questions when it can.

Citizenship   (7)
One's status as a person who owes allegiance to the United States and is entitled to all the rights and privileges guaranteed and protected by the Constitution. Citizenship is usually obtained by birth on American soil. This is known as the rule of *jus soli.* This rule applies to anyone except children of foreign sovereigns or their ministers. There is also the rule of *jus sanguinis* or "law of blood," which applies when children of Americans are born abroad. Aliens may also be admitted to citizenship under a process known as naturalization. Congress is empowered to establish all rules and qualifications for naturalization. Citizenship may also be conferred by federal courts as authorized by Congress. Since the Civil Rights Act of 1866, all persons born or natu-

ralized in the United States are citizens of the United States. The Fourteenth Amendment reiterated that language in Section 1. The term *dual citizenship* refers to a person's status as a citizen of the United States and the state in which he or she resides, or to the holding of citizenship in two countries. *See also* PRIVILEGES AND IMMUNITIES, 29.

Significance   Citizenship is elaborated in two privileges and immunities clauses in the U.S. Constitution. The Constitution requires, for example, that citizens of a particular state have parity with citizens of all other states. The *Slaughterhouse Cases* (16 Wallace 36: 1873) emphasized the distinct character of federal and state citizenship. *Slaughterhouse* held that privileges and immunities conferred by state citizenship were outside federal reach through the Fourteenth Amendment. Such an interpretation took a very narrow view of the substance of federal citizenship. It covered only such things as interstate travel and voting. While subsequent decisions have extended the meaning of citizenship, *Slaughterhouse* is still controlling in that it precludes use of privileges and immunities language in protecting citizens by federal authority. Revocation of naturalized citizenship may occur following a formal denaturalization proceeding. The Court has imposed restrictions on the power of government to revoke citizenship, but there is a generally recognized right of expatriation that permits voluntary renunciation of citizenship.

Civil Law (8)

Law concerned with private rights and remedies. Civil law is different from criminal law in that it focuses on transactions of a private kind. Criminal law, on the other hand, prescribes and proscribes behavior in an attempt to protect society from harm. The role of the government is more limited in the area of civil law. The government's principal responsibility is to provide an impartial means for the resolution of private disputes. The government may be either a plaintiff or defendant in a civil action but typically is not a party at all; in criminal cases, the government will always function as a prosecutor. There are a broad range of disputes that fall under the civil law category, but among the more numerous are domestic relations, contract violations, and a variety of liability matters. *See also* CRIMINAL LAW, 12; DISPUTE RESOLUTION, 13; LITIGATION, 24.

Significance   Civil law regulates conduct that is essentially private. Civil law allows government to provide a forum for dispute resolution as well as a mechanism for the enforcement of civil judgments. Government's role in the enforcement of civil judgments, in turn, protects the integrity of private transactions. The processes established under civil law take the place of private means of dispute resolution. In doing so, civil law ensures that disputes will be settled in a lawful and peaceful manner. Unlike matters of criminal law, the government, when not a party to a case, has no interest in which party prevails in a civil suit. Rather, civil law protects the public interest by facilitating dispute resolution. Under certain circumstances, actions involving both civil and criminal law may arise. Violation of a criminal law can be punished. At the same time, the violator could be subjected to a civil action arising out of the same act in an effort to recover personal or property damages suffered by the victim or to implement government policy.

Code (9)

A collection of laws and regulations that are in effect in a particular political system. A code brings together statutes or other rules under some systematic arrangement, usually by subject matter. All operative federal statutes can be found in the United States Code. The code is kept current through a supplementing process with a revised edition produced every six years. Other codes exist at the federal level such as the Code of Federal Regulations, an annual compilation of federal agency regulations that have appeared in the Federal Register. There is also a Code of Military Justice, which contains all substantive and procedural law applying to those in the military. *See also* MILITARY JUSTICE SYSTEM, 61; STATUTE, 35.

Significance   Codes draw all laws of a particular kind into a single source. Codes classify laws and regulations. As a result, codes are invaluable reference resources. Codes can be easily supplemented; these supplements become the basis of periodic and potentially systematic legislative revision of laws. Most states have codified their statutes as well as judicial interpretation of them in volumes typically called Compiled Laws.

Common Law (10)

A body of principles that derive their authority from court judgments that embrace common customs and usages. Common law consists of all such principles that do not have their origin in statute or legislative mandate. Common law is a peculiarly English institution because it preserves and promulgates principles of law based on judicial decisions rather than on rules resulting from legislative enactments. Common law is judge-made law as distinct from statutory and administrative law. The tradition of common law evolved in large part because the English legal profession strongly resisted the establishment of a statutory system. Students of the law in England were trained more in the pragmatic applications of the law than they were in documentary systems of law enforcement. The legal profession was not so much interested in anticipating the adjudication of infractions of statute as it was in maintaining the precedent-setting value of actual controversies settled. This reliance on the value of precedent is perhaps the greatest legacy of the English common law system. Judges were placed in the position of either following the established precedent or distinguishing it. In either case, they became the arbiters of the existing law. No decision was made unless an actual dispute existed. Much that was fundamental to common law was recorded only in the opinions rendered by judges. *See also* JURISPRUDENCE, 20; PRECEDENT, 28.

Significance   Common law is law based upon prevailing usage. Use of common law invests judges with substantial flexibility in fashioning responses to specific case needs, although precedents established by judges reduce its flexibility. Once a decision is made, its root principles are drawn upon in subsequent cases of a similar kind, thus making the particular legal principle common to other related situations. Common law forms the basis of many legal processes in the states. While there is no federal common law as such, federal judges do utilize state common law in diversity of citizenship cases. Common law must yield to statute where conflict exists, but statutory law is generally founded upon common law principles. As a consequence, few major substantive conflicts arise. Furthermore, courts tend to interpret statutory law using common law traditions, which further diminishes the likelihood of incompatibility between statutes and common law principles.

Constitutional Law (11)

The aspect of public law that deals with the organic or fundamental law of a political system. Constitutional law addresses itself to the basic organizational framework of the government and the authority of those occupying governmental positions. Constitutional law sets forth in a general way the manner in which public matters are to be administered. This usually includes the statement of basic principles which will govern the relationship between the government and individual citizens. In the United States, there is a national constitution as well as a constitution for each of the 50 states. Constitutions usually take the form of written documents, but the fundamental law of a political system may be unwritten, as in Great Britain. The U.S. Constitution and those of the states are all set forth in writing. Constitutions are very general, and require regular interpretation. Constitutional law not only includes the provisions of a document but also the thousands of court decisions rendered over the years that contain interpretative rulings. The rulings have the same force as the words of the document. *See also* JUDICIAL REVIEW, 18; PUBLIC LAW, 31; STATUTE, 35.

Significance   Constitutional law is the highest form of law and all other laws and governmental actions must conform to it. It not only defines the power of a government but also the limits placed upon that government. Constitutions are either general or specific, long and involved or very brief. Many issues are addressed through application of the general provisions. Final authority on the meaning of the U.S. Constitution resides with the U.S. Supreme Court. The highest state court performs a similar role with state constitutions. Under provisions of the Supreme Clause of Article VI of the U.S. Constitution, no provision of state law (even state constitutional provisions) may conflict with the national constitution. Neither may legislative enactments known as statutes conflict with constitutional provisions. Courts safeguard the integrity of constitutions from improper legislative or executive action through the use of the power of judicial review. Judicial review empowers courts to invalidate actions that are in conflict with constitutional provisions.

Criminal Law   (12)

Law that deals with formally forbidden conduct. Criminal law both declares what conduct is illegal and sets forth the penalties for violations. The purpose of criminal law is the prevention of harm to the community and the protection of public safety. Criminal law is the opposite of civil law, which essentially governs individual conduct with respect to private matters. A wide range of conduct has been prescribed. The most serious offenses are classified as felonies and may be punishable by prison sentences in excess of one year. Such offenses as murder, arson, assault, and armed robbery are examples of felonies. In many states, the individual who commits the felony of first-degree murder may receive capital punishment. Less serious offenses are called misdemeanors and generally carry lighter punishments such as jail time up to a year in length or monetary fines. Certain traffic violations, shoplifting, and disorderly conduct are among those infractions typically defined as misdemeanors. Our federal system empowers both the national and state levels to define criminal conduct. Most criminal law is enacted at the state level, although the body of federal criminal law has increased since the early 1980s as the federal government has become more active in such areas as drug enforcement. Substantive criminal law in effect either nationally or in a particular state is typically compiled into a single criminal code. *See also* CIVIL LAW, 8; CODE, 9; LEGAL POSITIVISM, 22.

Significance   Criminal law is enacted by legislative bodies. It is positive law in that it reflects the views of a legislative majority on socially unacceptable conduct. Not only do governments set the rules, but they also play an extensive role in rule enforcement. The government is responsible for both the apprehension and prosecution of offenders. This latter function reflects the view that criminal behavior injures the society at large, and that it is a public responsibility to seek punishment on behalf of the individual victim. It is for this reason that criminal cases are usually entitled "People" or a named state against the defendant. In order to insure that government does not act arbitrarily in its law enforcement function, a number of procedural safeguards are established by both constitutional and statutory provisions.

Dispute Resolution (13)

Judicial function aimed at producing settlement of conflict. Dispute resolution is the primary function of the judicial system. The courts are a forum provided by government through which parties to a dispute may bring arguments and supporting evidence. The process encourages the resolution of conflicts by negotiation, but if this is not possible, the courts have the capacity to adjudicate matters in dispute and render authoritative decisions. The kinds of conflicts that enter the judicial process are either criminal or civil disputes. The conflict in criminal matters is between an individual and society. The judicial process must assess the societal injury stemming from the individual's deviant behavior and the punishment for that conduct. Civil disputes, on the other hand, typically involve conflict between two or more private parties, although some level of government is often a party to a civil action. Such disputes require the judicial process to define or redefine the relationship of the parties and possibly allocate (or reallocate) items or value among them. *See also* ADJUDICATION, 1; ARBITRATION, 4; JUDICIAL FUNCTION, 16; LITIGATION, 24; MEDIATION, 25.

Significance   One of the means by which courts engage in dispute resolution is litigation. Litigation is a lawsuit that utilizes one set of processes a court can bring to dispute resolution. This set is fully adversarial. Both parties to a lawsuit advance their arguments, almost always through trained attorneys. These arguments are presented to an impartial trier of fact (either a judge or jury), which ultimately determines which party's "facts" have been best supported. The process of litigation is complex and costly. In addition, there is often a lengthy waiting period before the case can be adjudicated. As a consequence, many disputes are resolved in alternate ways. Direct negotiation between the parties may bring about settlement. Intervention in the form of mediation or arbitration may also produce resolution of conflict. While these activities take place outside the court system as such, they can be viewed as part of the larger dispute resolution process, which operates in a fashion that fully complements the processes of courts.

Due Process of Law (14)

Legal concept representing the normal and regular administration of law. Due process is founded on the principle that government may not act arbitrarily or capriciously. It means that government may only act in ways established by law and under such limitations as the law imposes to protect individual rights. There are constitutional provisions at both the federal and state levels designed to ensure that laws will be reasonable both in substance and in means of implementation. Due process language is contained in two clauses of the U.S. Constitution. The Fifth Amendment prohibits deprivation of "life, liberty, or property, without due process of law" and sets a limit on arbitrary and unreasonable actions by the federal government. The Fourteenth Amendment contains parallel language aimed at the states. Due process requires that actions of government occur through ordered and regular processes. It subjects those processes to constitutional and statutory limits in the protection of individual rights. There are two kinds of due process. The first is *procedural due process,* which focuses on the methods or procedures by which governmental policies are executed. It guarantees fairness in the process by which government imposes regulations or sanctions. Procedural due process requires that a person be formally notified of any proceeding in which he or she is a party, and he or she be afforded an opportunity to an impartial hearing. Additional procedural rights have been enumerated in the Bill of Rights. Through the process of incorporation, most Bill of Rights protections have been applied as limitations on the states through the due process clause of the Fourteenth Amendment. *Substantive due process* represents the second kind of due process. It involves the reasonableness of policy content. Policies may deny substantive due process when they do not relate rationally to legitimate legislative objectives or when they are impermissibly vague. The distinction between procedural and substantive due process directly involves the nature of judicial review. When the U.S. Supreme Court examines a policy for procedural fairness, it makes only a limited review. It does not engage in consideration of legislative motive or the wisdom of the enactment. Appraisal of the reasonableness of substance, however, allows the Court to act as an extension of the legislative process. Since most state enactments impinge on property interests, the due process clause has provided the Court with a comprehensive method by which to judge state regulatory measures. *See also* INCORPORATION, 308; JUDICIAL REVIEW, 18; PROCEDURAL DUE PROCESS, 30; SUBSTANTIVE DUE PROCESS, 37.

Significance   Due process of law pursues fairness by demanding an orderly course of legal proceedings. A critical element is the right of a party to be heard by an impartial tribunal with jurisdiction over the dispute. The two due process clauses in the U.S. Constitution have frequently been used to challenge governmental actions as lacking either procedural or substantive fairness. The due process clause of the Fifth Amendment restricts the federal government. While utilized to some degree to contest federal economic regulation, those regulations were infrequent early in our history. As federal power was used more extensively, constitutional challenges tended to focus on the particular federal legislative power source, such as the interstate commerce power. Claims of due process violations backed up many of these challenges, but were not featured elements. That has not been the pattern with the due process clause of the Fourteenth Amendment. This clause has provided the mechanism by which Bill of Rights guarantees have been applied to the states. The Fifth Amendment counterpart has not had to function as a conduit since the enumerated Bill of Rights protections apply directly to the federal level. Nationalization of the Bill of Rights through the due process clause of the Fourteenth Amendment increased in impact through the 1960s. The importance of the Fourteenth Amendment due process clause as the focus of state economic policy has also been extensive.

Prior to the Civil War, the vested rights issue, which dominated many of the early contract clause cases, began to enter the U.S. Supreme Court's handling of various legislative enactments through the concept of due process. The argument was that the due process clauses could be used to protect property and economic interests. Initially, the Court rejected these contentions and deferred to state legislative enactments as in the *Slaughterhouse Cases* (16 Wallace 36: 1873). In such cases, the Court opted for an entirely procedural view of due process. In subsequent cases like *Munn v. Illinois* (94 U.S. 113: 1877), the Court also emphasized the sovereign authority of state police power, which entitled states to legislate for the health, safety, morals, and the general well-being of its citizenry. Strong substantive due process dissents were entered throughout this period, and eventually that position prevailed. The substantive due process majority sought to strike down state legislation it considered unreasonable. The argument was that substantively unreasonable regulation was as much a deprivation of due process as actions that used arbitrary methods. Under this approach, the Court addressed itself to the wisdom of state policies. Elements of the laissez-faire economic view were drawn into due process cases in this manner. One such element was the doctrine of liberty of contract. The doctrine held that if two parties entered into a lawful agreement, the state had no authority to interfere. The liberty of contract argument was used to invalidate a number of state regulations on hours of work, as in *Lochner v. New York* (198 U.S. 45: 1905). The period of substantive due process subsided in the 1930s at the same time the Court became more deferential to the exercise of power at the federal level. Over time, the Court essentially abandoned economic due process. At its height, however, the clause permitted the Court to perform an almost legislative role. Since most state laws touched property or contract interests, the opportunities for active intervention by the courts was great. Since the 1940s, the Court has generally turned its due process inquiries to noneconomic issues. At times, the activist substantive focus of earlier courts can be seen in cases involving individual freedoms and equality.

Equity (15)

Decisions based on a judge's sense of fairness rather than strict common law standards. The equity model permits judges to issue remedies in civil cases based on equitable principles that are outside or that supplement common law. Some of the flexibility of equity jurisdiction, however, has been lessened by the tendency of judges to follow precedents established in earlier equity cases. Cases in equity differ from other civil actions at law or common law because of the nature of the relief or remedy sought. In equity actions, damages are not readily remedied by monetary damage awards (although equitable relief may be supplemented by awards of monetary damages). Equitable relief may, for example, be appropriate in situations like environmental contamination or school discrimination where money may be insufficient, in itself, to arrest or repair the injury. In such cases, the plaintiff carries a heavier burden than in other civil cases because it must be shown that injury is permanent and therefore irreparable by mere payment of damages. *See also* COMMON LAW, 10; EQUITY JURISDICTION, 49; INJUNCTION, 226; IRREPARABLE INJURY, 229.

Significance   Considerations of equity in American courts protect against unjust results stemming from too rigid application of common law principles. Although courts of equity are structurally separate in Great Britain, equity jurisdiction in the United States is placed in the same courts that possess jurisdiction over statutory and common law. Equity relief is normally provided by a court in one of two ways, an injunction or court order. Injunctive relief is designed to preserve the status quo until such time as the merits of the cases can be adjudicated. Such remedy begins as a temporary order but may become permanent upon completion of a trial or other formal proceeding. The court order, on the other hand, requires a party to perform a certain act. Such a court order is actually the positive form of an injunction. Orders of this kind are more likely in the school discrimination action while the injunction is more likely in an environmental protection suit.

Judicial Function   (16)

The roles performed by the courts in the political system of the United States. Several judicial functions are prominent. The first and most common is dispute resolution. The courts provide a forum for the presentation of arguments and processes by which disputes may either be settled or adjudicated. This function is not only essential for the parties to the suit but generally allows the government to better manage conflict in the society. Second, the courts perform a socialization function. They attempt to influence behavior of individuals by penalizing unacceptable conduct. This is especially evident with criminal penalties, although it occurs in civil situations as well. While deterrence through threat of sanction is more frequent, the courts may also reinforce proper conduct. Third, courts authoritatively distribute benefits and sanctions. Courts render decisions that actually impose punishments of imprisonment or require one party to pay another party large sums of money. These judgments are fully enforceable through the exercise of governmental power. Finally, courts play a role in the shaping of public policy. This is especially true at the appellate level where the courts are required to render interpretive judgments on issues that arise in the application of law. *See also* ADJUDICATION, 1; CIVIL LAW, 8; CRIMINAL LAW, 12; DISPUTE RESOLUTION, 13; LITIGATION, 24.

Significance   Insights into the operations of courts are based on an understanding of the functions of courts and the specific processes designed to perform those tasks. Courts generally exist to facilitate dispute resolution. Many disputes are not actually brought to court but rather are resolved by agreement of the disputants. The courts should, as a consequence, be viewed as but one mode of dispute resolution and a mode of last resort at that. The kinds of issues brought to courts may be categorized as either civil or criminal. Civil disputes generally involve private parties and their relationship to one another. Most civil litigants are individuals or businesses, although the government may also be a party in a civil suit. The judicial function in a civil dispute is to establish or adjust the relationship of the parties. The court may also have to redistribute resources among the parties. In a criminal case, on the other hand, the conflict that requires resolution is between society at large and a misbehaving individual. The court then authoritatively determines the outcome by imposing formal sanctions, such as imprisonment.

Judicial Immunity (17)

Insulates judges from civil suits for actions done in the performance of their judicial functions. The doctrine of judicial immunity was intended to protect judges from fearing civil lawsuits commenced by unhappy litigants. It was felt that threat of such suit might intimidate judges from making controversial or difficult decisions. The doctrine was aimed at serving the public interest by having judges who could function with "independence" and "without fear of consequences." *See also* LIFE TENURE, 102.

Significance   The Supreme Court first established the doctrine of judicial immunity in *Bradley v. Fisher* (13 Wallace 335: 1872). The immunity doctrine created in that case was extensive and applied to actions even when they might be "in excess of their jurisdictions" or "maliciously or corruptly" motivated. Only acts that are "non-judicial" are not covered by the immunity doctrine. This broad definition as well as some criteria for determination of "judicial" acts was incorporated into the Court's decision in *Stump v. Sparkman* (435 U.S. 349: 1978). The *Stump* case involved a judge approving the sterilization of a minor. The judge of a general jurisdiction court was approached by the mother of the minor with a petition authorizing the process. The judge approved the petition without assigning the matter a docket number, giving notice to the minor, or appointing counsel to represent her. The Court ruled that having jurisdiction to sign the petition was determining in the case. Where judicial immunity is at issue, the "scope of jurisdiction must be construed broadly." Furthermore, immunity exists even if the action taken by the judge was "in error, was done maliciously, or was in excess of his authority" so long as he or she had not acted in "clear absence of jurisdiction." Clearly, said the Court, all judicial acts must be protected and no flaw in the judge's performance makes a ruling "any less a judicial act." The Court used two criteria in determining the action here was a judicial one. First, responding to the petition was a function "normally performed by a judge." Second, response from the judge was obtained consistently with the "expectation of the parties" that they are dealing with the judge in his or her "judicial capacity."

Judicial Review (18)

The power of courts to examine governmental actions to determine whether they are within constitutional limits. Judicial review varies depending upon whose actions are under review. One situation involves review of administrative actions. Such review is both common and relatively limited in policy impact. Two more significant types of review were cultivated by Supreme Court Chief Justice John Marshall in the early 1800s. The first involves the Supreme Court's role as arbiter of the federal-state relationship. This kind of review allows the courts of the national government to review actions of the constituent states and invalidate those that collide with national authority or interfere with other states. The power to perform this kind of review can be derived from the Supremacy Clause of Article VI of the U.S. Constitution and the Judiciary Act of 1789. The other significant kind of judicial review involves judicial capacity to review actions of coordinate branches. Such a power carries the potential of placing the courts in a position of policy dominance. The argument for such a power is that the integrity of the Constitution must be safeguarded from actions that conflict with it. Judicial review is not mentioned in the Constitution, although it was debated at length by the framers. *See also* JUDICIAL ACTIVISM, 309; JUDICIAL SELF-RESTRAINT, 311; STATUTORY CONSTRUCTION, 36.

Significance   Judicial review authorizes courts to examine governmental actions, including those of the legislative and executive branches, and declare them unconstitutional if necessary. Review of legislative or executive actions may ultimately uphold such actions because most judges subscribe to the principle of judicial self-restraint. The courts seldom engage in judicial review as such. Rather, they engage in statutory construction, or the interpretation of what a law means. The power to review the constitutionality of actions by the other branches, a action most commonly called judicial review, was discussed extensively at the Constitutional Convention, but it was ultimately not included in the expressly delegated judicial powers. The Supreme Court first asserted the power in the case of *Marbury v. Madison* (1 Cranch 137: 1803). In *Marbury*, the Court determined that a section of the Judiciary Act of 1789 unconstitutionally expanded the original jurisdiction of the Supreme Court. The Court asserted that it must, under such circumstances, be able to void enactments that collide with the Constitution. Chief Justice John Marshall considered judicial review to be the "very essence of judicial duty." The arguments for judicial review of this kind became so firmly rooted in American jurisprudence that the doctrine became one of the principal means by which courts participate in the shaping of public policy.

Judiciary (19)

The governmental branch that possesses judicial authority. The term *judiciary* can refer either to the court system generally or to the judges in aggregate who sit on the various courts. It is the function of the judiciary to interpret or construe the law as distinct from creating or executing it. The related term, *judicial,* refers to that which belongs to the position of a judge, such as the authority to render judgments in formal processes. The judiciary in the United States is divided between the national and state levels of government. The power of particular courts, both federal and state, is defined by each court's jurisdiction. Usually, courts possess either original jurisdiction or appellate jurisdiction, but in some cases both. The former allows a court to hear a case first, while the latter allows a court to review the proceedings of a lower court. The judiciary is created either by specific provision of federal or state constitutions or by statutes enacted pursuant to constitutional mandate. The Supreme Court is created by terms of Article III of the U.S. Constitution. Article III also conveys power to Congress to establish inferior federal courts. The first Congress established the district and circuit courts in the Judiciary Act of 1789. A number of judiciary acts have followed, including the Act of 1891 (also known as the Evarts Act), which created the U.S. Court of Appeals. *See also* ADJUDICATION, 1; JUDGE, 91; JUDICIAL REVIEW, 18; JUDICIARY ACT OF 1789, 55.

Significance   The judiciary is one of the three basic functional elements of the American system of government at both the national and state levels. An independent judiciary that possesses power approaching or equivalent to the executive and legislative branches is an essential component for implementing both the separation of power and checks and balances concepts. It is the function of the judiciary to interpret the law in order to preserve the functional boundaries among the branches and levels of government. Through the power of judicial review, the courts can check the improper or excessive exercise of power by another branch. The judiciary also acts to resolve disputes between private and public parties as well as to preside over the procedures devoted to fact-finding and interpretation of law.

Jurisprudence (20)

The science and philosophy of law. Jurisprudence has come to include the examination of legal ideas, theories, and analyses based on inquiry developed in anthropology, philosophy, politics, psychology, and sociology. Jurisprudence as a mode of thought has its genesis in the thinking of Plato and Aristotle. Neither distinguished between legal and social theory, arguing that no polity could exist without law. Several centuries later, Roman thinkers saw jurisprudence as the science of knowing what is right and wrong. Jurisprudence thus can be viewed as the repository of thoughts and the body of sources from which the law emanates. Many Western legal thinkers have devoted attention to rules that should govern the behavior of individuals in relation to each other and to the state. Jurisprudence has been classified into schools of thought. While each category may assert claims of independence from each other, there is some overlap among jurisprudential schools. Indeed, the evolution of the various schools is dialectic in character as one view reacts to that which has come earlier. Nonetheless, identification of several broadly distinctive categories is useful. The view that was first to appear was natural law. According to natural law jurisprudence, laws that govern all things have their origin in nature. Natural law is common to all persons of all times and places. As a consequence, if law enacted by government violates one of the fundamental natural laws, the man-made law is immoral and invalid. Legal positivism sees law as separate from the moral abstractions of natural law. Rather, positivists focused on the concept of state sovereignty, enacted laws, and their purely logical application. Sociological jurisprudence rejected the abstractions and mechanistic logic of positivism and held that law and legal processes can only be understood as part of society. Closely akin to sociological jurisprudence is legal realism. Realists recognize the salience of social factors, but they go further and focus more tightly on the responses to these social forces by those functioning in the legal process. Within the more general category of legal realism fall political and behavioral jurisprudence. *See also* BEHAVIORAL JURISPRUDENCE, 5; LEGAL POSITIVISM, 22; LEGAL REALISM, 23; NATURAL LAW, 26; POLITICAL JURISPRUDENCE, 27; SOCIOLOGICAL JURISPRUDENCE, 33.

Significance Jurisprudence is the amalgam of philosophical thought, historical and political analysis, sociological and behavioral evidence, and legal experience. The study of jurisprudence fosters the view that ideas about law do not develop in an intellectual vacuum. Rather, they evolve from critical thinking in a number of disciplines. Jurisprudence enables people to understand how law has ordered both social institutions and individual conduct. It also allows a fuller appreciation of the scope of the responsibility held by those who make law, administer law, and render equitable decisions about the law.

Law (21)

A rule of conduct issued or embraced by the authority of government. Law is a manifestation of sovereign power and must be obeyed by all who are subject to it. Laws are enforced in the courts, and sanctions may be imposed for violations of the law. Law has several origins. The primary source is a constitution. Law may also derive from acts of legislative bodies or rulings of administrative agencies. Custom or tradition is also a source of law, including common law or remedies of equity. Several kinds of law take their name from the sources or origins identified above. Law established by a constitution is called constitutional law, for example. There are other categories of law as well. Law that concerns itself with content is called substantive law. Such law, for example, defines inappropriate conduct and establishes punishments that may be imposed for engaging in the proscribed conduct. Procedural law, on the other hand, speaks to processes of law or the manner in which the law is applied. Criminal law and civil law are two other classes of law. Criminal law deals with conduct formally proscribed by government. Criminal law usually comes in the form of statute and substantively defines a broad range of crimes. Constitutions and statutes set forth safeguards for processing those accused of criminal behavior. Civil law reaches noncriminal conduct between or among individuals or groups. Civil law focuses largely on such matters as property, legal injury, and contracts. *See also* CONSTITUTIONAL LAW, 11; JURISPRUDENCE, 20; STATUTE, 35.

Significance Law is a body of rules and standards coming from government. In a democratic political system, law not only sets the standards but establishes the processes through which enforcement occurs. Law may establish standards by prohibiting certain conduct because it directly harms persons or property. Other actions may be proscribed even though they do not directly cause harm. Laws requiring the feeding of parking meters or prohibiting the running of a private lottery are of this kind. Law may also extend benefits to certain people. Defining eligibility for food stamps, particular tax deductions, or agricultural subsidies reflects the authoritative "allocation of value" function of law. In addition, law creates regularity and predictability. Such regularity helps to deter arbitrary conduct by private parties as well as public officials.

Legal Positivism (22)

A jurisprudence that sees law as a body of man-made rules. Key to legal positivism is the concept of sovereignty and the exercise of sovereign power. Positive law sets out rules of conduct based on the relationship between those who rule and those who are ruled. To the positivist, law is a body of rules adopted and enforced by the state as it seeks to administer justice. In a representative democracy, positive law is a rule based on the will of the majority. The foremost exponent of legal positivism was John Austin, an English jurist of the nineteenth century. Austin rejected natural law jurisprudence. Instead, he saw law as a body of content quite separate from moral abstractions and social forces. While those factors exist, they do not directly bear upon the "science" of positive law. Because Austin provided the broadest theoretical framework for positivism, legal positivism is often referred to as Austinian Positivism. Legal positivism is also referred to as analytical jurisprudence. *See also* LEGAL REALISM, 23; NATURAL LAW, 26.

Significance Legal positivism has had a substantial influence on American legal thought. Prior to Austin, positivistic thought was apparent in William Blackstone's *Commentaries on the Law of England,* although it was interwoven with elements of natural law jurisprudence. Blackstone argued that laws must not contradict the laws of nature. At the same time, he saw law emanating from the state as a secondary law of nature with principles that are certain and unchangeable. Blackstone stressed fixed legal principles and logic and saw law as the perfection of reason. The legal theory of Blackstone largely shaped the attitudes of American colonists and were strongly represented at the Constitutional Convention in Philadelphia. Positivism has also had an impact on defining the role of the judiciary in American law. The judicial process to the positivist is virtually mechanical. Judges examine the circumstances of a dispute in relation to the law that emanates from the power of the state and render decisions through the application of sheer logic. Notwithstanding arguments advanced to the contrary, by behavioral and political jurisprudents for example, the idea of judges discovering law through wholly neutral principles and logic remains a central element of American legal thought.

Legal Realism (23)

A school of jurisprudence that stresses behavioral and political factors as the most critical to judicial decision making. Legal realism minimizes the impact of abstract legal rules and principles on deciding particular cases. Leading legal realists, such as Oliver Wendell Holmes, Jerome Frank, and Roscoe Pound, believed that law does not have a transcendental quality but rather is a product of social forces and the behavior of people in the legal process responding to those forces. Legal realism is, in some respects, similar to sociological jurisprudence, although realists are more inclined to view law primarily in terms of official conduct. Legal realists do not subscribe to the rules fashioned in legal precedents because law is neither that certain nor that clear. Rather, decisions are based on judges applying the "right" rules and offering a written rationale for the decision, ideally a rationale grounded on empirical bases. *See also* JUDICIAL ACTIVISM, 309; JURISPRUDENCE, 20; SOCIOLOGICAL JURISPRUDENCE, 33.

Significance   The legal realist believes that law is largely the product of human behavior. The exercise of discretion in the application of law is viewed as both inevitable and productive. Since legal judgments are not governed by abstract legal principles, other factors such as personal values shape decisions. Accordingly, legal realists seriously engage in the study of legal institutions and processes as well as the environment in which they operate. They seek to explain conduct of those operating in the legal processes, and attention is focused on the political, sociological, and psychological dimensions of behavior. Legal realism prompted substantial quantities of legal research, and it greatly heightened our understanding of the legal system, especially the lower courts. The legal realist impact can also be seen in the content of texts and courses in contemporary legal education.

Litigation (24)

A lawsuit that is contested in a court. Litigation is a civil legal action initiated for the purpose of enforcing a legal right or securing some kind of legal remedy. Litigation is a controversy that is taken all the way to trial and is decided on the basis of evidence presented to a judge or a jury. The objectives of litigation are reflected in the kinds of relief or remedy sought in court. A large number of litigants want to restore something to a previous status. Such litigation typically involves return of money or property that previously belonged to the plaintiff. Damages, which attempt to obtain some kind of compensation for a loss, are closely related . If a person is injured in some kind of accident, compensation may be recovered for losses suffered beyond the medical costs. Damages may also be sought for injury to reputation or for mental suffering. In addition, litigation may take place in an effort to require someone to take some action or stop certain action. An action seeking to restrain a company from emitting pollutants or infringing on a patent are examples of this kind of litigation. Finally, litigation may seek to define or clarify legal rights. For example, litigation may be instituted to stop enforcement of a law that a group feels is interfering with its constitutional rights. *See also* DISPUTE RESOLUTION, 13; JUDICIAL FUNCTION, 16.

Significance   Litigation is one mode of dispute resolution, but it has its drawbacks and seldom do cases filed with the courts progress all the way to the trial stage. Litigation is costly, and other methods of dispute resolution may be sought for that reason. In addition, actual trial of a dispute places an "all or nothing" decision in the hands of a third party, a judge or jury. Taking a lawsuit to conclusion also reduces the possibility that the parties can maintain any kind of relationship following litigation. Alternatives to litigation exist, such as private negotiation, mediation, or arbitration, and the data suggest that the alternatives are attractive to litigants and potential litigants. While the number of case filings has increased dramatically since the early 1970s, the actual number of contested trials has not increased proportionately. These data clearly show that cases are increasingly likely to be resolved or settled without taking litigation full course.

Mediation (25)

Intervention intended to promote a settlement by a third party in a dispute. Mediation is generally nonadversarial in character and is conducted informally. The process may ultimately produce resolution of the dispute, but it may not be that successful. Instead, mediation may only yield a clarification of the issues in a dispute, a function which is nonetheless helpful to subsequent efforts to resolve the dispute. Unlike the arbitration process, a third party may only try to lead the parties to a settlement; a mediator has no power to render a binding decision. Mediation processes have been established under both federal and state law. The Federal Mediation and Conciliation Service, for example, was created in 1913 to provide services aimed at resolving labor disputes. Similar agencies can be found at the state level, especially in the large industrialized states. The term *conciliation* is often used interchangeably with the term *mediation. See also* ARBITRATION, 4; SETTLEMENT, 244.

Significance　　Mediation is a dispute resolution alternative to the courts. If successful, it reduces the case demands on the judiciary and provides quicker and less expensive results for parties to a dispute. Mediation has been particularly effective in domestic disputes. Indeed, many urban or other large jurisdictions have created mediation or conciliation agencies within the court itself. Additional incentive for use of mediation is provided under the Dispute Resolution Act of 1980, which directs federal funding to states that establish or improve their nonjudicial dispute resolution processes.

Natural Law　　　　　　　　　　　　　　　　　　　(26)
Jurisprudential view that laws which govern all things have their origin in nature. The natural law concept is that such laws are both eternal and unchanging. Natural law jurisprudence asserts that fundamental rules governing human behavior derive from basic characteristics of a human nature common to all. Natural law jurisprudence has produced in volume more writing than any view of law. Early conceptions of natural law can be seen in the thinking of Aristotle, but the first comprehensive statement of natural law is most commonly attributed to the Greek Stoics and such Roman thinkers as Cicero. The most systematic framework for natural law theory was developed by Thomas Aquinas in the Thirteenth Century. Natural law is opposite from the positivistic theories of private and public morality. Natural law and natural rights are common to all persons of all times and places. As a consequence, if law is created by man (government) that violates one of the fundamental natural rules, the man-made rule is immoral and invalid. Positivistic theories, on the other hand, deny such a universal basis for fundamental rules of conduct and assert that such fundamental rules cannot be known in any objective or authoritative way and that all law is based on human agreement. *See also* COMMON LAW, 10; LEGAL POSITIVISM, 22.

Significance　　The development of natural law and natural rights was an attempt to clarify how people should deal with arbitrary governmental conduct. The concept of natural law provided the foundation for social contract theory which, in turn, was to become a key element in American political thought. John Locke's *Second Treatise on Government*, for example, provided the theoretical basis for the American Revolution and constitutional movement. Natural law theories also provided the rationale for such declarations as the English Bill of Rights, the French Declaration of the Rights of Man and Citizen, and the United Nations Universal Declaration of Human Rights. Natural law also underlies many acts of civil disobedience. If one believes that a law is morally wrong, the person has an obligation to conduct acts of civil disobedience to heighten social consciousness on the issue. The late Dr. Martin Luther King, Jr., used this approach in his efforts to combat the immorality of discrimination. The critical question is whether human rights are grounded "in nature," and if so, whether such a view can be defended without a carefully defined justification. In the absence of such justification, the notion of human rights as products of natural law may provide a rationale for self-serving conduct and a circumstance approaching anarchy where people claim a right to do what they please regardless of the social consequences.

Political Jurisprudence (27)

An approach to the study of law and courts that features the political character of judicial processes. Political jurisprudence is a conceptualization of law with its roots in legal realism generally and sociological jurisprudence more specifically. The political approach emerged in the 1940s in an attempt to produce theory that could explain the Supreme Court decisions rendered in the wake of President Franklin Roosevelt's plan to "pack" the Court. Political jurisprudence generally embraced the realist positions but recast them in political terms. The human element, it argues, is key. Judges do not mechanically apply abstract legal norms, but rather are influenced by their individual views of justice. As a consequence, law and legal processes must be examined in a political context. *See also* BEHAVIORAL JURISPRUDENCE, 5; JURISPRUDENCE, 20; LEGAL REALISM, 23; SOCIOLOGICAL JURISPRUDENCE, 33.

Significance Political jurisprudence developed, logically enough, from within the discipline of political science, a discipline heavily grounded in law and legal doctrine. After the turn of the century, many political scientists began to subscribe to the thinking of the legal realists. For some, however, the theories of the realists were not quite adequate. This inadequacy was underscored in the events of the 1930s. President Roosevelt attempted to transform his mandate from the 1932 election by establishing public policy aimed at economic recovery. His initiatives were largely stymied by the Supreme Court's narrow interpretations of federal authority, especially the taxing and commerce powers. Roosevelt was returned to office in 1936 and immediately sought to enlarge the Supreme Court. It was a thinly veiled attempt to "pack" enough justices onto the Court to ensure a favorable response to the hamstrung New Deal proposals. The plan had no real chance of adoption by Congress, but it seemed to drive the swing votes on the Court to Roosevelt's position. Although the membership on the Court did not change, after the "packing" proposal the Court changed its positions on the pivotal constitutional law issues associated with the New Deal. The approach known as political jurisprudence was developed to explain such outcomes. Political jurisprudence would later splinter, with a portion of its number becoming judicial behaviorists. Notwithstanding, most contemporary research on the courts appears to be a product of those holding the political jurisprudential view.

Precedent (28)

A previous court ruling on a question of law. A precedent is recognized as providing a basis for resolving identical or similar cases coming before courts at a later date. Precedents are regarded as a principal source of common law. A precedent may be established when a court considers a novel legal issue or offers an interpretation on statute. Under the doctrine of *stare decisis* ("let the decision stand"), courts attempt to resolve present and future cases on the basis of legal principles established through precedent. Precedents can be overturned in making later decisions, but this occurs only rarely. *See also* COMMON LAW, 10; *OBITER DICTUM*, 276; *RATIO DECIDENDI*, 282; *STARE DECISIS*, 34.

Significance Courts are expected to follow precedents because they are established legal doctrine. To do so heightens the stability and predictability of the law. Precedents also serve a pragmatic function for courts. Reliance on past practice reduces whatever risk may be associated with new legal directions. The portion of a precedent that courts utilize in subsequent cases is the basic principle necessary to resolve an issue. This element is called the *ratio decidendi*. Other discussion in an opinion is called *obiter dictum*, and it has no legal relevance. The existence of legal precedent does not eliminate all judgment in legal interpretation. Most cases before appellate courts involve questions that suggest more than one line of precedents, and it is often possible to find precedents that support both sides of a case. Indeed, legal disputes are commonly contested over which precedents control

a particular question in a case. Precedents that are marginally different from an immediate case may be distinguished and held not to
apply. If a particular precedent becomes obsolete or is shown to be
unworkable, a court may modify or abandon it and replace it with a
new precedent.

Privileges and Immunities (29)

Legal benefits flowing from one's status as a citizen. A privilege is a
benefit or an advantage, while an immunity frees a person from an
obligation or a penalty. Certain privileges and immunities exist for a
person by virtue of his or her citizenship. The U.S. Constitution contains two references to privileges and immunities. Article IV, Section
2, provides that the "Citizens of each State be entitled to the Privileges and Immunities of citizens of the several States." The purpose
of this clause was to ensure that out-of-state citizens receive the same
treatment as a state's own citizens. The clause established parity
across the states. The Fourteenth Amendment also provides that "No
State shall make or enforce any law which shall abridge the privileges
or immunities of the United States." This section of the Fourteenth
Amendment, adopted in 1868, was a specific response to the Black
Codes, which in many Southern states had the effect of restoring
pre-Civil War conditions of slavery. *See also* CITIZENSHIP, 7; DUE PRO-
CESS OF LAW, 14.

Significance   The protection of privileges and immunities was se-
verely limited by the *Slaughterhouse Cases* (16 Wallace 36: 1873), in
which the Supreme Court distinguished between federal and state citizenship. The Court placed most key civil and political rights within
the state citizenship category. That limited the privileges and immunities of federal citizenship to such rights as interstate travel, protection while abroad, and participation in federal elections. The
protections afforded by federal citizenship through the Fourteenth
Amendment have expanded substantially over the years since
Slaughterhouse, but the expansion has taken place under the due process and equal protection clauses rather than the privilege and immunities clauses.

Procedural Due Process (30)

A procedural review that focuses on the means by which governmental actions are executed. Procedural due process guarantees fairness
in the ways that government imposes restrictions and punishments.
It demands that before any deprivation of liberty or property can

occur, a person must be formally notified and provided an opportunity for a fair hearing. Procedural due process differs from substantive due process. The former focuses on how government should function while the latter stresses what government can reasonably do. *See also* DUE PROCESS OF LAW, 14; SUBSTANTIVE DUE PROCESS, 37.

Significance   Procedural due process must be accorded persons accused of crimes. It includes access to legal counsel, the ability to confront witnesses, and a trial by jury. Procedural due process also applies to regulation of property. Constitutional protection against loss of liberty or property is guaranteed in two constitutional amendments: the Fifth, which is directed at the federal government, and the Fourteenth, which is directed at the states. When the Court was first asked to use the Due Process Clause of the Fourteenth Amendment to invalidate state economic regulatory initiatives, it adopted a largely procedural approach. In the *Slaughterhouse Cases* (16 Wallace 36: 1873), for example, the Court refused to examine the reasonableness of a state-granted slaughterhouse monopoly. This approach was also seen in *Munn v. Illinois* (94 U.S. 113: 1877), where the Court allowed a state rate regulation on businesses "affected with a public interest." Within a decade of *Munn*, the Court embraced the substantive due process approach and found most economic regulations to be unreasonable and therefore unconstitutional. Substantive due process eventually fell into decline beginning with such post-Depression decisions as *Nebbia v. New York* (291 U.S. 502: 1934) and *West Coast Hotel v. Parrish* (300 U.S. 379: 1937), and the Court essentially abandoned the substantive due process approach with respect to commercial regulations.

Public Law   (31)
Law that generally concerns the activities of the state as it exercises its sovereign power. Public law is a classification that includes such elements as constitutional, criminal, and administrative law. It extends to the structural organization of the political system. The authority of government as well as the constraints under which government must act are defined by public law. Public law applies to the people as a whole rather than selectively to individuals or small groups. In other words, public law protects or advances a public as distinct from a private interest. Public law is also a designation applied to international law or the law that extends to relationships among political systems. *See also* CONSTITUTIONAL LAW, 11; STATUTE, 35.

Significance   Public law is essentially concerned with authority, obligations, and rights. The substance of public law is most commonly contained in constitutions and legislative enactments. The provisions protecting free speech and authorizing regulation of interstate commerce are illustrative of public law derived from the national constitution. Public law in the form of statutes is more extensive, although it is subordinate to constitutional directives. Statutes governing, for example, taxation, immigration, business regulation, or consumer protection or defining criminal conduct fill volumes. A large proportion of this body of law is related to the development of the administrative state. Those rules that emanate from administrative agencies are also part of the body of public law.

Separation of Power (32)

The doctrine and practice of dividing the powers of government among several coordinate branches to prevent the abusive concentration of power. The distribution of powers embodied in the U.S. Constitution distinguishes functionally between government and people, and between executive, legislative, and judicial branches. While the Constitution creates three separate branches, it assigns them overlapping responsibilities that make them interdependent and that encourage the operation of a checks and balances system. The Congress is assigned the responsibility for passing laws, but these laws must be implemented by the president and the executive branch and can be interpreted, even declared unconstitutional, by the Supreme Court. The president is head of the executive branch of government, but the laws he or she is responsible for implementing and the money necessary for doing so come from the Congress. The Supreme Court also has the power to declare his or her actions unconstitutional. The framers used the doctrine of checks and balances to protect against absolute power coming to reside in any one of the branches. The doctrine of checks and balances is a device that simultaneously softens and augments separation of powers. Checks and balances soften the separation of powers because they require the concurrence of one branch in the work properly assigned to another branch, and they implement the separation of power because they specify the controls each part of government has over the other parts. *See also* CONSTITUTIONAL LAW, 11; DUE PROCESS OF LAW, 14; FEDERALISM, 51.

Significance The principle of separation of power is designed to limit the abusive exercise of governmental authority by partitioning authority to several locations. Coupled with the checks and balances features of American constitutional law, governmental power is decentralized and restricted. This structural distribution of power creates different points of access as each branch tends to respond to different kinds of political stimuli. The key factor, however, is that none of the branches dominates the processes of government for a protracted period of time. The separation of power may create fragmentation or disunity for government if there exists sufficient inter-branch conflict. Such conflict can often be found when the executive and legislative branches are controlled by different political parties. It has become the function of the courts to umpire the functional lines of separation among the branches and the territorial lines between the federal and state levels of government.

Sociological Jurisprudence (33)

A view that law and legal processes can only be understood as part of society at large. Sociological jurisprudence had its origin in the work of those who argued that law is part of the historical tradition of a society. This perspective suggested the need to compare legal systems, an objective to which the social sciences easily lent themselves. Among those who provide the foundation for sociological jurisprudence was the legal realist Roscoe Pound. Pound saw the traditional view of law as too "mechanical." Rather, law should be seen as reflecting contemporary social needs. Law is to provide a set of rules, established through accepted processes, dedicated to the resolution of disputes between and among the various interests in society. Law, thus, is not abstract principles, but rules that are applied through a legal system that possesses sufficient discretion to maximize the possibility of conflict resolution. This orientation emphasized the "realities" of the law, but also strongly urged empirical sociological research. *See also* LEGAL REALISM, 23; POLITICAL JURISPRUDENCE, 27.

Significance   Sociological jurisprudence had a substantial impact on legal thinking in the United States. It departed from the positivist orientation that viewed the judicial function as applying law from legislatively adopted principles. Application of the sociological approach first developed national visibility in the early 1900s as Louis D. Brandeis sought to defend a state law establishing minimum wages and maximum hours of work. He used what was called the "Brandeis brief" to supplement legal arguments with socio-economic data to support the reasonableness of the law. The Supreme Court legitimized the approach by upholding the state law in *Muller v. Oregon* (208 U.S. 412: 1908). Brandeis was eventually appointed to the U.S. Supreme Court, where he was later joined by Benjamin Cardozo, who was also a leading exponent of sociological jurisprudence. In his writings on the judicial process, Cardozo consistently emphasized the social character of law. While recognizing logic and precedent as playing a key role in judicial decision making, Cardozo also argued that judges must respond to societal needs and, in doing so, be fully cognizant of social science measurement of such need. The sociological jurisprudents were the first to break from the ranks of traditional legal thinkers and were responsible for establishing a new course for American legal thought.

Stare Decisis (34)

Latin for "let the decision stand." *Stare decisis* holds that once a principle of law is established for a particular legal situation, courts should adhere to that principle in similar cases in the future. The case in which the rule of law is established is called a precedent. Indeed, the doctrine holds that a previous decision is binding on any question subsequently arising under the rule of law established by it. Precedents are the source of common law. A precedent may be established when a court considers a novel legal issue or offers an interpretation on a statute. *See also* COMMON LAW, 10; PRECEDENT, 28.

Significance   *Stare decisis* creates and maintains stability and predictability in the law. It creates a large body of settled usages that define common law. Precedents may be modified or abandoned if circumstances require, but the expectation is that rules from previously adjudicated cases will prevail. In addition to heightening stability and predictability, *stare decisis* also serves a pragmatic function for the courts: reliance on past decisions reduces whatever risk may be associated with new legal directions.

Statute (35)

Law enacted by the legislative branch of government. Statutes are enacted by legislatures under power authorized and means prescribed by federal and state constitutions. Resolutions adopted by legislative bodies are not considered statutes. Law adopted by government at the local level is typically called an ordinance rather than a statute. Statutes may be either public or private. A public or general statute establishes a policy that applies to everyone. A private or special statute, on the other hand, is directed at particular persons or classes. A private bill, for example, could deal with a citizenship matter or land title of a particular individual. When a legislative body enacts a private law, it is often required to make an almost judicial determination in order to resolve the private issue. Statutes may be either mandatory or directory in character. A mandatory statute requires a particular action while a directory statute leaves compliance optional. In other words, a directory statute offers mere direction, and there is no consequence for failure to take the direction. *See also* LAW, 21; LEGAL POSITIVISM, 22; STATUTORY CONSTRUCTION, 36.

Significance   Statutes are enacted for a variety of reasons. Among these are to define criminal conduct and establish penalties for violations, to appropriate public funds, or to create administrative agencies. Statutes are the major source of positive law, or law reflective of the will of the legislative majority. Statutes can essentially provide for anything so long as they do not conflict with constitutional law. Courts may, through the exercise of judicial review, determine if a statute is incompatible with constitutional provisions. Those statutes that are found in conflict are nullified. More likely, courts will be asked to render interpretations of what statutory provisions mean. This process of statutory construction clarifies law through application and fills in any gaps that may exist in the general provisions of a statute. Statutes are compiled and codified on a subject matter basis. Currently applicable federal law is found in the United States Code, which is regularly supplemented and revised.

Statutory Construction   **(36)**
Interpretation of legislative enactments by the courts. Statutory construction is one of the primary interpretative functions of the judiciary. A statute is seldom enacted that anticipates every possible application. Thus it is necessary for courts to determine how a statute applies. Courts engaged in statutory construction may refer to records of various stages in the legislative process, such as committee hearings or floor debates, as a means of determining legislative intent. If such intent can be identified, it will govern the application of the law. If the legislative objectives are less than obvious, it becomes the province of the courts to fashion an interpretation that will cover the application. Statutory construction is different from judicial review in that it does not usually extend to nullification of an enactment as unconstitutional. Rather, statutory construction focuses upon determining which of two or more contending interpretations of a statute is to prevail. In such cases, the constitutionality of the statutory provision is not often in doubt. *See also* JUDICIAL FUNCTION, 16; JUDICIAL REVIEW, 18; STATUTE, 35.

Significance   Statutory construction is one of the basic functions of the judiciary. The need to interpret provisions of enactments arises frequently because legislatures typically choose to respond to policy issues in relatively general terms. Legislatures intend that detail will be forthcoming through application. What gaps exist in the general provisions are filled in by the courts (or administrative agencies) as provisions of statutes are applied to specific situations. In some instances, judges find sufficient guidance from legislative records that make intent reasonably clear. Where such clarity does not exist, it is left to the courts to choose from different possible interpretations. Exercise of interpretive power in these situations is one of the ways the courts have come to directly influence the substance of public policy. If a court interprets a law in a way that is unacceptable to the enacting legislature, that body may take "corrective" action and replace the judicial interpretation with language it prefers.

Substantive Due Process (37)

A substantive review focusing on the content of governmental policy and actions. Substantive due process is distinguished from procedural due process, which attends to the means by which policies are executed. Judicial review of the reasonableness of legislative enactments allows the courts to actively intervene in policy judgments more than they could if review were confined to procedural considerations. The use of substantive due process to invalidate economic regulation is illustrated by the Supreme Court's decision in *Lochner v. New York* (198 U.S. 45: 1905). *Lochner* involved an attempt by the State of New York to limit the work week of bakers to 60 hours. The Court held that there is "no reasonable ground for interfering with the liberty of a person or the right of free contract by determining the hours of labor in the occupation of a baker." The Court made a substantive judgment that the regulation of work hours for bakers was sufficiently unreasonable to constitute a denial of due process of law. *See also* DUE PROCESS OF LAW, 14; PROCEDURAL DUE PROCESS, 30.

Significance Use of the substantive due process approach places considerable policy monitoring power in the hands of the courts. In *Meyer v. Nebraska* (262 U.S. 390: 1923), for example, the Supreme Court struck down a statute prohibiting the teaching of a foreign language to any pre-ninth grade student, public or parochial. The Court ruled that the statute was "arbitrary and without reasonable relation to any end within the competency of the State." Substantive due process review also occurs when statutes are stricken for reason of vagueness. When the Court voided a city ordinance in *Coates v. Cincinnati* (402 U.S. 611: 1971), an ordinance that prohibited public annoyance by assemblies of three or more persons standing on public sidewalks, it did so because the ordinance was arbitrary. It conveyed no discernible standards of conduct. Another example of substantive due process is the striking down of state statutes prohibiting abortion. Over the years, guarantees of procedural due process have been invoked by the Supreme Court far more frequently than guarantees relating to substantive due process.

Tort (38)

A private or civil injury to a person or property. An injured party may bring suit, but tort actions do not represent a major portion of civil case filings. Rather, such claims are typically resolved prior to the filing of a lawsuit. The potential for litigation, however, is high since there are so many personal injury situations. A tort action must include the legal obligation of a defendant to a plaintiff, violation of that obligation, and a causal relationship between the defendant's conduct and the injury suffered by the plaintiff. *See also* LITIGATION, 24; SETTLEMENT, 244.

Significance　　A tort is any civil wrong except breach of contract. A lawsuit alleging the negligence of an automobile driver is a tort action, for example. An assault is a tort. So is a trespass. A current tort issue of growing importance involves the liability of governmental units for injury stemming from actions of government employees. As a general rule, governments are not responsible for injuries committed by employees performing purely "governmental functions." The Supreme Court, however, ruled in *Maine v. Thiboutot* (448 U.S. 1: 1980) that suits may be brought for alleged denial of rights under any federal statute under provision of Section 1983 of Title 42 of the United States Code. The decision in *Thiboutot* to allow Section 1983 suits alleging violation of any federal law may prove to have a substantial impact on federal-state relationships. Given the extent to which federal statutes, especially those involving entitlement programs, intertwine with state governmental activities, state officials now become subject to direct legal action as a result of *Thiboutot*. Thus state governments and their officials have become subject to greater tort liability through lawsuits commenced in the federal courts.

Writ (39)

A written order from a court requiring the recipient of the order to do what is commanded. Numerous kinds of writs exist, but they generally are directed either toward commencement or furtherance of a lawsuit, or they require some particular action to be performed. The first of these types of writs is akin to the original writ of practice, which was issued from chancery court. A writ of this kind could, for example, require a civil defendant to repair some injury or appear in court to answer to civil claims. A summons is the kind of writ currently used for this purpose. The second kind of writ may be called a prerogative writ. These are discretionary orders reserved for unusual or extraordinary circumstances. Writs of *mandamus, habeas corpus,* or *certiorari* are among the class of prerogative writs. *See also* CERTIORARI, 261; HABEAS CORPUS, 270; INJUNCTION, 226.

Significance   The issuance of a writ is one of the means by which courts exercise judicial power. There exists a wide range of writs, but they are typically issued to facilitate operation of the judicial process or to enforce a decision rendered within that process. A writ may be issued, for example, to compel a citizen to appear at a judicial proceeding. A writ of *mandamus* directs a public official to perform an official act; it is an affirmative command. Its preventive counterpart is an injunction. When a court entertains a petition for *habeas corpus,* the state is required to appear and justify the detention of an individual. If a person is judged to be in custody improperly, the court can issue a writ of *habeas corpus* ordering the state to release the person. A writ of *certiorari* is used when a court wishes to review an action of an inferior court and orders pertinent records to be delivered. Most of the cases considered by the U.S. Supreme Court are reviewed through *certiorari.*

2. Judicial Organization

Understanding the activities occurring in courts requires a familiarity with the structural organization of the judicial system. Structure involves more than an organizational chart and matters of a technical character. Indeed, the organization of the judicial system has direct consequences on substantive policy and affects the outcomes of the disputes processed by the courts.

The United States has a dual court system with multiple courts in each. That is, we divide the judicial functions between the federal government and the states. Within both the federal and state court systems, jurisdiction—a court's power to act—is divided among several courts. The federal and state systems do overlap geographically, but the courts of each system are structurally separate. The kinds of cases a court may hear is governed by its jurisdiction. Jurisdiction defines whether a case should be heard by federal or state courts. The area of overlap between federal and state courts is small.

The separation of courts into federal and state systems has some noteworthy consequences. Each system has its own structure and operates based on rules established by its own constitutions and statutes. The existence of fifty-one sovereign entities, each operating its own court system, creates some diversity of rules and substantive policy. This autonomy carries over to personnel, and each system has its own court staff. Further, cases do not move from one system to another. Generally, when a case is commenced in a particular court, the courts of that system carry the case through to disposition.

The jurisdiction of a court is defined by federal and state law. Jurisdiction generally assigns power to courts to hear cases based on subject matter, the parties to a suit, the residency of the parties, or the location of a particular incident. The overall jurisdiction of the federal courts extends to essentially three kinds of cases. First, federal courts can hear cases deriving from the U.S. Constitution, from federal statutes, or from treaties. This category of jurisdiction is based on the substantive legal question. Second, federal courts possess jurisdiction for any case involving the federal government or one of its officers or agencies. Third, federal courts may hear diversity cases or conflicts involving citizens of different states or foreign nations. Any issue not fitting these categories falls within the jurisdiction of state courts.

As a general pattern, the court system divides courts into one of two functional categories, trial and appellate. The trial courts deal with questions of fact while the appellate courts review the actions of lower courts and examine questions of law or procedure. By comparison to the state judicial systems, the organization of the federal judiciary is fairly straightforward. An organizational chart of the United States court system is provided in Figure 2-1. The principal trial court in the federal system is the district court. Each state has at least one federal district court, with some having more depending on case demand and population. The district court possesses general jurisdiction, which means the docket contains a wide range of cases. Certain very narrow categories of issues go to a small number of specialized federal courts such as the Court of International Trade.

Structurally sitting atop the district and specialized courts are two levels of federal appellate courts. The intermediate court is the Court of Appeals, which is typically the court providing the first appellate review. The courts of appeals are divided into twelve geographic units known as circuits. All but the circuit for the District of Columbia are made up of several states. A particular court of appeals hears the cases originating in the district courts located in the states of its geographic circuit. The Supreme Court is the other appellate court of the federal system, although it does possess original jurisdiction in certain special cases. The Court has national geographic jurisdiction and may also review cases from the state courts if the cases pose a substantial federal question.

The configuration of courts at the state level varies widely, but a general pattern does emerge. Like its federal counterpart, a state system divides courts between the trial and appellate functions. While some states have as many as ten trial courts, there are usually two basic types. The first is a court of general jurisdiction, which hears a broad range of cases. Typically, these cases involve felony or serious misdemeanor-level criminal charges or civil cases having substantial value at stake. The second category of trial court is the more specialized or limited jurisdiction court. These courts respond to the great numbers of less serious conflicts or focus on a particular area such as money

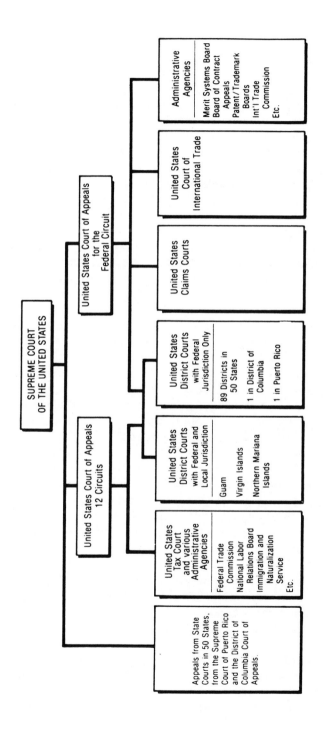

Figure 2-1. The United States Court System

claims against the government, domestic relations, or matters involving juveniles.

Many states have a two-tier appellate process much like the federal system. The intermediate appeals courts provide a first and often final round of review for cases arising from the trial courts. These courts are usually distributed across a state and review cases from the trial courts of their discrete geographic areas. Only a small proportion of cases go beyond these intermediate courts to the courts of last resort, commonly called supreme courts. Some states permit direct appeal to the supreme courts for at least some case categories, while other states first require a ruling from an intermediate court. States that use intermediate appellate courts for screening purposes restrict bypass possibilities and usually allow the supreme courts to set their own dockets; that is, the state supreme court must agree to review the cases that appear before it. Cases not reviewed remain as decided by the intermediate court. In some of the small states, there are no intermediate level appellate courts, and all appeals are routed through the supreme courts. The federal and state systems do converge at the top where the U.S. Supreme Court may review cases from state systems. Any state case reviewed by the U.S. Supreme Court, however, must meet the threshold jurisdictional requirements for a federal case.

Administrative Office of the United States Courts (40)

Agency that manages the daily operations of the federal courts. The Administrative Office of the United States Courts was established by Congress in 1939. The office is an agency of the Judicial Conference of the United States, although the director is selected by the Supreme Court. The administrative office performs basic management duties for the federal courts. It also collects and processes data on federal court activities. The office acts as staff for the judicial conference and functions as a clearinghouse for information obtained by the conference and its many committees. Finally, the office provides liaison among the federal judiciary, the conference, and the legislative and executive branches. The office represents the conference before Congress, conveying budget requests, advocating additional judgeships, and recommending changes in court rules and other matters of consequence to the federal courts. *See also* JUDICIAL CONFERENCE OF THE UNITED STATES, 54.

Significance   The establishment of the Administrative Office of the United States Courts was an outgrowth of President Franklin Roosevelt's criticism that the federal courts were not managed efficiently. Roosevelt proposed that a court administrator be appointed with extensive administrative authority over the federal courts. Because the judiciary wished to retain more control over the courts than the Roosevelt proposal allowed, it offered its own counterproposal for the administrative office. Neither the office nor its director was given any policy making authority, but were to function largely as the administrative arm of the judicial conference. This proposal was adopted, and it remains in effect. Finally, the office has not been altogether successful in securing congressional support for various proposals affecting the court system, especially in its attempts to obtain more money for judicial branch expansion.

Appellate Jurisdiction (41)

The power of a court to review decisions of lower courts. Appellate jurisdiction empowers a superior court to affirm, set aside, or modify a lower court decision. Appellate jurisdiction is conveyed through constitutional or statutory mandate. Federal appellate jurisdiction is granted by Article III of the U.S. Constitution, which states that the Supreme Court possesses such jurisdiction "both as to law and fact, with such exceptions and under such regulations as the Congress shall make." Parallel provisions exist regarding appellate jurisdiction in state judicial systems. Appellate jurisdiction is generally assigned to the courts on two levels. One is an intermediate appellate court that handles the initial appeal. The second level is a superior or supreme court. The United States Court of Appeals is the intermediate appellate court in the federal system, while the United States Supreme Court is the appellate level superior to that. Appellate jurisdiction is distinguished from original jurisdiction. The latter refers to trial courts with authority to hear cases in the first instance. *See also* INTERMEDIATE APPELLATE COURT, 53; ORIGINAL JURISDICTION, 62; UNITED STATES SUPREME COURT, 76; UNITED STATES COURT OF APPEALS, 71.

Significance   The exercise of appellate jurisdiction is undertaken for two basic reasons. First, it allows the process to correct errors that may have occurred at lower levels. Second, it permits appeals courts to interpret constitutions and statutes and set forth the principles by which the law is to be applied. This function clarifies the law and fosters consistent application. An appeals court has several options in reviewing a decision of a lower court. It may *affirm*, which means the lower court result is correct and must stand. It may *modify* the lower court by retaining portions of the decision while changing others. The appellate courts may also *reverse* or *vacate*, which is to set aside the lower court decision. Lower court judgments that are vacated are typically returned or remanded to the court from which they came for further action. Exercise of appellate jurisdiction may be mandatory or discretionary. Where mandated, an appellate court has no option but to review the case. The intermediate appeals courts have mandatory review. Other appeals occur at the discretion of the appellate court. Where review is discretionary, an appeals court may reject application for review. The writ of *certiorari* is a discretionary avenue of access to the United States Supreme Court, for example.

Bankruptcy (42)

A process for freeing persons from some liability for debts. Bankruptcy proceedings are governed by federal law, specifically the Bankruptcy Act and amendments to it. Commencement of the bankruptcy process may come at the initiative of the debtor or a group of creditors. Such proceedings are conducted by bankruptcy courts, which are an arm of the United States district courts. Bankruptcy referees have historically been selected by district court judges. In 1984, Congress enacted new legislation that leaves bankruptcy matters with the district court but provides that bankruptcy judges be appointed to 14-year terms by the court of appeals for the circuit in which the district is located. Some cases under the Bankruptcy Act are handled as "straight" bankruptcy, where a trustee liquidates certain specified assets of the debtor and distributes the proceeds among the creditors. The act also has what are called "rehabilitative" provisions (Chapters 11 and 13), which allow a debtor to reorganize instead of liquidate in hopes of paying off accumulated debts with future earnings under reorganization. The act protects the debtor during the course of such an attempt. *See also* LEGISLATIVE COURT, 59; UNITED STATES DISTRICT COURT, 75.

Significance   Bankruptcy proceedings allow persons or businesses to free themselves from accumulated indebtedness they could never pay off. Such protection has existed in some form since early in American history when a number of states enacted insolvency laws. While states may still legislate in the area, federal law supercedes state law at any point of conflict. Bankruptcy matters under the several federal Bankruptcy Acts (1898, 1933, 1978, and 1984) historically were handled by the U.S. district courts as part of their equity jurisdiction. As the volume of cases grew, district judges delegated these cases to referees. In 1978, Congress sought through the Bankruptcy Reform Act to create an independent bankruptcy court using the Article I power to create legislative courts. This act was struck down by the Supreme Court in *Northern Pipeline Construction Company v. Marathon Pipe Line*

Company (458 U.S. 50: 1982). The Court ruled in this case that the task assigned to bankruptcy judges by the act could only be performed by judges possessing the independence associated with constitutional or Article III-derived courts. A revised version of the law was eventually passed in 1984, which created bankruptcy courts as sub-units of the district courts. Under the law, bankruptcy judges are now selected by the court of appeals and generally have exclusive control over bankruptcy cases. In certain situations, bankruptcy judges submit their findings to district judges who, in turn, enter final judgments. Nonetheless, the role of the bankruptcy judge has broadened, and the change represents dispersing some powers of the district courts to other units.

Circuit Court (43)

A federal court that, until 1911, possessed both original and appellate jurisdiction. The circuit court was created by provision of the Judiciary Act of 1789 and was one of the original components of the federal judicial system. The court was to convene twice a year in each of the districts within its geographic circuit. These courts devoted much of their time to cases of an interstate character. There were three circuit courts initially, with each composed of two Supreme Court justices and one district court judge. Within several years, there were proposals to establish separate circuit court judgeships. The Judiciary Act of 1801 provided for the creation of sixteen new judgeships, elimination of circuit-riding by Supreme Court justices, and expansion of the jurisdiction of both the district and circuit courts. It was this act that provided President John Adams with the opportunity to appoint the famous "midnight judges" at the end of his tenure. This was viewed as a blatantly partisan attempt by the Federalists to retain control of the federal judiciary. The act was repealed at the urging of the Jefferson administration and replaced with the Circuit Court Act of 1802. While circuit-riding was resumed under the act, single district court judges were permitted to conduct circuit court business, a change that gradually reduced the role of the justices on the circuit court. This system remained largely intact until after the Civil War, when the heavy appellate caseload of the Supreme Court prompted system reform. The first response was to shift some of the Supreme Court's appellate caseload to the circuit courts. The problem was not fully solved, however, and in 1891 the Congress established the circuit courts of appeal. These new courts were given appellate jurisdiction to review cases from district courts, a function previously held by the circuit courts. While the circuit courts remained in existence, they had by this action become somewhat redundant and largely obsolete. The new appellate court possessed their appellate jurisdiction, and their trial jurisdiction substantially duplicated that of the district court. As a result, the circuit courts were formally abolished by Congress in 1911. *See also* JUDICIARY ACT OF 1789, 55; UNITED STATES COURT OF APPEALS, 71; UNITED STATES DISTRICT COURT, 75.

Significance   The circuit courts were a major element in the first federal court system. The fundamental political issue of the time was the relative strength of the federal and state levels of government. Under the Articles of Confederation, there had been no federal judiciary. Instead, state courts functioned as both state and federal courts. The Anti-Federalists preferred continuation of such a system under the new Constitution. The issue was not resolved at the Philadelphia Convention, but was left to the first Congress to decide. The Judiciary Act of 1789 resolved the question in favor of an independent federal court system. When Chief Justice John Marshall later asserted the doctrine of federal judiciary supremacy, the impact on American federalism was substantial. As important as the circuit court was to the initial federal system, it was structurally defective from the beginning. Among the main defects was the excessive "circuit-riding" obligation of the Supreme Court justices. It required them to travel to the various circuits twice a year, keeping them on the road for a minimum of nine months a year. The structure also required Supreme Court justices to sit in judgment of their own trial level decisions if they were appealed. These defects first led to modifications of the circuit court's jurisdiction and composition. Failure to fully remedy the design difficulties ultimately prompted Congress to reassign most of its functions and later abolish the court altogether.

Circuit Judicial Council   (44)

Entity designed to maximize the efficiency of federal courts within the geographic circuits. A circuit judicial council consists of the court of appeals judges from the circuit as well as a small number of district court judges. While council policies are typically followed voluntarily, councils are empowered by federal law to order judges within their respective circuits to comply with their directives. The councils watch the district court caseloads and the assignment of judges in an effort to ensure that trial courts remain as current as possible. Each circuit also has its own judicial conference. These circuit conferences are required by law to meet at least once a year. The conferences facilitate discussion of topics of mutual concern among the district court and court of appeals judges in the circuit. *See also* JUDICIAL CONFERENCE OF THE UNITED STATES, 54.

Significance   The circuit judicial councils are located in the middle levels of federal court administration. While certain management benefits do result, two major drawbacks can be identified. First, the councils seem unable to establish and enforce uniform standards. This is true because the councils are drawn from regional geographic bases, which encourages decentralization, autonomy of circuits, and localism. Second, court of appeals judges on the councils do not perceive themselves as administrative overseers of the trial courts. On the contrary, they see themselves as professional colleagues and seldom engage in real supervision.

Concurrent Jurisdiction (45)

Authority of both federal and state courts to hear the same kinds of cases. Where concurrent jurisdiction exists, litigants are able to choose between state or federal courts as the better location to file suit. The most common concurrent jurisdiction situation is the civil action involving citizens of different states. So long as the value of the dispute exceeds $10,000, federal courts have jurisdiction to hear the case. State courts are also empowered to hear such cases. State courts may also hear some cases involving federal law such as civil rights, commerce, or Social Security disputes. There are also crimes that violate both federal and state laws, and these may be prosecuted in courts at either level. Federal and state jurisdiction also intersect in cases involving prisoner petitions from persons convicted of state crimes. These are typically cases where a petitioner is attempting to invoke federal *habeas corpus* provisions. *See also* DIVERSITY JURISDICTION, 47; FEDERALISM, 51; *HABEAS CORPUS*, 270.

Significance   Concurrent jurisdiction permits certain kinds of controversies to be heard by federal or state courts. The presence of concurrent jurisdiction gives plaintiffs in civil actions the opportunity to locate in the court they believe will be most favorable to them because of differences in procedural rules, court caseload, or judicial attitudes. Concurrent jurisdiction also creates the possibility that policy decisions of the state and federal courts will be different. This may occur, for example, when state courts establish and apply legal standards that are more demanding than those used in federal courts. Concurrent jurisdiction is the opposite of exclusive jurisdiction, which specifically assigns an issue only to either a federal or a state court. Occasionally, one may see reference to overlapping jurisdiction. This typically refers to situations where more than one court in the same judicial system may hear the same case. Such overlap will occasionally occur in a state system when a new limited jurisdiction court is added to the system without carefully defining its boundaries with respect to already existing courts. The term concurrent jurisdiction is reserved for those points of overlap between federal and state courts.

Constitutional Court (46)

A court established under language contained in Article III of the federal constitution. Constitutional courts exercise judicial power granted from that article and are limited to the jurisdictional boundaries set forth there. Judges of constitutional courts are protected from decreases in compensation during their service and may hold tenure "during good behavior." Constitutional courts are distinguished from legislative courts, which are established under powers conferred to Congress in Article I. Constitutional courts can only respond if an issue takes the form of a bona fide case or controversy, but may, under terms of the Declaratory Judgments Act of 1934, issue declaratory judgments. Examples of constitutional courts are the U.S. district courts and the U.S. court of appeals. *See also* DECLARATORY JUDGMENT, 265; LEGISLATIVE COURT, 59.

Significance The constitutional courts established under Article III mandate are the most important federal courts. This category of court provides the basic judicial function in the federal system and decides the overwhelming majority of constitutional issues entering the federal courts. These are the courts that were intended from the outset of our constitutional history to receive insulation from the other branches of government to ensure their functional independence and the judicial role in the checks and balances system.

Diversity Jurisdiction (47)

A federal civil case with a plaintiff and a defendant from different states. Diversity jurisdiction deals with the problem of diversity of citizenship. The description of federal court jurisdiction in Article III of the Constitution provides that "federal judicial power shall extend to cases between citizens of different states" or between citizens and aliens. Since the Constitution did not establish inferior federal courts, and since only Congress is permitted to confer such jurisdiction, diversity jurisdiction lies wholly within the control of Congress. Diversity jurisdiction was first conferred upon lower federal courts in the Judiciary Act of 1789, but a $50 controversy had to exist before federal courts could enforce their jurisdiction. The amount in contro-

Significance   Diversity jurisdiction is periodically debated in Congress among those who would abolish it altogether, those who would reduce it dramatically, and those who would retain it as is. Proponents of abolition point to the cost to federal taxpayers, the intervention of federal courts in state law matters, and the redundancy and uncertainty that exist when a dual system of courts addresses the same issues. Opponents of change argue the possibility of home party bias against nonresidents, the value of two-system interaction, and the multiplicity of civil actions the federal courts, for procedural reasons, are better equipped to handle. Diversity jurisdiction exists where there is a diversity of citizenship or where there is an interstate aspect to a legal action. Suits below the dollar threshold that involve no substantial federal issue are conveyed to state courts. Diversity of citizenship cases constitute about 30 percent of the current civil caseload of the U.S. district courts. The potential substantive conflict between federal and state law litigated in federal courts under diversity jurisdiction was minimized by the Supreme Court's decision in *Erie Railroad Company v. Tompkins* (304 U.S. 64: 1938). The Court held that state statutory or common law is always to be applied in diversity cases decided in federal courts and that no general federal common law exists.

Dual System (48)

Refers to the parallel judicial structure located at the federal and state levels. The dual system for courts is an element of the American federalism where authority is divided between the two levels. Generally, the two judicial systems are separate. Each has its own system of courts that performs trial and appellate functions. Once a case begins in either the state or the federal system, it typically remains there. The vast majority of lawsuits are litigated in the state courts. Most criminal prosecutions, domestic matters like divorce actions, and common financial recovery disputes are governed by state law. Federal jurisdiction, on the other hand, is limited to matters involving federal constitutional, statutory, or treaty matters, or cases where the parties are citizens of other countries or different states. Concurrent jurisdiction, which exists for several narrow categories of questions, permits litigants to initiate cases in either federal or state courts. The principal point of linkage between the two court systems is the U.S. Supreme Court. Provided federal jurisdictional requirements are satisfied, decisions of state courts of last resort may be reviewed by the

United States Supreme Court. Otherwise, the two systems are essentially independent. The administration of the two levels of courts is similarly independent. *See also* CONCURRENT JURISDICTION, 45; FEDERALISM, 51; STATE SUPREME COURT, 66; UNITED STATES SUPREME COURT, 76.

Significance The dual court system is a structural manifestation of American federalism. There are two principal consequences of having this dual judicial system. One is that it promotes diverse policies and legal doctrine. While states may have similar constitutional provisions, statutes, and common law traditions, the state courts do not interpret them in exactly the same way. Different local attitudes as well as different social conditions account for some of the variation. Much of the diversity, however, is the product of a nonunified court system. Second, the dual system also provides strategic alternatives to litigants wishing to bring certain kinds of actions. Where jurisdiction is concurrent, a plaintiff may file the case in the court expected to offer more favorable response. The plaintiff in a civil rights action, for example, might find the federal courts a more favorable forum. At the same time, partisan election disputes that meet federal jurisdiction requirements might be more favorably litigated by the locally dominant party in its own state courts.

Equity Jurisdiction (49)

The power of a court to grant relief or remedy to a party seeking court assistance outside the principles of common law. Equity jurisdiction permits judgments based on perceptions of fairness that supplement common law doctrines. Relief is assistance extended by a court to an injured or aggrieved party that is justified by equitable considerations. A remedy is the specific means, such as an injunction, by which a court intervenes to protect a legal right or interest through its equity jurisdiction. In *Brown v. Board of Education II* (349 U.S. 294: 1955), for example, the Supreme Court mandated that lower federal courts issue relief decrees shaped by equitable principles. The Court characterized equity as having a practical flexibility in its approach to constructing remedies. The lower courts were to reconcile public and private needs with decrees framed by perceptions of fairness and justice. A show cause proceeding is a process in equity jurisdiction with the rules of equity applying. A show cause order may be issued by a court to require a party to appear and explain why an action should not take place. Anyone opposed to the action has an opportunity to express his or her position and produce supporting evidence. If the affected party does not appear or present acceptable reasons, the proposed show cause action will take place. The burden of proof is on the party required to show cause. *See also* APPELLATE JURISDICTION, 41; ORIGINAL JURISDICTION, 62.

Significance   Equity jurisdiction is needed because in some cases the law is too rigid or unjust in its application. Equity jurisdiction is the power to hear certain kinds of civil cases using processes developed in the old chancery courts. Equity jurisdiction in the United States is placed in the same courts that possess jurisdiction over statutory and common law. In Great Britain, courts of equity are structurally separate from courts having jurisdiction over legal matters. As states adopted uniform rules of civil procedure, chancery courts disappeared as separate entities in the United States. Considerations of equity in American courts protect against injustices occurring through proper but too rigid application of common law principles or where gaps exist in the common law.

Federal Judicial Center (50)

The research and development mechanism for the federal courts. The Federal Judicial Center was established by Congress in 1967 to perform several kinds of functions. First, the center is heavily involved in research on the federal judicial system. The center has a research division with staff representing various academic disciplines. The division either conducts research itself or contracts with experts outside the center on particular projects. The results of the research are made available to federal judges and court personnel as well as the academic community. The center offers recommendations aimed at the improvement of federal court management. Finally, the center engages in educational activities. In addition to publishing various materials for judicial personnel, the center conducts training programs. Noteworthy are the New Judges Seminars, where various materials are provided to newly appointed federal judges. The seminars are also excellent opportunities for new judges to meet and communicate with other judges. *See also* ADMINISTRATIVE OFFICE OF THE UNITED STATES COURTS, 40; JUDICIAL CONFERENCE OF THE UNITED STATES, 54.

Significance   The Federal Judicial Center is not directly involved in the management of the federal courts. Rather, the center gathers and disseminates information on judicial operations. The center essentially functions as a "think tank." The center is managed by a director who is selected by the chief justice. The center also has an advisory board of directors chaired by the chief justice. The center has a small staff, but also contracts with private parties or other government agencies to conduct research on specific questions.

Federalism (51)

The practice of joining several political entities into a larger political whole while preserving the basic political integrity of each. Federalism divides authority between a central government and constituent unit governments with each level governing the same people and the same territory. In a federal system, authority may be shared and exercised concurrently. More commonly, each level is supreme within its own sphere of authority. A federal system or federation is opposite from a "unitary" system, where the central government possesses sovereignty exclusively. The American federal system is generally defined by the U.S. Constitution. By provision of Article VI, conflicts arising from the exercise of federal and state power are resolved in favor of the central government through the Supremacy Clause. Powers of the national government are specified, and powers not assigned to the federal level are "reserved" for the states by the Tenth Amendment. *See also* CONCURRENT JURISDICTION, 45; DUAL SYSTEM, 48; INCORPORATION, 308.

Significance   In the United States, federalism is a principal component of constitutional democracy. The geographical separation of powers discourages the concentration of power. Federalism permits local matters to be addressed by local rules and practices. At the same time, issues common to all states may be resolved at the national level. It is federalism that produces a dual system of courts in the United States, one at the federal level and one at the state level. Among the consequences of such a structural configuration is that laws and legal doctrines differ from state to state. In other words, independent state judicial systems allow, if not promote, substantive as well as procedural diversity. Provisions of the U.S. Constitution have come to limit some of this diversity. Through a process known as incorporation, most federal Bill of Rights provisions have been extended to the states by means of the due process clause of the Fourteenth Amendment. This means that federal constitutional protections of individual rights limit the actions of government at both the national and state levels.

General Jurisdiction Court (52)

A trial court that has the power to respond to a broad range of issues. The term jurisdiction defines a court's authority, and courts with general jurisdiction may properly hear civil and criminal cases of various kinds as well as act in an appellate capacity in specified situations. U.S. district courts are the federal trial courts of general jurisdiction. Every state judicial system will have one (possibly more) general jurisdiction trial court, typically located at the county level. *See also* JURISDICTION, 56; LIMITED JURISDICTION COURT, 60.

Significance   The general jurisdiction court is the workhorse of any judicial system. A general jurisdiction court is distinct from a court of limited or special jurisdiction, which is a court that entertains a highly particularized docket. Commonly, a court system has multiple courts with a general jurisdiction court and several courts of limited jurisdiction. Rather than categorize under general and limited jurisdiction labels, some characterize courts as either major or minor. A major trial court will hear felony criminal cases, civil cases involving money values in excess of a certain level (usually $10,000), and possibly possess some appellate authority. Minor courts, on the other hand, deal with misdemeanor cases, traffic matters, small claims, and other civil questions of limited monetary value.

Intermediate Appellate Court   (53)

An appeals court structurally located between trial courts and a court of last resort. The jurisdiction and organization of intermediate appellate courts varies from state to state. Typically, these courts review decisions from the general jurisdiction trial courts and specified administrative agencies. A number of states have only one intermediate court, while others, generally the larger states and the federal government, separate their intermediate courts geographically into regions or districts. The federal intermediate appellate court, the U.S. court of appeals, is divided regionally into units known as circuits. There is also some variation in the jurisdiction of the intermediate courts. Some states, for example, authorize one intermediate court to review civil cases, while another hears criminal appeals. The entire membership of an intermediate appeals court may review a case, in which case the court sits *en banc.* More often, however, judges are assigned to panels of three for the review of individual cases. *See also* APPELLATE JURISDICTION, 41; MANDATORY JURISDICTION, 275; UNITED STATES COURT OF APPEALS, 71.

Significance   Intermediate appellate courts have been established to reduce the volume of cases seeking review by courts of last resort. It was to unburden the Supreme Court that Congress established the U.S. court of appeals in 1891. The jurisdiction of most intermediate courts is mandatory; they have no discretion over the cases they review. In the United States, litigants are entitled to one round of appeal. Making review mandatory is intended to satisfy this obligation at the intermediate level. Indigent criminal defendants wishing to exercise the right to one appeal are entitled to assistance of counsel at this level. Establishment of intermediate courts has reduced Supreme Court caseloads, but only modestly and typically not for the long term. Rather, after a period of time, the presence of a new intermediate court tends to prompt the filing of more appeals.

Judicial Conference of the United States (54)

Principal administrative policy making mechanism for the federal judicial system. The Judicial Conference of the United States meets at least twice a year and is composed of the chief justice of the United States Supreme Court, the chief judges of the twelve judicial circuits, and a district judge from each of the circuits. The key function of the conference is the fashioning of rules to govern federal criminal and civil procedure. The conference also discusses such issues as operating budgets, judicial transfers, caseload issues, and other matters of importance to the functioning of the federal judiciary. Most of the work of the conference is conducted through an extensive committee structure. Each committee focuses on a specific topic and offers reports and recommendations to the full conference. The conference also possesses supervisory authority over the Administrative Office of the United States Courts. *See also* ADMINISTRATIVE OFFICE OF THE UNITED STATES COURTS, 40; CIRCUIT JUDICIAL COUNCIL, 44.

Significance The Judicial Conference of the United States allows federal judges to participate in both the development of policy for the federal courts as well as their administration. The number of judges involved in the process is increased substantially through the committee structure. Involvement by so many federal judges enhances the legitimacy of the conference and its activities. At the same time, the participation of large numbers of judges tends to reinforce local influences and keeps the conference from becoming the unifying or centralizing authority many feel is needed to more effectively administer the federal judicial system. Further, notwithstanding the breadth of judicial representation in the conference, it lacks authority to compel compliance with its own policy decisions.

Judiciary Act of 1789 (55)

The federal law that created the lower federal court system. The Judiciary Act of 1789 was based upon the power conveyed to Congress by Article III of the Constitution. The act provided that the Supreme Court would consist of six justices. It also established general jurisdiction trial courts called district courts in each state. Each district court was allocated one judgeship. Three circuit courts were also established, with each composed of two Supreme Court justices and one district court judge. This structuring of the circuit courts required Supreme Court justices to travel to those locations where the courts would sit, a practice known as "riding the circuit." Finally, the act defined in detail the jurisdiction of the newly created courts as well as a number of matters regarding the appellate jurisdiction of the Supreme Court. *See also* CIRCUIT COURT, 43; JUDICIAL REVIEW, 18; UNITED STATES DISTRICT COURT, 75.

Significance The Judiciary Act of 1789 has been changed numerous times since its enactment, but the principal element of the act was its reflection of the position of federal supremacy. That thrust clearly remains. Section 25 of the act, for example, tied state courts directly to federal appellate power, at least when state court judgments failed to recognize federal supremacy. Thus the act represented a political victory for the Federalists. The Judiciary Act of 1801 increased the size of the lower courts to provide the Federalists with a place for the "midnight judges," those judges appointed to the federal courts barely in advance of the incoming Jefferson administration. The act also altered lower-court jurisdiction, solidifying the opportunity for the Federalist-controlled judiciary to withstand the loss of the White House and Congress to the Jeffersonians. The Circuit Court of Appeals Act of 1891 established the courts of appeal and finally ended the "circuit-riding" practice.

Jurisdiction (56)

The power of a court to act, including its authority to hear and decide cases. Jurisdiction defines the boundaries within which a particular court may exercise judicial power. Judicial power is specifically conveyed through the assignment of jurisdiction. The jurisdiction of federal courts is described by Article III of the Constitution in the case of the Supreme Court, and by acts of Congress in the case of the lower federal courts. In either case, federal jurisdiction may extend only to issues that Article III specifies as lying within the judicial power of the United States. Federal judicial power may extend to cases defined in terms of substance and party as well as to cases in law and equity that stem directly from the federal Constitution, federal statutes, or treaties, or to cases that fall into the admiralty and maritime category. Federal judicial power also extends to cases involving specified parties. Regardless of the substance of the case, federal jurisdiction includes actions (1) where the federal government itself is a party; (2) between two or more states; (3) between a state and a citizen of another state; (4) between citizens of different states; (5) between a state and an alien; (6) between a citizen of a state and an alien; and (7) where foreign ambassadors are involved. *See also* APPELLATE JURISDICTION, 41; DIVERSITY JURISDICTION, 47; EQUITY JURISDICTION, 49; ORIGINAL JURISDICTION, 62.

Significance   Jurisdiction conveys authority to courts to act in particular cases, to, in effect, "say the law." Federal court jurisdiction is defined in provisions of the Constitution and federal statutes. Jurisdiction routes particular kinds of issues or parties to the appropriate judicial forum. While the authority of courts may overlap to some degree, the lines of differentiation are usually quite clear. The independence of federal and state court jurisdictions was designed to maintain the respective sovereignty of the two levels of government. State constitutions and statutes usually define the jurisdiction of state courts. They often do so in terms of the amount of money sued for in civil actions or the maximum punishment allowed in criminal actions. Jurisdiction also refers to the location of parties and the court. A court located in a particular county may be the only court that has jurisdiction in a lawsuit involving two residents of that county, or it may be the only court that has jurisdiction to hear a criminal case when the crime occurred within that county. The concept of location of jurisdiction is technically a question of venue, however, and not one of jurisdiction. If the power of a court is questioned on the basis of location, it is usually because the court lacks the proper venue. If an issue is properly before a court, a judgment may be rendered. A judgment is the final ruling of a court on a matter properly before it. The judgment of a court may also be called its decision or decree. On occasion, judgment also refers to the reasoning underlying a decision, but more typically the rationale of a decision is called the opinion. One such judgment may be to dismiss, which is to dispose of a case with no further consideration of it. The court may also issue a stay, which suspends some action or proceeding until a further event takes place.

Justice Department (57)

Executive department responsible for the enforcement of federal laws. The Justice Department was established by Congress in 1870. The head of the department is the Attorney General of the United States, who, by virtue of office, is a member of the president's cabinet.

Prior to 1870, the attorney general held cabinet rank, but did not head an executive department. The principal functions of the Justice Department are to enforce federal laws and provide legal counsel to the various agencies and officers of the federal government. The department houses the solicitor general, who is responsible for conducting all cases before the Supreme Court. The department is divided into a number of divisions. The criminal division is involved in criminal prosecutions, a function typically performed by federal prosecutors known as U.S. attorneys. The department also supervises the federal prison system and federal prisoner parole. The Federal Bureau of Investigation (FBI), the national police agency, and the Drug Enforcement Administration (DEA) are also located in the department. Other divisions include antitrust, civil, tax, and civil rights. The last is designed to provide effective enforcement of federal civil rights laws. *See also* ATTORNEY GENERAL OF THE UNITED STATES, 80; SOLICITOR GENERAL, 117; UNITED STATES ATTORNEY, 120.

Significance   As the federal government assumes a larger law enforcement function, the role of the Justice Department expands accordingly. This is especially evident with respect to new federal initiatives in the area of drug enforcement. The Justice Department is responsible for all federal criminal prosecutions and more generally coordinates appearances by the executive branch in the federal courts. It is through the Justice Department that key law enforcement policy priorities are implemented nationally. If, for example, a presidential administration wishes to direct more resources toward combating drug trafficking or enforcement of civil rights law, the attorney general can direct U.S. attorneys to make such adjustments, and they will occur throughout the country. The Justice Department thus is the medium through which federal enforcement policy is executed at the national level.

Juvenile Court   (58)

State level court that hears matters involving minors. Juvenile courts have jurisdiction over minors accused of criminal conduct and minors who may be the victims of abuse or neglect. Some states place their juvenile jurisdiction in a separate court, while other states create family courts that also hear domestic relations issues. Each state specifies a maximum age for persons under the jurisdiction of juvenile court. The line is typically established as either 16 or 18 years of age. The juvenile courts conduct delinquency hearings to determine if minors are guilty of criminal conduct. Delinquency hearings have become quite formal and in many ways now closely resemble an adult criminal trial. The charges in such proceedings essentially duplicate adult criminal charges, e.g., burglary, auto theft, assault. Juveniles found to be delinquent then have a dispositional hearing where treatment or remedy is determined. In some cases, juveniles may be institutionalized, in which case the outcome resembles a prison sentence for an adult offender. Juvenile court authority over a person terminates when the designated age is reached. If a juvenile has an extensive record, is approaching the age boundary, and is accused of serious criminal conduct, the juvenile court may relinquish jurisdiction and have the person prosecuted as an adult. Juvenile authorities also engage in supervision of those juveniles involved with status offenses. Those are offenses, such as truancy or incorrigibility, that stem from juvenile "status." There are no adult counterparts for such offenses. *See also* LIMITED JURISDICTION COURT, 60; SPECIALIZED COURT, 65.

Significance   The roots of the juvenile court go back to the English legal system. The separate and specialized treatment of juveniles was built on the concept of *parens patriae*—that the state acts as the parent of the country. Accordingly, the state ought to treat juveniles as a benevolent parent rather than in the adversarial manner it treats adults. As a result, juvenile courts were to be nonadversarial in character and juvenile proceedings informal. Juvenile proceedings came to be regarded as civil and largely free from due process expectations. Indeed, the *parens patriae* approach led to insensitivity to legal procedures. The U.S. Supreme Court dramatically modified these practices beginning in the mid-1960s with a series of decisions that extended constitutional protections to juvenile proceedings. The major case was *In re Gault* (378 U.S. 1: 1966), which held that delinquency proceedings that may lead to detention must provide juveniles with access to counsel (appointed counsel in the event of indigency), adequate notification of charges, the right to confront accusers, and the privilege against self-incrimination. The procedural requirements have been formalized to the extent that juvenile courts provide most of the constitutional protections afforded adults, although certain differences remain.

Legislative Court   (59)
A court created by Congress under authority conveyed by Article I of the United States Constitution. A legislative court will function as a court, but it is also designed to perform functions not exclusively judicial in character. These courts are created by Congress in exercise of its powers found in the legislative article of the Constitution (Article I) to "constitute tribunals inferior to the Supreme Court." Legisla-

tive courts are usually established to fulfill particular administrative functions in addition to, or as part of, their assigned judicial responsibilities. Legislative courts include the United States Claims Court, the United States Tax Court, and the United States Court of Military Appeals. In addition, the territorial courts in, for example, Guam were created by Congress to exercise federal jurisdiction as well as to handle matters that normally appear in state courts. These territorial courts were established from powers conveyed to Congress in Article I to govern territories. Legislative courts are distinct from constitutional courts, which are created from power granted to Congress under Article III, the judicial article. *See also* ADVISORY OPINION, 200; CONSTITUTIONAL COURT, 46.

Significance   The creation of legislative courts accomplishes two objectives. First, these courts have highly focused jurisdiction and add a dimension of specialization to the federal judiciary. Second, legislative courts create flexibility in the federal system and relieve the workload of other federal courts, especially the district courts. Unlike constitutional courts, legislative courts may render advisory opinions, which are rulings on legal issues without the presence of a real case. Judges of legislative courts also differ from constitutional court judges in that they do not possess the tenure safeguards enjoyed by Article III judges. While not required to do so, Congress may convey life tenure to legislative court judges. While such protection has been extended to most legislative court judges, territorial court judges serve limited terms. There are limits to congressional authority to establish legislative courts. In 1982, for example, Congress attempted to create a bankruptcy court as a legislative court. The Supreme Court invalidated the proposal in *Northern Pipeline Construction Company v. Marathon Pipeline Company* (450 U.S. 50: 1982), ruling that the nature of the new court's functions required Article III constitutional status.

Limited Jurisdiction Court (60)

Trial court whose authority to act is restricted to particular categories or cases. Limited jurisdiction courts are the opposite of courts possessing general jurisdiction and may be referred to as "minor" trial courts. Courts of limited jurisdiction are found at both the federal and state levels. At the state level, these courts may have such names as district, municipal, metropolitan, magistrate, domestic relations, or justice of the peace courts. Such courts typically have their jurisdiction limited in one of two ways. First, they may hear only criminal or civil cases of a less serious variety. For example, a court may be limited to misdemeanor-level criminal offenses or to civil actions having a money value of less than five or ten thousand dollars. Second, limits may be established by defining the categories of questions a court is empowered to hear. Examples would include small claims, traffic, or juvenile courts. The federal system contains several specialized courts of limited jurisdiction, including the Tax Court and the Court of International Trade. Limited jurisdiction courts tend to serve smaller geographic areas than general jurisdiction courts and are typically quite decentralized. *See also* GENERAL JURISDICTION COURT, 52; SPECIALIZED COURT, 65.

Significance   Upwards of 80 percent of matters litigated in state courts are heard by limited jurisdiction courts. These are high volume courts, and they deal with criminal or civil questions that are not particularly serious. Several consequences stem from this situation. First, limited jurisdiction courts are often criticized as engaging in "short-cut" or "mass production" justice. Given current funding, few courts at this level can afford the luxury of lengthy case-processing time. Virtually no cases at this level are actually tried, and a large number of these are not even contested. Second, where courts of limited jurisdiction are not part of an integrated state system of justice, some judges may have limited formal legal training. Third, the large numbers of courts at this level are substantially responsible for the fragmented character of some state court structures. Finally, these courts are seldom courts "of record." That is, no record is kept of the proceedings. This produces uneven if not haphazard attention to procedural standards. It also means that if a case is appealed from one of these courts, it must be heard again in its entirety (*de novo*). While some of these criticisms are serious, it is clear that courts of limited jurisdiction dispose of the vast bulk of matters entering the American court system.

Military Justice System   (61)
Court established for proceedings involving military personnel. The military justice system is provided for in the Code of Military Justice. The code also defines offenses and punishments, and it sets forth the procedural standards and due process safeguards that apply to defendants. The central element in the system is the court-martial, a tribunal in which prosecution of military personnel accused of crimes takes place. The system also contains a Court of Military Review, which provides automatic review of any court-martial cases where the sentence is confinement of at least a year. In addition, there is the United States Court of Military Appeals, which was established by Congress

to review certain cases from the military justice system and is composed of three civilian judges. Congress recently authorized that cases from the Court of Military Appeals be reviewed by the Supreme Court on direct appeal. *See also* UNITED STATES COURT OF MILITARY APPEALS, 75.

Significance   The military justice system has jurisdiction over American military personnel under virtually any circumstance. It parallels the civilian judiciary and is governed by the Code of Military Justice. Concerns about both the substantive and procedural fairness of the military justice system led Congress to adopt a new and more comprehensive code in 1950. The revised code contains more extensive procedural safeguards than previously and provides to those undergoing court-martial many, though not all, of the constitutional protections afforded civilians. Appellate review was also made more extensive so that no sentence of a court-martial more severe than a year's incarceration may be executed unless the findings and sentence are affirmed by the Court of Military Review. Major issues concerning the military justice system involve questions of military versus civilian jurisdiction and the rights of military defendants.

Original Jurisdiction (62)

The authority of a court initially to hear and determine a legal question. Original jurisdiction is vested with trial courts rather than appellate courts, although Article III extends limited original jurisdiction to the Supreme Court. Various trial courts are assigned specific original jurisdictions, which are defined in terms of subject matter or party. Original jurisdiction in civil cases is often divided on the basis of the monetary value of the action. Cases involving large amounts of money generally are assigned to the principal court of general jurisdiction while lesser amounts typically are given to courts of limited jurisdiction. Similarly, felony-level criminal matters are usually heard by general jurisdiction courts while misdemeanors are adjudicated by the limited jurisdiction courts. A felony is a criminal offense for which punishment may be death or imprisonment for more than a year. A misdemeanor is a minor criminal offense punishable by imprisonment in local jails for up to a year. Since the U.S. District Court is the only trial court of broad jurisdiction in the federal system, it has original jurisdiction over all federal criminal matters. *See also* APPELLATE JURISDICTION, 41; GENERAL JURISDICTION COURT, 52; LIMITED JURISDICTION COURT, 60.

Significance   Original jurisdiction establishes which court will first respond to a case or controversy. The trial courts possess original jurisdiction in the American system and preside over the resolution of all fact disputes. This may occur either by trial or settlement. Original jurisdiction is particularly important because comparatively few cases are appealed from courts of first instance. Appeals typically involve only questions of law as distinct from questions of fact. The latter are essentially the exclusive province of the trial court and are generally resolved with finality by the court of original jurisdiction.

Probate Court (63)

A state court with jurisdiction over wills and estates. Probate courts may also have the power to appoint guardians as well as to perform certain functions with minors. Probate courts operate at the county level and can be found in most of the larger states. Where separate probate courts do not exist, the matters comprising that jurisdiction are absorbed by other state trial courts. Probate courts are occasionally called surrogate courts. The principal concern of probate courts is the proper distribution of assets from an estate. Several interests must be protected. First, there are the interests of beneficiaries. This becomes a difficult problem in the event that a will does not exist. In that event, the probate court must apply the principles of state probate law that govern inheritances. Second, courts must be sure that inheritance taxes have been paid. Finally, creditors must have their claims covered. In most instances, the function of probate courts is largely administrative and does not involve adversary proceedings. *See also* LIMITED JURISDICTION COURT, 60.

Significance Probate courts play a role in estate supervision, a function reflective of the societal interest in protecting property rights. While the probate court is technically a trial court, there is seldom a need for actual fact-finding. Nonetheless, the probate process is prone to delay, especially in situations where disputes do exist. In particular, the process has extensive notice requirements accompanied by lengthy waiting periods. As a result, it is not unusual for the process to take in excess of one year. The substantive law of probate varies widely across the states, and there is an effort being led by the American Bar Association to adopt a uniform and streamlined probate code. Most probate courts are empowered to appoint guardians to administer the affairs of persons determined to be incapable of conducting business for themselves. In some jurisdictions, probate courts supervise the adoption of children and may also engage in supervision of minors.

Small Claims Court (64)

A court designed to provide an accessible and quick forum for the resolution of small claims. Generally, the maximum amount of a small claims court controversy is in the $1000 to 2000 range, and legislatures often adjust the limits to allow for inflation. Small claims courts operate quite differently from the conventional trial process. Neither lawyers nor juries are found in small claims actions. Lawyers are never required and commonly not allowed (except when they represent themselves). The proceedings are quite informal, with the presiding judge acting as the finder of fact. Since standard rules of evidence do not apply, judges may be more assertive in eliciting information. Decisions are generally rendered at the time the cases are heard and orders entered immediately. Appeals stemming from small claims proceedings are heard by general jurisdiction trial courts. In such instances, trials are conducted anew (*de novo*) since small claims courts are not courts of record. *See also* LIMITED JURISDICTION COURT, 60.

Significance Small claims courts are designed to allow rapid and inexpensive processing of small claims. Such courts were initially established to allow consumers and the disadvantaged to help themselves through the court system. The reality is that citizens are not commonly plaintiffs in small claims actions. Rather, actions are brought by retailers and finance companies who find small claims court an efficient and inexpensive method to collect debts. Frequently, representatives of retailers or loan companies bring claims forward in quantity, sometimes 100 or more at a time. For a variety of reasons, plaintiffs prevail in an overwhelming proportion of small claims cases. Often judgments are won by default because the small claims defendant fails to appear. Because this is so, alternatives are being suggested to provide additional avenues for disposition of small claims.

Specialized Court (65)

A court having narrow or highly focused jurisdiction. A specialized court is established to reduce the caseload of general jurisdiction courts and to heighten the expertise of judges working in a highly technical legal area. While specialized courts operate in a manner generally like other trial courts, their narrow focus makes them resemble administrative agencies in some respects. Judges of such courts, for example, tend to adopt strong policy positions as a consequence of the specialized issue focus. Among the specialized courts within the federal court system are the United States Court of International Trade, the United States Claims Court, the United States Tax Court, and the United States Court of Appeals for the Federal Circuit. As with the decisions of other trial courts, appellate review may occur. *See also* LEGISLATIVE COURT, 59; LIMITED JURISDICTION COURT, 60; UNITED STATES COURT OF INTERNATIONAL TRADE, 74.

Significance   Specialized courts have been used at both the federal and state levels to perform narrowly focused, often highly complex functions. Such courts not only relieve general jurisdiction court case-loads, but also become extensions of legislative bodies in dealing with the fine detail of certain policy areas. Another advantage is the expertise of judges who focus so narrowly. Further, diverse legal doctrines are avoided because a single court is making pronouncements rather than having such decisions come from general jurisdiction courts throughout the country. Specialized federal courts may be either constitutional or legislative courts. That is, they may be created by Congress using power conveyed by the Constitution through either the judicial article (Article III) or the legislative article (Article I). The United States Court of International Trade and the United States Court of Appeals for the Federal Circuit are both constitutional courts, while the United States Tax Court and United States Claims Court are legislative courts. Notwithstanding the advantages of specialized courts, legislators are somewhat hesitant to create such courts for fear they fall victim to the influence of those interest groups whose issues appear regularly before specialized courts.

State Supreme Court   (66)

The court of last resort in state judicial systems. Almost every state calls this court the supreme court although several have other names such as the supreme court of appeals. Regardless of name, this court functions as the final appellate authority within the state system. It differs from the United States Supreme Court in that many state supreme court judges are elected rather than appointed. There is some variation in the structure and jurisdiction of state supreme courts. They range in size from five to nine justices, and, like the U.S. Supreme Court, they generally sit *en banc* rather than in panels. The appellate jurisdiction of state supreme courts depends substantially on whether the system contains an intermediate appellate court. Where an intermediate court exists, the supreme court typically possesses extensive discretion over the cases it reviews. This discretionary jurisdiction allows state supreme courts essentially to control substantive law questions on their dockets. If the system does not have an intermediate court, the state supreme court provides the first level appellate function and is often required to review at least certain categories of cases. *See also* DISCRETIONARY JURISDICTION, 266; INTERMEDIATE APPELLATE COURT, 53; UNITED STATES SUPREME COURT, 76.

Significance   State supreme courts have jurisdiction in all matters of state law and act as the final authority on matters involving the interpretation of the state constitution or state statutes. Accordingly, each functions to clarify state law through pronouncement of procedural and substantive principles. Such authority gives state supreme courts an extensive policy making role. In addition, state courts of last resort engage in the review of lower court actions and will, where necessary, correct errors made by inferior courts. Finally, state supreme courts typically have administrative responsibilities over the state judicial system as a whole. This includes basic management of budgetary matters and caseloads. State supreme courts also have authority to issue court rules that govern the operation of state courts, a role that commonly involves oversight of judicial discipline as well.

Territorial Court   (67)
Trial court established by Congress to function in U.S. territories. The territorial courts are a unique form of specialized court, although they are part of the federal district court system. These courts handle all the federal judicial matters in the territories of Guam, Virgin Islands, and the Northern Mariana Islands. Since there are no state or local courts in these territories, these courts possess that jurisdiction as well. The Commonwealth of Puerto Rico operates with its own U.S. district court rather than a territorial court. *See also* LEGISLATIVE COURT, 59; SPECIALIZED COURT, 65; UNITED STATES DISTRICT COURT, 75.

Significance   The territorial courts were created by Congress using authority conveyed in Article IV, Section 3, to "make all needful rules and regulations respecting the territory or other property belonging to the United States." The people living in the territories are American citizens, and the territorial courts provide them with a local system of law virtually identical to that in the United States. Although analogous to district courts, the territorial courts have a local jurisdiction unlike their counterparts in the states. Further, unlike district court judges, territorial court judges do not have life tenure; rather, they are appointed for eight-year terms.

Three-Judge District Court   (68)
A special U.S. district court created to try certain kinds of cases. The

three-judge district court was authorized in 1903 and was designed to hear Sherman Anti-trust and Interstate Commerce Act cases filed by the U.S. attorney general. Soon after, the jurisdiction of this court was expanded to include citizen challenges of the constitutionality of federal law. In such suits, three-judge courts were empowered to issue injunctions against enforcement of the questioned statute. A three-judge district court is established on a per case basis and is dissolved when a particular case is concluded. A three-judge court is typically composed of two district judges and one of the circuit's court of appeals judges. Appeals of decisions of the three-judge courts go directly to the Supreme Court. *See also* SPECIALIZED COURT, 65; UNITED STATES DISTRICT COURT, 75.

Significance   The three-judge district court was intended to take certain cases having unusual policy importance out of the hands of single judges. The direct appeal to the Supreme Court also had the effect of expediting important cases through the judicial process. Prior to 1960, the process worked reasonably well, although it was rarely used. The volume of civil rights litigation began to dramatically increase the number of three-judge courts convened in the 1960s. The demand for such courts increased because such congressional initiatives as the Civil Rights Act of 1964 and Voting Rights Act of 1965 specified use of such courts. The direct appeal feature eventually created severe caseload problems for the Supreme Court, and in 1976 Congress passed legislation limiting the use of three-judge courts to certain kinds of civil rights litigation and legislative apportionment cases.

Unified Court System   (69)

A court system organized around sets of one or two consolidated trial courts. The unified court system has certain structural and administrative characteristics and is an approach designed to reduce the historical fragmentation of state courts. This fragmentation was a consequence of the nineteenth century practice of creating courts with narrow jurisdiction on an *ad hoc* basis. The state government was partially responsible for funding these courts, but often the principal control unit was located at the county or municipal level. The existence of a number of independent courts with blurred and overlapping jurisdictional lines created a fragmented condition. The legal profession, under the lead of Roscoe Pound, sought to counter this fragmentation with a movement for unification. A number of organizations, most notably the American Judicature Society, have continued to urge unification since the early 1900s. The unification proposals generally focus on two elements. The first is the consolidation of trial courts into a single set of state courts. The second involves centralization of court funding and management at the state level. Over the years, unification has taken place in most state judicial systems. *See also* GENERAL JURISDICTION COURT, 52; STATE SUPREME COURT, 66.

Significance   The concept of the unified court system rests on some key propositions. The first is that a fragmented system is highly inefficient. The second relates to control; unification advocates contend that courts are ineffective when control is divided between the state and local levels. A third element is that courts ought to be administered by professionals. While the merits of these arguments seem compelling, opposition to such reform existed because it disturbed the status quo and the groups who were in power under the fragmented system. There was also resistance to loss of control at the local level. Many argued that control over trial courts was more appropriately located at the local level rather than the state level. Currently, there is no real uniformity in the structure of state courts, but the unified system has become the most frequently used model.

United States Claims Court (70)

Hears claims from private parties against the federal government. The Court of Claims was established in 1855 to address claims stemming from war debts. The court was renamed by the Federal Court Improvement Act of 1982. Examples of the kinds of cases currently heard by the claims court include claims arising out of governmental contracts, injuries caused by official negligence, and claims by either civilians or military personnel for back or retirement pay. The court originally possessed appellate jurisdiction over cases coming from the Indian Claims Commission. This appellate authority was reassigned in 1982 to the United States Court of Appeals for the Federal Circuit. A number of cases are referred directly by Congress. The court consists of 16 judges appointed by the president for staggered fifteen-year terms. The judges preside over cases individually except in cases that are congressional referrals. The court is headquartered in Washington, D.C., although it may convene anywhere in the country. *See also* LEGISLATIVE COURT, 59.

Significance   The United States Claims Court provides a means by which claims against the federal government may be resolved. Since the federal government is immune from this kind of suit without its consent, these actions require an unusual process. The claims court is an alternative to congressional consideration of these matters. If the court finds that a party is entitled to an award, however, Congress must specifically appropriate the funds to pay the claim. Final judgments of the claims court may be appealed to the U.S. Court of Appeals for the Federal Circuit.

United States Court of Appeals (71)

The intermediate appellate court of the federal judicial system. The U.S. Court of Appeals was established by Congress in 1891 to provide a first appellate review of cases brought from federal trial courts and certain administrative agencies. The objective was to decrease the number of cases seeking appellate review from the Supreme Court. These courts were first called the circuit courts of appeal. The United States is divided geographically into 12 regions called judicial circuits. Each state is assigned to one of 11 circuits. The twelfth is a separate circuit for the District of Columbia. All appeals from lower courts within one of these regions go to the court of appeals for that circuit. The cases reviewed by the court of appeals come almost exclusively from the U.S. district courts. The exception is the court of appeals in the District of Columbia, where almost half of the cases originate with federal administrative agencies. Accordingly, the types of cases on the dockets will closely reflect the activities of the district courts. Territorial courts are assigned to specific circuits as well. There is also a U.S. Court of Appeals for the Federal Circuit, which has national jurisdiction over highly specialized substantive matters such as patent and copyright issues and over rulings of such agencies as the International Trade Commission and the Merit System Protection Board. *See also* APPELLATE JURISDICTION, 41; CONSTITUTIONAL COURT, 46; INTERMEDIATE APPELLATE COURT, 53; MANDATORY JURISDICTION, 275; UNITED STATES COURT OF APPEALS FOR THE FEDERAL CIRCUIT, 72.

Significance   The United States Court of Appeals reviews issues of law in more than 30,000 cases annually. As an appellate court, the court of appeals engages in law interpretation and has substantial policy impact. The court has no authority to hear a case in the first instance and has mandatory jurisdiction on cases seeking review. That is, it cannot refuse to hear any case seeking appeal. The courts were established by Congress under authority from Article III, making this a constitutional court. It was first empowered to screen cases for the Supreme Court. That screening function has been performed, and only a relatively small proportion of cases decided by the court of appeals seeks further review from the Supreme Court. Although some of the court's cases do proceed to the Supreme Court, the court of appeals is typically the point of both first and final appellate review for most cases. Court of appeals judges are appointed for life by the president with the advice and consent of the Senate. Each circuit has from 4 to 23 permanent judges, depending on case demand. Each of the courts usually reviews cases in divisions or panels of three judges, but will occasionally sit *en banc* with all the judges in the circuit participating.

United States Court of Appeals for the Federal Circuit   (72)

Established in 1982 to function as the successor to the Court of Customs and Patent Appeals. The Court of Appeals for the Federal Circuit is an Article III or constitutional court with national jurisdiction. It hears appeals from district and territorial courts in patent, trademark, and copyright cases. It also hears appeals from final decisions of the United States Claims Court and the United States Court of International Trade. The court may also review administrative rulings of the Patent and Trademark Office, the International Trade Commission, the secretary of commerce, and the Merit System Protection Board. *See also* CONSTITUTIONAL COURT, 46; INTERMEDIATE APPELLATE COURT, 53; UNITED STATES COURT OF APPEALS, 71.

Significance   The U.S. Court of Appeals for the Federal Circuit is similar to the other courts of appeal except that it has a specialized substantive jurisdiction, and it can hear cases from across the country rather than from smaller regions or circuits. Like the other courts of appeal, it sits between a court or agency having original jurisdiction and a higher court. It examines matters of law and procedure, but the substance of the cases is highly specialized. This court has 12 circuit judges appointed by the president with the advice and consent of the Senate. It typically reviews cases with three-judge panels. While the court sits in Washington, D.C., it may hear cases wherever one of the other 12 courts of appeal sits.

United States Court of International Trade   (73)

A specialized court dealing with matters arising out of tariff laws and the imposition of duties and imposts. The court was created in 1980 and replaced the Customs Court. It is composed of a chief judge and eight associates. The judges are appointed by the president with the advice and consent of the Senate. No more than five of the judges may be affiliated with any one political party. The Customs Court was given constitutional status by Congress in 1956; thus the court's judges have life tenure and are protected by the Article III bar against reducing salaries. The court is headquartered in New York City, but it has authority to hear and decide cases at any major port of entry in the United States. A panel of three judges typically sits for each case before the court. Decisions of this court may be appealed to the U.S. Court of Appeals for the Federal Circuit. *See also* LEGISLATIVE COURT, 59; SPECIALIZED COURT, 65.

Significance   The United States Court of International Trade is the trial court for private citizens and corporations to litigate issues involving duties, valuation of imports, and regulations on imported merchandise. The Customs Court Act of 1980 changed the name of the court and defined its jurisdiction over civil cases arising out of import transactions. The court has the power of law and equity comparable to a U.S. district court. This court relieves the district court, which would hear such cases in its absence, from hearing frequent and highly specialized matters involving import classifications and valuations.

United States Court of Military Appeals   **(74)**
A legislative court established in 1950 to review all appeals from military court-martial cases. The Court of Military Appeals consists of three civilian judges appointed by the president for 15-year terms. The court is exclusively an appeals court and reviews criminal cases coming from the military justice system. The court must review decisions involving top-level military personnel (generals or flag officers) and cases where the death penalty is invoked. It retains discretion to review on petition any other case from the military courts. *See also* LEGISLATIVE COURT, 59; MILITARY JUSTICE SYSTEM, 61; SPECIALIZED COURT, 65.

Significance   Establishment of the Court of Military Appeals was an outgrowth of serious concerns about the military justice system. In 1950, Congress enacted the Uniform Code of Military Justice, which integrated many of the rights accorded civilians into the court-martial process. Creation of an appeals court composed exclusively of civilians was an important element in the tightening of the military justice system. Decisions of the United States Court of Military Appeals may be reviewed by the Supreme Court through use of the writ of *habeas corpus*.

United States District Court   **(75)**
The federal trial court of general jurisdiction. District courts are the

primary federal courts of original jurisdiction, disposing of about 300,000 cases per year. The jurisdiction of the district courts, defined pursuant to Article III, includes all federal criminal cases, civil actions arising under the federal Constitution, statutes, treaties if the amount in controversy exceeds $10,000, cases involving citizens of different states (with the same $10,000 minimum), admiralty and maritime cases, and review of certain administrative agency orders. A portion of district court cases (about 15 percent) are criminal, but most criminal prosecutions occur in state courts. The remaining cases on district court dockets are civil. Three categories of civil matters stand out. A large number of cases involve application of the U.S. Constitution or federal statutes. These cases may have substantial public policy consequences. This category includes cases involving protection of civil rights. Second, there are the diversity jurisdiction cases where parties from more than one state are involved. Third are the prisoner petitions. In these cases, state and federal prisoners assert that their imprisonment violates some constitutionally protected right. Most of these cases come through the court's power to issue writs of *habeas corpus.* Congress may alter the jurisdiction of the district courts. All district judges are appointed by the president with the advice and consent of the Senate and possess life tenure. *See also* MAGISTRATE, 103; ORIGINAL JURISDICTION, 62; TERRITORIAL COURT, 67; THREE-JUDGE DISTRICT COURT, 68.

Significance   The United States district courts conduct the great majority of business in the federal judicial system. As a result, they are designed to be the principal points of entry into the federal system. Each state has at least one district court with some of the larger and more populous states having as many as four. There are 89 district courts in the 50 states plus one for the District of Columbia and one for the Commonwealth of Puerto Rico. There are also territorial courts in Guam, the Virgin Islands, and the Northern Mariana Islands. Unlike district court judges, territorial judges serve eight-year terms and handle, in addition to federal matters, local issues that would normally fall to a state court. The district courts vary in size, ranging from one to 30 judges depending on the caseload of the court. Congress may add district court judgeships at its discretion. Currently there are nearly 600 district court judges. Cases decided by the district courts may be appealed to the court of appeals for the appropriate circuit, although certain cases are taken to the U.S. Court of Appeals for the Federal Circuit.

United States Supreme Court (76)
Highest court in the federal judicial system. The Supreme Court is

the only federal court directly established by provision of the judicial article of the U.S. Constitution (Article III). It is principally an appeals court, although it has been assigned original jurisdiction over cases involving ambassadors, consuls, public ministers, and matters where a state is an actual party. The Court exercises appellate jurisdiction "with such exceptions, and under such regulations as the Congress shall make." Appellate jurisdiction has been granted to the Court through various statutes, beginning with the Judiciary Act of 1789. Congress has also conferred rule-making authority to the Court, allowing it to oversee the processes used by the lower federal courts. The Court is headed by the chief justice of the United States, who presides over the eight associate justices. The size of the Court is set by Congress and has ranged from as few as five to as many as ten justices. All justices are nominated for life tenure by the President with the advice and consent of the Senate. *See also* APPELLATE JURISDICTION, 41; *CERTIORARI*, 261; JUDICIAL REVIEW, 18.

Significance   The Supreme Court has extensive power to make or influence the substance of public policy. Through the exercise of its power of judicial review and statutory interpretation, the Court can define the meaning of the Constitution as well as the parameters of legislative, executive, and judicial power. The Supreme Court receives its cases from two principal sources, the United States Court of Appeals and state courts of last resort. With certain exceptions, the Court has control over which cases it reviews. Most cases get to the Court via the writ of *certiorari*, issued wholly at the discretion of at least four of the justices of the Court. Approximately five thousand cases seek review annually, with only about two hundred actually receiving a full review yielding a decision with an opinion.

United States Tax Court   (77)
A specialized judicial agency that hears disputes concerning decisions of the Internal Revenue Service (IRS). The United States Tax Court was established in 1924 as an agency of the executive branch. It was originally called the United States Board of Tax Appeals. Its name and status as an Article I court of record was changed in 1969. The Tax Court has jurisdiction in under- or over-payments of income, gift, and estate tax and holding company surtax cases following rulings made by the IRS. In 1969, the court was given jurisdiction to redetermine excise taxes and penalties. In 1974, the court was granted power to render declaratory judgments relating to retirement plans. The court is composed of 16 judges, but frequently utilizes senior judges and special trial judges who may be assigned at the court's dis-

cretion. Judges are appointed by the president and serve staggered 15-year terms. The court is located in Washington, D.C., but conducts its business throughout the United States. *See also* LEGISLATIVE COURT, 59; SPECIALIZED COURT, 65.

Significance   The United States Tax Court was designed to provide a means of appealing IRS decisions more effectively. Prior to 1969, this court functioned as an administrative agency, but the Tax Reform Act designated the agency an Article I legislative court. The court relieves the district courts from the large number of suits resulting from administration of the tax code. The court is empowered to handle "small" tax claims of under $5,000 through an informal hearing process that expedites disposition of such cases. Except for small tax cases, the decisions of the court are subject to review by the court of appeals. Decisions in the smaller cases do not set legal precedents and cannot be appealed.

3. Judicial Process Personnel

The activities of courts are influenced by the informal and ongoing relationships among those who have a role in daily court operations. The various people who hold positions in the court system may be referred to in the aggregate as the courtroom work group. The work group includes the judges, prosecutors, defense counsel, attorneys appearing in civil cases, and the court support staff. This chapter will present terms and concepts relating to the functions of those in the work group, the ways judicial personnel are recruited, and some characteristics of the legal profession from which many members of the work group come.

The principal roles in the judicial system are performed by attorneys. All attorneys share the common experience of legal education, which usually means graduation from law school. Law school is a socializing process where prospective attorneys learn the law and become familiar with the expectations and practices of the profession. Law students learn the accepted way of resolving conflicts and legal questions; they learn a preferred approach to thinking and problem solving. They also come to embrace concepts of value to the profession such as adherence to legal precedent or previously decided principles of law. While this process does not affect all law students identically, this socialization process is manifest in virtually every activity an attorney eventually undertakes.

A lawyer engages in one or more kinds of activity in the practice of law. Some attorneys are litigators. That is, they actually take cases to court. While only a small proportion of lawyers try cases, this is a highly visible aspect of the profession. More often, attorneys counsel clients on legal options or represent clients before governmental agencies other than courts or in conflict situations with other parties.

The objective in these instances is to comply with regulations or resolve problems before litigation becomes necessary. Lawyers also protect clients' interests by developing needed documentation. Most lawyers pursue a private practice. While the proportion has declined over the past several decades, upwards of three-quarters of all lawyers work in private practice. A small segment of this group work in the very large law firms that represent much of the corporate world. Most private practitioners work by themselves or in small groups or partnerships. A minority of lawyers, about 15 percent, work for the government. This number includes lawyers in the executive and legislative branches as well as those associated with the federal and state judicial systems.

The recruitment of judicial system personnel varies considerably by position. Obtaining assistance of legal counsel is largely a private matter, and selection is made by the client. This is true for virtually all legal services a lawyer may provide, including litigation. Economic resources often determine the selection of an attorney. The Constitution, however, requires assistance of counsel in criminal cases, and local jurisdictions must provide lawyers for those financially unable to retain their own. Attorneys who represent indigent criminal defendants are typically recruited under the auspices of the trial courts of the local jurisdiction. In places where a public defender system is used, trial judges formally select the public defender.

Attorneys representing the public are selected by executive appointment or by election. Most state attorneys general and virtually all local prosecuting attorneys are selected in partisan elections. Several states have the governor appoint the attorney general in much the same way the president appoints the U.S. attorney general. Federal prosecutors, known officially as U.S. attorneys, are also appointed by the president. These appointments are typically conducted on a partisan basis.

The methods used for judicial selection vary more widely. Executive appointment is used for all federal judges with the advice and consent of the Senate. The federal judicial selection process involves more participants than the constitutional provisions might suggest. It also varies depending on the level of the federal court having the vacancy. Several states also use executive appointment as the formally designated selection method. The number is misleadingly low, however, because executive appointment is used in most elective states to fill all unexpired judicial terms. In addition to executive appointment, there are a few states that use a legislative appointment process. More than half the states use elections to select judges, splitting almost equally between partisan and nonpartisan ballots. Finally, there is the

Missouri Plan, which combines gubernatorial appointment, election, and substantial influence by the legal profession.

The judicial selection processes do not differ that markedly in practice. They are all subject to political pressures and state governors tend to play a strong role in the various processes, including the elective, because of the power to fill vacancies that occur before a term expires. While none of the states grant life tenure to judges as the federal system does, incumbents are virtually certain of reelection or reappointment in state systems. In addition, there seems to be no real difference in the kinds of judges selected by the various techniques when compared, for example, on the basis of education or previous judicial experience. If there is a difference in impact, it may be seen in the behavior of judges once they take the bench. There is some evidence that suggests that judges in election states are more attentive to public opinion.

Advice and Consent (78)

Power given the United States Senate to approve treaties and federal appointments. The advice and consent power is conveyed by language in Article II, Section 2, and besides treaties, applies to presidential nominations for "ambassadors, other public ministers and consuls, judges of the Supreme Court, and all other officers of the United States whose appointments are not herein otherwise provided for, and which shall be established by law." Senate consent on treaties requires a two-thirds vote. Confirmation of appointments occurs by simple majority. The Senate's advice and consent role emerged from the Constitutional Convention as a compromise between those who favored executive appointment and those who advocated selection by Congress. Like many of the other compromises struck at the convention, advice and consent was grounded in the checks and balances concept. However, the language of compromise did not resolve all the questions about federal judicial selection. Many argued that judicial appointment was fundamentally a presidential prerogative with the Senate's role a mere formality. The process has been highly political from the outset, and often the preferences of the nominating president and the Senate have not coincided. As a result, almost 25 percent of the nominations for the Supreme Court have not been confirmed by the Senate. Advice and consent allows the Senate to assert political power over the president, but the power is wholly negative and rejection of a presidential nominee does not permit the Senate to propose an alternative. *See also* EXECUTIVE APPOINTMENT, 89; SENATE JUDICIARY COMMITTEE, 115; SENATORIAL COURTESY, 116.

Significance   The advice and consent language of Article II explicitly governs Supreme Court nominees. The Constitution establishes no other federal courts. Rather, it leaves the establishment of inferior federal courts to Congress. This raises questions about whether the advice and consent provisions apply to nominees for those judgeships. Over the years, several practices have developed with respect to nominees for those courts. The most important is senatorial courtesy. The practice applies to nominees for any federal positions in a particular state and requires the president to confer with senators of his or her party from that state before making any nomination. What this normally means is that the Senate member(s) will actually recommend one or more specific names to the president. Failure of the president to accept and appoint such nominees will bring about defeat of the nomination. Senatorial courtesy thus transfers selection prerogatives for particular offices, including U.S. District Court judgeships, from the executive to members of the Senate. The Senate consents or not by a vote of the entire body. The key preliminary work is done by the Senate Judiciary Committee, which gathers information, conducts hearings, and ultimately recommends confirmation or rejection to the Senate. Typically, the committee's recommendation is upheld.

American Bar Association (79)

A voluntary association of lawyers in the United States. The American Bar Association (ABA) was founded in 1878 to improve the legal profession. The initial concern of the ABA was the absence of quality controls on legal education and admission to the profession. The ABA took the lead in tightening accreditation standards for law schools. Demonstration of proficiency by passing a bar examination as a requirement for entry to the profession was also an area where the ABA was active. Its activities eventually were extended beyond professional quality and development to include fostering greater public understanding of the legal system. The main governing body of the ABA is the House of Delegates, but the bulk of the preliminary work of the organization is done through an extensive network of highly specialized sections, divisions, task forces and standing committees. The ABA puts out a number of publications including the *American Bar Association Journal* (monthly) and *Washington Summary* (a weekly newsletter). A variety of affiliated organizations, such as the American Bar Foundation, provide research and publications helpful to the profession. *See also* CODE OF PROFESSIONAL RESPONSIBILITY, 83; SENATE JUDICIARY COMMITTEE, 115; STATE BAR ASSOCIATION, 119.

Significance The American Bar Association is the largest professional association, with membership in excess of 330,000. The ABA works closely with state bar associations in pursuing objectives related to professional competence and responsibility. As the national representative of the profession, the ABA has been effective in its support of proposals aimed at improving the American justice system. For example, it has sought or supported reforms that would improve the provisions of child welfare services and enhance delivery of legal services, especially to those unable to afford it. In general, the ABA is sensitive to procedural issues associated with government operations or policies. In addition, the ABA sets and enforces performance standards for the profession. Contained in the *Code of Professional Responsibility*, which was developed under the auspices of the ABA, are canons of professional conduct and ethics to which all lawyers are expected to subscribe. Failure to do so can bring discipline through state bar associations. The ABA also plays a critical role in the selection process for federal judges. A standing committee of the ABA formally examines each nominee for all federal courts and offers its evaluation to the Senate prior to its discharge of the advice and consent function. The ABA is also occasionally consulted about the qualifications of potential nominees prior to their nomination by the president.

Attorney General of the United States (80)

The cabinet member who heads the Department of Justice. The Attorney General of the United States is the chief law officer at the federal level. The attorney general acts as the principal legal counsel to the president and is responsible for representing the United States in all legal matters. The attorney general has a number of critical executive functions. All federal criminal prosecutions are initiated by the Justice Department through United States Attorneys. The priority assigned to enforcement of particular laws is a judgment of the attorney general. The Justice Department also supervises the federal prison system and the parole of federal prisoners. Also falling under the control of the attorney general are the two principal police agencies at the federal level, the Federal Bureau of Investigation (FBI) and the Drug Enforcement Administration (DEA). The attorney general also possesses substantial discretion in such policy areas as civil rights, immigration, and internal security. Formal opinions by the attorney general on federal questions govern agencies but can be challenged in court. *See also* JUSTICE DEPARTMENT, 57; SOLICITOR GENERAL, 117; STATE ATTORNEY GENERAL, 118; UNITED STATES ATTORNEY, 120.

Significance   The position of attorney general is one of the most powerful in the federal government. The attorney general is a political appointee of the president and is typically a trusted political ally. As head of the Justice Department, the attorney general is in a position to implement a president's program in the politically sensitive area of law enforcement. If, for example, a presidential administration wishes to intensify the war against drug trafficking, the attorney general can make enforcement changes through the DEA and U.S. attorneys. In other words, the Justice Department is the medium through which federal law enforcement policy is executed. The role of the federal government in law enforcement has grown substantially in the 1980s, and the influence of the attorney general has expanded accordingly. Finally, the attorney general plays a key role in federal judicial selection. As part of the presidential administration, the attorney general is personally responsible for identifying appropriate Supreme Court nominees for a president. A deputy is generally assigned responsibility for identification of prospective nominees for the lower federal courts, but the attorney general participates in defining the general characteristics of any candidate. It was, for example, at the direction of first William French Smith and later Edwin Meese that President Ronald Reagan was able to ideologically reshape the lower federal judiciary during his two terms as president.

Bailiff   (81)
A court officer responsible for keeping order in the court. In most local courts, the bailiff is a member of the Sheriff's Department, assigned to a court to provide a uniformed presence during all proceedings. The bailiff also has official custody of the jury, which means he or she insures the security of jury deliberations. The bailiff is usually also responsible for the custody of criminal defendants while they are in court. *See also* COURTROOM WORK GROUP, 87.

Significance   The bailiff is a familiar figure in courts. While the bailiff's functions are largely ministerial, he or she contributes to the smooth conduct of court business. In addition to keeping order, the bailiff also announces the entrance of the judge and often administers the oath to witnesses.

Chief Justice (82)

The highest judicial officer of the federal or state government. The responsibilities of state chief justices vary, but most have substantial administrative duties. The chief justice of the United States functions as the head of the entire federal court system. Some state chief justices perform a similar function in their state courts. Many chief justices also have powers that influence a court's decision making. The chief justice of the United States is illustrative. First, the chief justice is responsible for developing the "discuss" list, a list of those petitions from parties seeking review of their cases. This gives the chief justice the largest though not the exclusive role in determining which cases will be set aside without discussion and which will receive full consideration. Second, the chief justice presides over conference discussion. This allows the chief justice to direct discussion and often shape options for the Court. Third, the chief justice can assign the opinion writing responsibility when he or she is on the majority side. The chief justice of the United States is appointed for life by the president upon consent of the Senate. The chief justice is appointed to the specific position of chief justice; the position is unrelated to seniority. Chief justices of state supreme courts reach those courts by the various selection methods used by the state. Once on the state supreme court, a chief justice is selected by seniority, vote of colleagues, or some rotation scheme. The term of virtually all state chief justices is limited. *See also* STATE SUPREME COURT, 66; UNITED STATES SUPREME COURT, 76.

Significance Chief justices have some formal powers not held by their colleagues. They all enjoy heightened visibility because they hold the position. The influence of any particular chief justice, however, seems to be a function not of additional authority, but rather of the leadership skills the justice brings to the position. Some chief justices possess such skills and have an interest in trying to lead. In addition, a chief justice may sit on a court where colleagues are more receptive to strong leadership. Variations in the leadership performances of chief justices seems to be a product of the interplay of these factors. Chief Justice Earl Warren was a comparatively strong leader largely because of his political instincts and conciliation skills. Chief Justice Warren Burger, on the other hand, was not able to develop the support of his associate justices, and was not as successful a leader. Some chief justices are able to use the opinion assignments to pursue ideological or policy objectives. The opinion in major cases can be as-

81

signed to justices who are ideologically compatible or retained by the chief justice himself or herself. Opinion assignment can be crucial to maintaining the initial majority, or to defining the scope of the ruling. Use of opinion assignments in this way can involve a degree of risk if the chief justice's vote on the merits is intended to retain assignment power. Such action may be viewed as "illegitimate" by associate justices and can undermine the chief justice as court leader.

Code of Professional Responsibility (83)

Rules that govern the conduct of attorneys. The Code of Professional Responsibility was written and is periodically revised by the American Bar Association. The code contains general provisions on ethical conduct as well as more detailed rules that apply to particular situations. The rules contained in the code, also known as the Canons of Professional Ethics, speak to several categories of issues. One category addresses the lawyer-client relationship. Lawyers are admonished to represent their clients "zealously" but within the limits of the law. Another canon urges the exercise of fully independent judgment on behalf of a client. A lawyer is advised to avoid multiple client or business relationships that impair the capacity to make independent professional judgments for a client. Lawyers are also instructed to preserve the confidence of clients. This rule creates the attorney-client "privilege," which prevents lawyers from disclosing at trial the content of communications with a client. The code also speaks to the lawyers' obligation to the public. Attorneys must assist in maintaining the integrity and competence of the profession, in making legal representation as available to the public as possible, and in improving the legal system in general. *See also* AMERICAN BAR ASSOCIATION, 79; LAWYER-CLIENT RELATIONSHIP, 95.

Significance The Code of Professional Responsibility dates back to 1907 with revisions having been made several times since. Provisions of the code, or language closely parelleling the code, have been adopted in every state, typically through order of the state supreme court. There are sanctions for violations of code provisions. Charges of lawyer misconduct are primarily judged by other lawyers. Enforcement of the adopted code language is the responsibility of the state supreme courts, but much of the disciplinary process has been delegated to state bar associations. Special committees of the state bar respond to complaints or grievances filed against particular lawyers. These grievances typically come from clients, but can come from others. Following an investigation, the bar committee may bring formal charges against a lawyer and conduct a hearing. The committee may recommend disciplinary action, including suspension or permanent disbarment. Action on such disciplinary recommendations must be taken by the state supreme court. A wide range of sanctions is available. The least severe is a private reprimand, with suspension or disbarment reserved for serious misconduct. Recent concern about legal ethics and attorney performance has prompted law schools to require courses in legal ethics. In addition, a number of states have established special funds to compensate victims of unethical attorneys.

Court Administrator (84)

A nonjudicial official responsible for the management of a particular court or court system. Court administrators are used at both the federal and state levels to manage the day-to-day work of the courts. This includes such functions as budget preparation, recruitment and supervision of court personnel, and management of the court's docket. The last function is especially important because it involves the movement of cases through the court. At the federal level, the chief justice of the United States formally heads the court system. Power over policy and management matters is vested in the Judicial Conference of the United States and the regional judicial councils. Day-to-day management of the federal courts falls to the Administrative Office of the United States, whose performance is overseen by the judicial conference. Management of state courts is somewhat more complex. At the state level, a state court administrator usually is located within the state supreme court. The state court administrator generally oversees the state judicial system and also engages in data collection and long-range planning. State court systems, however, tend to be decentralized and much of the management of courts occurs at the local level. Most large urban jurisdictions employ court administrators to manage the operations of trial courts. *See also* ADMINISTRATIVE OFFICE OF THE UNITED STATES COURTS, 40; JUDICIAL CONFERENCE OF THE UNITED STATES, 54.

Significance The professional court administrator is a central character in the efforts to improve or "reform" the courts. Judges have historically been responsible for court administration, but many judges lack the specialized management training to administer their courts well, especially in multi-judge urban jurisdictions. One response to the management problem was to designate a chief judge in a jurisdiction as the primary administrative officer. While some chief judges have demonstrated a capacity for managing their courts, this approach does not generally provide adequate administration. Most court clerks do not have the formal training necessary to manage a court satisfactorily. Use of professional administrators is the most creative and effective approach to court management. Indeed, specialized graduate programs in court administration have been established in several major universities throughout the country. At an operational level, however, court administrators can function only if the judges for whom they work delegate sufficient authority to allow them to actually apply their management skills. This is especially troublesome with respect to case scheduling. A new centralized case assignment process, for example, might increase dispositions but be perceived by the judges of the court as impinging on their judicial authority. Notwithstanding problems such as this, jurisdictions continue to use or turn to professional court administrators to manage courts.

Court Clerk (85)

A court officer primarily responsible for maintaining a court's calendar and keeping the records of court proceedings. Court clerks file pleadings and motions and often issue formal writs and process documents of a court. Attorneys communicate with court clerks on all matters related to scheduling. Court clerks also collect fines and court costs in criminal cases. Once judicial proceedings are completed, court clerks are generally responsible for maintaining the evidence introduced in cases. *See also* COURT REPORTER, 86; COURTROOM WORK GROUP, 87.

Significance The court clerk generally handles the management functions necessary for the effective operation of a court. The position of court clerk is part of the trial court structure. The court clerk is either elected by the public or appointed by the chief or senior judge of the court. In the latter instance, the position is usually a reward for political party service. In some states, the county clerk serves as the court clerk. The county clerk is responsible for all legal recordkeeping in the county and simply extends this function to the courts. The court clerk has little policy influence, but does does have an impact on the efficiency and effectiveness of local judicial operations.

Court Reporter (86)

Person responsible for recording court proceedings. Court reporters typically use special stenotype machines to make a verbatim record of all proceedings. Taped recordings are used in some jurisdictions instead of court reporters. Transcripts from stenotype tapes are produced for all cases pursuing some issue on appeal. *See also* COURT CLERK, 85; COURTROOM WORK GROUP, 87.

Significance   Court reporters are court employees and part of the courtroom work group. Court reporters are salaried staff, but are separately compensated for transcribing court records for appeals. It is the transcript of a proceeding that provides the record of asserted mistakes or errors claimed by the party pursuing appeal. For example, if a criminal defendant claims a jury instruction was prejudicial, the transcript of the judge's instruction becomes the focus of appellate court review. In some jurisdictions, the reporter is responsible for the care of physical evidence used in a case. Once the case concludes, ongoing responsibility for the preservation of evidence is transferred to the court clerk.

Courtroom Work Group   (87)
The judicial officers and support personnel who function in the courts on a regular basis. The concept of the courtroom work group is most often found in the literature on the criminal process, but applies to the full range of judicial activities. The principal members of the courtroom work group are the judge, the prosecuting (or plaintiff's) attorney, and counsel for the defense. These three members perform the functions that constitute the essence of the adversary model. In addition, the courtroom work group includes such personnel as the court reporter, court clerk, and bailiff. The work group members are the courthouse "regulars" who operate the processes of the judicial system and make the substantive judgments that determine which cases move through the process and how they emerge at the conclusion. Work groups form because of the ongoing interaction of the regulars. While parties to suits change, the regulars remain a constant. Though the regulars do not all work for the same agencies, each is drawn to cases to perform particular functions. More important, each member of the work group must work with the others; no member can perform in isolation. The work group members come to share similar goals or interests, especially the movement of cases through the judicial system. If the work group members cooperate, they all benefit by heightening case dispositions. In other words, the work group members exist in a relationship of interdependence despite the differences in their individual roles. *See also* BAILIFF, 81; COURT CLERK, 85; COURT REPORTER, 86; DEFENSE ATTORNEY, 88; JUDGE, 91; PROSECUTING ATTORNEY, 110.

Significance   Understanding courtroom work group relationships is essential to understanding how the judicial process operates, particularly with criminal cases. The work group is important in several ways. First, the work group modifies formal authority patterns. Decisions formally assigned to one member become joint decisions. Sentencing, for example, is a judicial function, but judges often accept plea agreements negotiated by the prosecutor and defense attorney. These agreements are likely to contain sentencing considerations. In other cases, judges may defer to the recommendations of prosecutors or probation officers. Second, predictable behaviors are produced by the work group network. Members come to share norms of conduct and performance. This establishes a firm framework within which all interaction takes place. Cooperation and trust are fostered in this way. Third, the work group socializes newcomers to the expectations of the members. In this way, the overall system is maintained. Enforcement of work group norms is informal but effective. Rewards and sanctions are such that most work group members find it imperative to comply.

Defense Attorney (88)

A lawyer who represents the defendant in criminal or civil cases. A defense attorney responds to the charges or claims of the other party and offers evidence and reasons that the prosecution or plaintiff should not prevail. While defense attorneys do appear in civil cases, the term defense attorney or defense counsel is generally used in referring to that small portion of lawyers who represent persons accused of crimes. Defense lawyers act both to represent and protect the defendant's interests and to advise the accused of legal and strategic options. Representation includes advocacy, which manifests itself in several ways. Defense attorneys must protect a defendant's legal rights. This may include filing motions challenging the sufficiency of searches or custodial interrogations. Advocacy also involves aggressive challenging of the prosecutor's case. Prosecution witnesses are cross-examined during trial in an attempt to diminish their impact on the defendant. In some instances, the defense will not only attempt to react to the state's case, but alternatively advance an affirmative defense as well. The defense attorney's role as counselor involves both advice on legal points and the informal norms of the local criminal justice community. Most defense attorneys are familiar with assistant prosecutors and local trial judges and frame strategies based on what they know of established patterns of behavior. This may be of particular importance in developing a negotiating strategy. Few criminal cases are actually tried, and few defendants walk away from criminal charges. The defense lawyer must typically resolve a case by negotiation, evaluating what the state can prove and seeking an outcome that might mitigate damage to the defendant. Winning in such situations is measured by avoiding long periods of incarceration rather than securing an outright acquittal. *See also* ASSISTANCE OF COUNSEL, 126; PROSECUTING ATTORNEY, 110; PUBLIC DEFENDER, 111.

Significance Assistance of defense counsel in criminal cases was seen as a fundamental right and was included in the Sixth Amendment to the United States Constitution. It was viewed as essential that a person charged with a crime be able to access the "guiding hand of counsel." The counsel protection was initially viewed as meaning that the state could not interfere with an accused's desire to consult counsel. Beginning in the 1930s, this protection was expanded in several ways. First, the Supreme Court developed an interpretation of the Sixth Amendment that held the states responsible for providing indigent defendants with lawyers. This requirement prompted establishment of public defender systems in a number of jurisdictions. Appointment of private lawyers on a case-by-case basis was used in the remaining jurisdictions. Second, the Court began to see many steps in the criminal process occurring both before and after the trial as stages "critical" to a defendant's interests. Thus counsel was required at such stages as station house interrogations, arraignments, and sentencing. Finally, the Court required that the right to access counsel be fully explained to the accused. The performance of defense counsel is key to the sufficiency of justice in our adversary system. The Supreme Court decisions expanding the scope of constitutional protections clearly underscore the fundamental role of defense attorneys.

Executive Appointment (89)

Nomination of public officials by the president or a state's governor. Executive appointment is established for federal judicial selection by language in Article II, Section 2, which requires the president to nominate justices of the Supreme Court among other officials. A president's nominee does not become a federal judge until confirmed by the U.S. Senate. Presidents may fill judicial vacancies while the Senate is in recess, but the judge must be confirmed by the Senate when it reconvenes. Executive appointment is also one of the methods of selecting judges of state courts. As at the federal level, most executive (gubernatorial) nominees must be confirmed by a legislative body or special review committee of some kind. In states that use elections as the principal method of judicial selection, governors are permitted to make interim appointments to fill vacancies. Executive appointment of judges is highly political. Presidents and governors alike tend to nominate persons of their own party or who are ideologically compatible. The competence of a prospective nominee is also important, and both presidents and governors take into consideration the evaluations conducted by screening committees established by the American Bar Association or state bar associations. *See also* ADVICE AND CONSENT, 78; INTERIM APPOINTMENT, 90; NOMINATING CRITERIA, 106; RECESS APPOINTMENT, 112; SENATORIAL COURTESY, 116.

Significance   Executive appointment of judges is a carryover from the colonial period. Delegates at the Constitutional Convention eventually compromised between executive and legislative appointment by adding the requirement of Senate consent to complete federal judicial selection. Presidents generally succeed when nominating justices to the U.S. Supreme Court, although more than 20 percent of the nominees have not been confirmed. The practice of senatorial courtesy applies for selection of lower federal court judges, particularly the U.S. district court. Senatorial courtesy transfers much of the nominating initiative to a home-state senator when he or she shares the president's party affiliation. With life tenure for federal judges, there are no interim judicial appointments. Presidents can make recess appointments, however. Executive appointment at the state level is somewhat more involved. Most states turned from executive appointment to popular election during the Jacksonian period. Despite various "reform" efforts, election remains the method of judicial selection in a majority of states. Only seven states use executive appointment as their formally designated method of choosing judges. However, executive appointments are common in every state that uses elections because of interim appointments. In an elective state, if a judge cannot complete a term, the governor appoints a successor who serves until the next general election, when he or she may run as an incumbent. Judicial terms tend to be long and vacancies frequent, so governors make many interim appointments. Furthermore, because incumbent judges are seldom defeated in elections, interim appointees usually retain judgeships. Thus, it can be said of many elective states that most of their judges first attained the bench through gubernatorial appointment rather than election. Governors also exercise nominating prerogatives in states that use "merit" selection, although choices are confined to a list of candidates recommended by screening commissions.

Interim Appointment   (90)

Process by which state judicial vacancies are filled between elections. An interim appointment is made by the state's governor and occurs only in states that use election as the formally adopted method of judicial selection. Interim appointments are highly partisan, although most governors take into account how prospective nominees are viewed by the legal profession. Judges appointed on an interim basis take office immediately upon appointment and possess full judicial power. In most states, however, these judges must face election either for a full term or the balance of the unexpired term at the next general election. *See also* EXECUTIVE APPOINTMENT, 89; RECESS APPOINTMENT, 112.

Significance   The interim appointment seriously compromises elective selection of judges. It allows governors to appoint many (if not most) judges in a state and gives governors a dominant role in judicial selection. This is true for at least two reasons. First, the opportunity for governors to make interim appointments is high. Judicial terms tend to be lengthy, usually six or eight years. The longer the term, the greater the likelihood of vacancy. Second, once interim judges are appointed, they enjoy all the advantages of incumbency. Data show they tend to retain these judgeships when elections do take place. Indeed, most of the appointed judges are not even opposed in the first election. As a consequence, high proportions of judges in election states are likely to have first attained the bench by appointment and not election. For the twenty-two states that elect at least some of their judges, it is necessary to recognize the overlap of elective and appointive selection techniques. Interim appointments do not occur at the federal level.

Judge (91)

An officer who presides over a court. A judge is the principal member of a court and is responsible for controlling the proceedings that take place there. The functions of judges vary by the kinds of courts on which they sit. Appellate judges, for example, review the record of proceedings at the trial level. The critical power of appellate judges is making decisions on rules of law. It is a decision making function exercised without assistance from others, such as executive branch officials or juries. The functions of trial judges are more diverse. Trial judges spend a substantial part of their time presiding over trials. Such trials are typically conducted with a jury, so the judge's role often is to supervise these proceedings rather than actually render a decision on the merits of the case. This function includes such tasks as applying rules of evidence, instructing juries, and maintaining order in the court. Judges perform these functions in trials without juries, but must act as fact-finder as well. While trials consume a great deal of time, very few cases are actually tried. A second function of trial judges is to facilitate settlement of disputes without having to go to trial. Often judges have pretrial conferences or use other methods of dispute resolution to promote agreements between the parties. Finally, trial judges perform various administrative functions. Generally, judges are responsible for the management of their courts. This involves preparing budget requests, recruitment of personnel, and supervision of court facilities. Judges are also responsible for managing case flow in their courts, a problem of major dimensions throughout the country. In many jurisdictions, the demands are sufficiently large and complex that professional court administrators are delegated many of these functions. *See also* COURT ADMINISTRATOR, 84; COURTROOM WORK GROUP, 87; DISCRETION, 140; MAGISTRATE, 103.

Significance Judges exercise discretion at a number of points in the legal process. In doing so, judges must make many subjective judgments. As a member of the courtroom work group, judges are influenced by other process participants. Nonetheless, judges are perceived as the most prestigious members of the work group and can ultimately make their own decisions if they choose. This independence is particularly evident in bail and sentence determinations. While rules governing pretrial release have been established by legislatures and court decisions, most judges develop operating practices based on their own perceptions of the functions of pretrial release or detention, the seriousness of the offense, and the defendant's prior record. It is fairly common that individual judges fashion their own bail rate schedules. Similarly, judges possess substantial discretion in criminal sentencing. Sentencing discretion may, however, be limited by the use of state guidelines that reduce or eliminate sentencing options. On balance, however, judges retain enough discretion to produce measurable disparities in sentences imposed. The differences prompt defense attorneys to attempt to "judge shop" in multi-judge courts. By using various procedural tactics, it may be possible to maneuver cases to get before a judge who is seen as more favorable. Thus, while the judge is only one member of the courtroom work group, he or she is located at the core of the judicial decision process.

Judicial Accountability (92)

The view that judges must be accountable to the public they serve. Judicial accountability becomes a critical issue in the choice of judicial selection methods. If accountability is assigned high priority, selection systems are chosen that allow the public to regularly evaluate judicial performance. On the other hand, if judicial independence is given priority, selection systems will be chosen that attempt to insulate judges from popular control or political influence. The framers of the U.S. Constitution sought to foster judicial independence. While the executive and legislative branches are involved in selection, federal judges are given independence by provisions of Article III, which grants life tenure and prohibits reduction of compensation. Most states used executive or legislative appointment selection methods until the 1830s. The election of 1828, however, brought Andrew Jackson to the presidency. With him came a desire for increasing popular control over all public officials. Independence, especially of judges, became less desirable. As a consequence, many states turned to partisan elections as the principal method of judicial selection. When parties themselves began to interfere with the exercise of popular control, a number of states turned to nonpartisan elections. The priority of accountability remained, however. One further reform came with "merit" selection, a method now in place in twenty states (at least for appellate courts if not all courts). However, retention elections are a principal component of the plan. Thus, even states wishing to depoliticize judicial selection with the "merit" approach embrace the priority of accountability. *See also* INTERIM APPOINTMENT, 90; JUDICIAL INDEPENDENCE, 93; MISSOURI PLAN, 104; NONPARTISAN ELECTION, 107; PARTISAN ELECTION, 108.

Significance   Judicial accountability can be achieved in more than one way. The other governmental branches, for example, may make courts indirectly accountable to the public. The appointive selection processes create some of these indirect controls. Similarly, if courts consistently make policy decisions that are incompatible with public sentiment, such "court-curbing" initiatives as scaling back on jurisdiction could occur. The technique most often advanced to provide direct control by the public is the election process. This has been the approach of preference among an overwhelming majority of the states; the public plays the central role in selecting and/or retaining judges. Elections, however, are not quite as effective at creating accountability as intended. This is true because judicial elections are typically not competitive (often not contested), judicial terms are long and elections infrequent, the public seldom has much interest in judicial elections, and voter turnout is generally very low. As a result, accountability in elective states is more often produced through the politics of the interim appointment process rather than by direct public participation in selection.

Judicial Independence   (93)

Extent to which judges are free from political pressure or control. Judicial independence is desirable because it allows judges to render decisions without fear of reprisal, insulating them from outside influences. Judicial independence may be fostered in a number of ways. One of the most important is to avoid judicial selection systems that feature popular participation. Judicial independence was a priority in structuring the federal courts. Not only are federal judges appointed rather than elected, but they also enjoy life tenure once confirmed. With life tenure, federal judges are never subject to popular control. Judicial independence is also furthered in ways not related to selection methods. Judicial immunity, for example, protects judges from civil suits arising out of actions taken in their official capacity as judges. It was felt that threat of civil suit might intimidate judges, and that the public interest would be best served by having judges who could function without fear of consequences stemming from their judicial conduct. The provision in Article III that protects the salaries of federal judges is similarly aimed at furthering judicial independence. *See also* JUDICIAL ACCOUNTABILITY, 92; JUDICIAL IMMUNITY, 17; LIFE TENURE, 102.

Significance   One of the central issues in choosing judges is whether a selection process furthers the end of judicial independence or judicial accountability. Most Western political systems have chosen selection methods that advance judicial independence. This was also the pattern in the United States for the first several decades of our history. With Andrew Jackson came a heightened interest in popular control of public officials, including judges. Many of the states that had previously used either executive or legislative appointment methods of judicial selection switched to partisan elections. In addition, limited terms of office were established for most judgeships, giving the electorate frequent opportunity to exercise control. While some states have subsequently moved to nonpartisan elections or some form of the Missouri Plan, the priority in virtually every state has remained on judicial accountability to the electorate. Federal judges, on the other hand, remain insulated from direct popular control. The federal judiciary is, of course, subject to the political dynamics associated with the principles of separation of power and checks and balances, but the federal judicial selection process is designed, in a general sense, to feature judicial independence.

Law Clerk (94)

A young lawyer who provides key support services for a judge. Law clerks function at all levels of the judiciary, but are most important at the appellate level. Illustrative are the several functions law clerks perform for the justices of the U.S. Supreme Court. The most critical is the screening of petitions from parties seeking review of their cases by the Court. The law clerks summarize the information in the petitions and court records, an invaluable function given the number of cases seeking review. Law clerks also do legal research on the issues contained in the cases selected for review. Law clerks are often given responsibility for drafting the opinions that accompany the Court's decisions. Each of the nine Supreme Court justices has three or four law clerks. The clerks are usually recent graduates of prestigious law schools. Law clerks generally have served as clerks with a lower federal court prior to appointment with the Supreme Court. Law clerks remain with a justice only a year or two before moving on. *See also* JUDGE, 91.

Significance   The impact of law clerks on the decision making of Supreme Court justices is considerable, but it varies with each justice. Some justices delegate a great deal of work to law clerks while other justices retain a greater amount for their own attention. It is clear, however, that law clerks have an impact in two important ways. First, justices depend on law clerks to screen requests for review of cases by the court. The sheer volume of cases precludes the justices from screening them all. Justice Stevens, for example, has his law clerks review all the petitions and pass on to him only the most substantial ones. He estimates this to be less than 25 percent of the total number of petitions. Other justices personally review greater numbers of petitions themselves, but consult extensively with their law clerks as they do so. Second, the availability of law clerks to outline or draft opinions encourages justices to file greater numbers of concurring or dissenting opinions. Furthermore, these individual opinions are likely to be more comprehensive and complex because of the availability of such high quality legal assistance.

Lawyer-Client Relationship   (95)

The interaction between an attorney and his or her client. The lawyer-client relationship is critical because the attorney represents the interests of another person. Clients depend on attorneys to make sound assessments and take appropriate action to safeguard their legal position. The ability of clients to make sure lawyers serve their interests varies. The one-time client, perhaps a criminal defendant, is in the least favorable position. Such a client is likely to have little legal knowledge and is in a poor position to evaluate a lawyer's performance. In addition, the one-time client does not constitute a substantial part of the lawyer's income and has little economic leverage. The corporate client, on the other hand, has greater control, especially the client who retains counsel on a long-term basis. Problems stemming from the lawyer-client relationship most often involve an attorney's competency and ethics. These are matters covered in the performance standards adopted by each state and applicable to every practicing attorney in that state. These standards closely parallel the canons of conduct contained in the American Bar Association's Code of Professional Responsibility. *See also* CODE OF PROFESSIONAL RESPONSIBILITY, 83.

Significance   The lawyer-client relationship directly affects lawyer performance. When clients delegate legal tasks to a lawyer, they expect competent performance. Licensure requirements that include completing law school and passing the bar examination are aimed at producing competent practitioners. Recognition of specialties through certification programs is also in place in many states. Canons of professional ethics also address competency and other representational issues. Lawyers are expected to exercise fully independent professional judgment on behalf of a client, and lawyers are directed to preserve the confidentiality of the attorney-client relationship. Attorney-client privilege is a rule of evidence that allows an attorney to refuse to testify about communications with a client. The lawyer-client relationship may also be affected by unethical or dishonest conduct by an attorney. In such a situation, a client may pursue a criminal complaint or bring a malpractice action against the lawyer. A client may also attempt to initiate sanctions available under processes adopted by state supreme courts. Following a hearing, disciplinary action may be taken by the state supreme court.

Legal Clinic   **(96)**
A law office that performs routine legal services at discount fees. Legal clinics largely serve middle-income clients who need legal assistance with wills or divorces. Clinics depend on high volume to be successful, and they engage heavily in media advertising to reach a wide clientele. Law clinics began to appear in the mid-1970s after the U.S. Supreme Court struck down many restrictions on lawyer advertising in the case of *Bates v. State Bar of Arizona* (433 U.S. 350: 1977). Removal of restrictions permitted clinics to advertise widely for prospective clients. Beyond volume, key to the financial success of legal clinics is efficiency. Greater efficiency comes from handling only certain kinds of cases, usually those that are quite straightforward. The economy of volume and efficiency allows clinics to charge lower fees. The low fees, in turn, provide the market appeal necessary to attract volume. *See also* LEGAL INSURANCE, 98.

Significance   Legal clinics attempt to draw clients from a population that would probably not use lawyers from the more traditional practices. Like legal insurance, legal clinics have made professional services more widely accessible, particularly to the economic middle class. Many are critical of the clinic approach to the marketing of legal services and are skeptical about the quality of services rendered. Advertising aside, concerns about quality may be misplaced. Legal clinics largely confine themselves to several particular kinds of common legal problems. It appears that an efficient, high volume approach is possible without compromising the quality of service.

Legal Education   **(97)**
Training required to prepare an individual to practice law. Legal education for most persons now entering the profession of law involves completing law school. This is a relatively recent development. Well into the twentieth century, prospective lawyers learned the law largely through apprenticeship. Most aspiring attorneys trained by clerking for a practicing lawyer. When they felt sufficiently prepared, they would seek admission to the bar before a local court. While law schools existed, they represented a seldom chosen path to the legal profession. Law schools became a more accepted option toward the end of the nineteenth century with the adoption of the case method of teaching law. Studying the underlying principles in appellate court cases made the study of law similar to other academic disciplines, and law schools connected to large universities began to appear more frequently. Not all law schools were of high quality, and the American Bar Association helped establish the American Association of Law Schools as an accrediting agency. Entrance standards for law schools were elevated as part of this process. These changes not only improved the quality of legal training, but produced greater uniformity of standards among the states. Currently, virtually every state requires graduation from an accredited law school as a prerequisite for taking the bar examination. *See also* AMERICAN BAR ASSOCIATION, 79; LEGAL PROFESSION, 99.

Significance   The legal education received from most law schools covers similar content. The curricula generally feature courses on such topics as contracts, criminal procedure, and constitutional law. The basis of study in these courses are appellate court opinions. The objective of these courses is to convey substantive principles of law as well as appropriate techniques of legal analysis. Some are critical of law school curricula, asserting that law students receive less practical preparation than is necessary to practice law. In response, a number of law schools have added clinical programs that allow students to gain some experience in local courts and in conducting negotiations on behalf of clients. The law school experience is a socializing process for prospective lawyers. Students learn to approach and solve problems in a particular way; they come to think in a similar way. Attitudes and values are also affected. Law students learn, for example, that use of nontraditional or unconventional approaches are generally unsuccessful. Law students also come to learn that particular specializations and association with large law firms carry the greatest rewards both in terms of professional status and income.

Legal Insurance (98)

Plans that allow persons to prepay legal services. Legal insurance plans are similar in design to insurance programs for medical services. Legal insurance may be available as part of an employee benefit plan, although persons may individually subscribe as well. The plans that are available vary considerably, but most entitle subscribers to a specific amount of attorney time annually. Insured persons are either able to consult any attorney of their choice or select a lawyer from a specified group. Current estimates indicate that between five and ten million people are covered by legal insurance plans in the United States. *See also* LEGAL CLINIC, 96; LEGAL SERVICES CORPORATION, 100.

Significance Legal insurance plans were devised to improve access of the nonindigent to legal services. Such insurance plans are not governmental programs, but rather come exclusively from private insurance companies. Persons who subscribe as individuals utilize plans more fully than do persons whose plans are provided as a job benefit. As a rule, these plans are used to respond to such legal problems as divorce, child custody and support, and wills rather than business matters. Legal insurance plans have been reasonably well received, although people generally attach less urgency to prepaid legal services than to medical insurance. At the same time, legal insurance represents one method by which the economic middle class can gain greater access to legal services.

Legal Profession (99)

Persons who are authorized to practice law. The legal profession consists of approximately 650,000 licensed attorneys. Generally, an attorney is a person appointed to act on another's behalf. The services performed by attorneys for their clients can be grouped into several broad categories. Lawyers act as official representatives of their clients. This may involve representation in court, but more often in other settings. An attorney may, for example, represent a client before a government agency to obtain a favorable outcome on a matter involving taxes or a local ordinance. If actual litigation develops, an attorney must be prepared to represent the interests of a client at a hearing or at trial. An attorney also frequently pursues settlements to disputes. Such settlements are typically negotiated rather than litigated. Negotiation is an activity common to the effective representation of both civil and criminal clients. Lawyers also provide clients with advice. That is, they counsel clients as to the actions they may take to best protect their interests. Finally, members of the legal profession prepare documentation for their clients. Documents such as contracts and wills secure the interests of clients into the future. *See also* AMERICAN BAR ASSOCIATION, 79; LITIGATION, 24; PRIVATE PRACTICE, 109.

Significance   The members of the legal profession are the central group in the administration of civil and criminal justice. Members of the legal profession are the only ones authorized to practice law either in or out of court. Persons must be admitted to the bar of a state before they can actually practice law there. Each state sets its own standards, but there are some common requirements. A prospective lawyer must graduate from a law school, pass a test known as a bar exam, and possess solid "moral character." Admission to the bar does not automatically authorize an attorney to practice in another state. While reciprocity does exist for many, persons may be required to take a state's bar exam as a condition of practicing in that state. Federal courts set federal standards. Although more stringent requirements do exist in some federal districts, a lawyer licensed in a state is typically able to practice before federal courts. The interests of the legal profession are generally promoted by bar associations, organizations established at the national, state, and local levels. Bar associations are interested in the economic well-being of attorneys, but they are also dedicated to high standards in the training of lawyers and legal ethics. Bar associations are involved in attempts to improve the legal services available to the public. Ten to fifteen percent of the legal profession practice law as salaried employees of government agencies, and another ten to fifteen percent are employed by private corporations. The remaining seventy percent are engaged in some form of private practice. A private practitioner may operate alone or in association with one or more other lawyers. Approximately fifteen percent of attorneys in private practice are members of firms with 20 or more lawyers.

Legal Services Corporation (100)

Federal agency established to underwrite some of the costs of legal counsel for the poor in noncriminal matters. Funding for legal aid to the poor was initially provided through the Office of Economic Opportunity (OEO). As OEO's poverty programs were eliminated in the 1970s, Congress created the Legal Services Corporation in 1974 to maintain at least some access to legal assistance for the poor. The corporation does not do legal work itself. Rather, it contracts with individual attorneys, law firms, organizations, and local governmental agencies to represent eligible clients. The corporation then funds those providing legal services through a grant process. Eligibility for legal services is based in part on income levels established by the corporation's governing board. Eligibility criteria are sensitive to several factors, including number of dependents and regional cost-of-living differences. In addition, the applicant for aid must have the kind of legal problem the local attorney is able to handle. A number of matters may be eligible for assistance, but most cases involve domestic matters, problems with government benefit programs, personal finances, and housing. *See also* LEGAL CLINIC, 96.

Significance The Legal Services Corporation was an outgrowth of the Johnson Administration's war on poverty in the 1960s. Its OEO forerunner was established at the time the Supreme Court was extending the constitutional protection of counsel to the indigent in criminal matters. It was the view of Congress that the poor needed legal representation in civil matters as well. At that time, the only civil representation for the poor was provided by local legal aid societies. These societies did what they could with volunteer attorneys, but invariably met only a small fraction of the need. Legal services available under the OEO program were often the means of social activism. Congress sought to prevent this when it created the Legal Services Corporation in 1974. Restrictions have been placed on the activities of attorneys associated with the corporation as well as the kinds of cases that can be accepted by funded lawyers. Various challenges to policies and agency actions have been prohibited, for example. Under the Reagan Administration, which sought to eliminate the corporation altogether, funding was decreased. In addition, Reagan appointed persons to the corporation's governing board who supported restricting its role. Nonetheless, the corporation has increased availability of legal services for the poor and remains a relatively visible means of providing counsel in civil matters. The need remains substantial, and in addition to counsel available through the corporation, other legal services can be obtained from locally funded agencies and from lawyers who donate their time *pro bono.*

Legislative Appointment (101)

A technique of judicial selection used in several states. The legislative appointment process involves the nomination of a prospective judge by the legislative body itself. If the nominee receives the votes of a majority of one or both chambers of the legislature, he or she stands appointed. The colonists had first-hand experience with a judiciary under the control of an arbitrary monarch, and following the War of Independence many wished to place judicial selection in the hands of the legislative rather than executive branch. Indeed, legislative selection was the method of preference among most states during the period 1776–1830, with almost half the states using it. The popularity of legislative selection (and executive appointment as well) diminished greatly in the wake of Jacksonian democracy. Many of the states wished to increase the role of the people in governance, and they replaced legislative selection with direct election of judges. Only South Carolina and Virginia continue to use legislative choice as their principle method of selecting judges. *See also* EXECUTIVE APPOINTMENT, 89; JUDICIAL INDEPENDENCE, 93.

Significance   The legislative appointment method of judicial selection could not withstand the pressure of popular sovereignty. Andrew Jackson sought to reform the judicial processes by making them more accountable to popular control. One of the consequences was that many states turned to election, initially partisan election, as the preferred method of judicial selection. In addition, people in some states became displeased with attempted legislative control. As state courts began to have an impact on state policies, some legislatures began to engage in power politics. Limits on judicial terms were enacted; more important, unpopular judicial decisions prompted attempts to remove judges. In short, many saw certain state legislative action as too strong, and steps were taken to curb such conduct. Taking judicial selection out of the hands of legislatures was one such step. Where legislative appointment was retained, two patterns emerged. First, prior legislative service became key to judicial appointment. Second, in legislative appointment states, party influence in judicial selection became substantial while the influence of the legal profession was minimal.

Life Tenure (102)

Term used to describe the effect of the constitutional language establishing the tenure of federal judges. Under terms of Article III, Section 1, all federal judges of constitutional courts "shall hold their offices during good behavior." This, in effect, means for the rest of their professional lives. The life tenure provision, as well as the Article III language forbidding Congress from diminishing the salaries of incumbent federal judges, was designed to promote judicial independence. The only way a federal judge may be removed is through the process of impeachment. Provisions exist under statute for sanctioning federal judges in ways less severe than removal from office. The life tenure protection exists only for federal judges. State judges, even those selected by executive or legislative appointment, serve terms of specified length. *See also* JUDICIAL INDEPENDENCE, 93.

Significance   The "good behavior" provision means that federal judges have virtual life tenure. Federal judges can be removed for misconduct, however, and Congress has the authority to implement removal procedures. The impeachment process requires the House of Representatives to bring charges, with a trial of those charges following in the Senate. The House has seldom brought impeachment proceedings against federal judges, and only five have been convicted and removed from office. Impeachment charges are usually for criminal conduct. In 1936, U.S. District Judge Halsted Ritter was accused of corruption and removed for bringing his court into "disrepute." The most recent removal of a federal judge occurred in 1986 when U.S. District Judge Harry Claiborne was impeached on charges related to income tax evasion. While the impeachment process has seldom been taken to conclusion, it may be used in leveraging a resignation from a judge who is unlikely to survive the process. In 1980, Congress enacted legislation authorizing the Judicial Council of each circuit to investigate complaints filed against judges. If the complaint has merit, the council may request that the judge retire, reprimand the judge, or order that no cases be assigned to the judge. In extreme cases, the council may recommend removal to the House of Representatives.

Magistrate   **(103)**
A quasi-judge who assists a judge in processing judicial business. Magistrates are attorneys who are appointed by judges to positions formally authorized under federal or state law. The Federal Magistrates Act of 1968 established the position of U.S. Magistrate, for example. The position was created to provide another tier of judicial officer in the federal courts. Under the 1968 Act, magistrates were assigned specific functions before and after both criminal and civil trials. Some of these duties, such as taking depositions, are comparatively routine. Other functions, however, require judgment such as hearing petty offense cases, issuing warrants, disposing of motions, and conducting

arraignments. Amendments to the Act in 1976 and 1979 enabled U.S. magistrates to hear additional pretrial matters and submit findings to the district court. U.S. magistrates are also empowered to preside at trials with the consent of the parties. If a magistrate presides at a trial, direct appeals go to the U.S. Court of Appeals. Full-time U.S. magistrates must be members of the state bar and are appointed to eight-year terms by judges of the U.S. District Court. Part-time magistrates serve four-year terms. There are about 600 full-time and part-time U.S. magistrates in the federal court system. Magistrates are also used in state courts, but seldom have the range of responsibilities of their federal counterparts. *See also* JUDGE, 91; REFEREE, 113; UNITED STATES DISTRICT COURT, 75.

Significance The use of magistrates is a response to the enormous caseload increases in the federal and state courts. Assignment of functions to magistrates is preferred by many over authorization of new judgeships or redefining the jurisdiction of existing courts. In the mid-1980s, U.S. magistrates handled about 400,000 matters that would have otherwise fallen to the U.S. District Court judges. The amendments to the Federal Magistrates Act in 1976 and 1979 were intended to clarify the authority of U.S. magistrates. The amendments expanded the power of magistrates, but did not produce the intended clarification. Questions remain about the legal status of magistrates. They perform judicial business and are structurally located in the judicial branch. At the same time, they are not judicial officers as Article III judges are. This paradox involves the growing legal issue of how much of the work of federal judges can be delegated to magistrates. In the meantime, the role of magistrates, especially in the federal system, is both substantial and growing.

Missouri Plan (104)

A technique of judicial selection that contains elements of both elective and appointive methods. The Missouri Plan originated in the early 1900s as judicial reformers sought ways to heighten judicial independence and competence. The plan, first advanced by the American Judicature Society as part of its more comprehensive package of reforms, was first adopted in Missouri in 1940. Eighteen states now use the Missouri Plan as their method of judicial selection for at least a portion, if not all, of their courts. The Missouri Plan, referred to as "merit" selection by its advocates, involves a number of steps to be fully implemented. The process begins with a commission that nominates judicial candidates. These commissions are typically composed of 9 to 15 members selected by the governor. The commissions tend to be dominated by representatives of the legal profession and are likely to include at least one sitting judge. The commission sends a list of nominees (usually three to five names) to the governor, who makes the appointment from the list. After a specified period (usually a year or so), a retention election is conducted and the electorate determines whether the judge is retained for a more lengthy period, at the end of which another retention election takes place. There is no opposition candidate in a retention election. Rather, the judge runs against his or her record on the bench. If a judge is not retained, a vacancy exists and the commission begins the process again. *See also* NOMINATING COMMISSION, 105; SELECTION PROCESS IMPACTS, 114.

Significance The Missouri Plan was designed to replace partisanship with professional merit as the decisive factor in judicial selection. Partisanship is not altogether eliminated, however, and manifests itself most commonly in the selection of commission members. At the same time, the deliberations of the commission function as a screen, and prospects with modest legal credentials are usually not advanced as nominees to the governor. The plan does strengthen the hand of the legal profession in judicial selection. The key step appears to be gubernatorial appointment. Data show that in excess of 98 percent of judges are retained at the election stage. In effect, Missouri Plan judges seem to acquire life tenure. The Missouri Plan is now the technique states adopt if they choose to change their selection process. Indeed, every state making a change over the past several decades has adopted some form of the Missouri Plan. A number of states are currently considering making the switch to such "merit" selection.

Nominating Commission (105)

A central element in the so-called "merit" selection of judges. The term nominating commission has generally been associated with federal judicial selection, but the commissions established for the lower federal courts function very much like Missouri Plan screening commissions. Federal nominating commissions have a comparatively short history. President Jimmy Carter brought to the White House a commitment to merit selection. Less than a month into his presidency, he established, by executive order, U.S. Circuit Judge Nominating Commissions for each of the then eleven U.S. Court of Appeals circuits. These commissions were citizen panels that would recommend names of prospective appointees whenever a judgeship became open in their geographic circuit. The members of each commission were chosen by Carter, and he was quite deferential to their recommendations. President Reagan did not share Carter's enthusiasm for the commissions and abolished the panels soon after taking office in 1981. A parallel effort was made to create nominating commissions for U.S. District Courts. Since these courts function wholly within one state, these commissions were created by U.S. Senate members on an individual basis. Some states have two commissions, one for each Senate member. Almost three-quarters of the states now have such commissions. While their operating processes vary somewhat, members are appointed by the senator who created a commission. The legal profession has tended to be heavily represented on these commissions, but the commissions remain relatively partisan. The District Court Nominating Commissions screen names and pass recommendations on to the senator who, in turn, recommends the name for nomination to the president. *See also* MISSOURI PLAN, 104.

Significance   The use of nominating commissions was designed to remove some of the politics from judicial selection while at the same time improving the quality of those nominated. The politics cannot be totally removed, however, because commission memberships are politically made, and the recommendations of the commissions are always subject to executive action and legislative confirmation. Where used, the commissions tend to impinge on the power previously exercised by individual senators. Indeed, it is for this reason that some senators have not wished to create commissions for U.S. District Court judges. In addition, the short-term record reveals that recommendations of commissions are virtually always of the same party as the president. This was the pattern for nominations before commissions were used. Where a difference does seem to exist is in the recruitment of minority and women judges. The record for the four years Carter used commissions in the selection of Court of Appeals judges shows that almost forty percent of the nominees were women, blacks, or Hispanics. Qualitative improvements from using nominating commissions are not apparent.

Nominating Criteria   (106)
Factors that govern executive choices for judicial nominations. Nominating criteria vary by executive, of course, and differ depending on the kind of judgeship under consideration. Despite the variance, some general patterns are apparent. When presidents are considering a Supreme Court nomination, the most important criteria seem to be professional competence and policy compatibility. Generally, presidents attempt to nominate lawyers of distinction. An important element is the absence of any taint with respect to ethical standards. Of critical concern to a president is the political orientation of the pro-

spective judge. A president brings to office an agenda, and no president will knowingly nominate someone to the Supreme Court who will make fulfillment of that agenda more difficult. While a justice may not always vote as the nominating president hopes, ideological compatibility produces judicial positions that are generally in accord with a president's policy preferences. Beyond these criteria, presidents are very cognizant of the practical political dimensions of a nomination. Presidents seek to make nominations that have no political "cost" in that confirmation will be virtually automatic. As a result, a president need not engage in any political "horse-trading" to obtain confirmation, which allows the president to conserve things to trade on other issues. Similarly, particular nominees may help a president with certain constituency groups. President Reagan's nomination of Sandra Day O'Connor was at least in part aimed at closing the so-called "gender gap," Reagan's relatively unfavorable standing with women. Finally, presidents may use even a Supreme Court nomination as a political reward, although this is a much more critical factor in the nomination of lower federal judges. Partisan reward is also a key factor with gubernatorial nominations at the state level. Since many state nominees will ultimately have to run in some form of election, likelihood of retaining the judgeship at the ballot box is a consideration, but it never, of course, comes into play with federal judgeships. *See also* EXECUTIVE APPOINTMENT, 89.

Significance   The nominating criteria that govern executive nominations of judges vary depending on the appointing official and the court involved. Historically, the ideological factor has been most important at the U.S. Supreme Court level, with partisan reward controlling lower federal court nominations. A generally similar pattern exists at the state level. The use of elections in so many states, however, makes electability a unique but critical factor at the state level. The traditional pattern in federal judicial nominations was not maintained by President Reagan, who used his nominating authority to reshape the ideological composition of the lower federal courts. Early in his tenure, Reagan established a Committee on Federal Judicial Selection made up of key people from the White House staff and the Justice Department. This group played an ongoing role in federal judicial selection and placed a premium on ideological and policy compatibility. It was through this committee, for example, that the Reagan Administration was able to honor its commitment to the "pro-life" position on the abortion issue. This approach is likely to be maintained during the presidency of George Bush. This approach did have the effect of making the federal judiciary much more conservative. By the end of Reagan's second term, more than half of the lower federal court judges had been nominated using largely ideological standards.

Nonpartisan Election (107)

An election in which the candidates run with no identification of their political party affiliation on the ballot. Nonpartisan elections are most commonly used to select judges and officials at the municipal level. Movement to nonpartisan elections was part of the progressive reforms early in the twentieth century. The objective was to purge politics from local government. The reformers believed that nonpartisan contests would minimize the impact of extraneous state and national issues from influencing elections. More important, it was believed that nonpartisanship would focus candidate qualifications and eliminate the influence of party machines and local political "bosses." Ballot access in nonpartisan elections is typically accomplished by petition. If more than two candidates file for an office, a nonpartisan primary is conducted to reduce the field to two. *See also* PARTISAN ELECTION, 108.

Significance   The nonpartisan approach to election has not produced a depoliticized electoral process. Rather, several kinds of patterns have emerged. First, political parties continue to dominate although they are disguised by the cloak of nonpartisanship. Parties continue to recruit and finance candidates, but not in an overt way. This is especially true in judicial elections, where candidates with previous partisan visibility have a distinct advantage. In the absence of other information, voters tend to vote for those who have established name recognition in the partisan political arena. It is for this reason that prosecuting attorneys, for example, are often sought as judicial candidates. Second, groups and coalitions perform the role of parties. These may be either coalitions that resemble those groups associated with the national parties or *ad hoc* independent community groups. In either case, slates of candidates are recruited and endorsed for each election. Yet another pattern is one where individual candidates establish their own organizations. Many people still favor nonpartisan elections, particularly with at-large elections used for judgeships at the state level, as a way of keeping state and local governments focused on the interests of the community rather than encouraging partisan or regional bickering. Those who oppose nonpartisan elections argue that they reduce voter turnout because parties have no incentive to encourage voting. They also see them as favoring the election of an upper-middle-class elite because without the encouragement of parties it is those from higher socio-economic situations who are most likely to vote, and they are most likely to vote for people like themselves.

Partisan Election (108)

Election in which the candidates run for office with party affiliation indicated on the ballot. Partisan elections first became popular in the 1830s during the height of Jacksonian democracy. Many states that had initially selected judges by means of executive or legislative appointment turned to partisan election in an effort to make judges and other office holders more accountable. A number of states subsequently opted to hold nonpartisan elections in an effort to reduce the influence of political party machines and bosses. The responsibility for candidate recruitment and campaign financing falls primarily to the parties in states with partisan elections. The party label often becomes the key factor when citizens make voting choices. Access to the ballot in partisan election states may be accomplished by petition, but typically the parties nominate candidates by caucus or at conventions. *See also* JUDICIAL ACCOUNTABILITY, 92; NONPARTISAN ELECTION, 107.

Significance Partisan elections tend to have higher turnouts than nonpartisan elections because there are mechanisms within the parties that prompt people to vote. Party labels simplify voter decision making but also tend to mask important candidate differences because many voters do not consider more than party affiliation. Incumbents in all elections are likely to be returned to office, but higher proportions of incumbents tend to be defeated in partisan election states than states using nonpartisan elections. If a minority party candidate happens to win a judgeship because of a presidential election or some other event influencing the election, that incumbent is more vulnerable in succeeding elections than an incumbent in a nonpartisan state. Twelve states use partisan elections for at least some of their judgeships. Each of these states permits its governor to make interim appointments when vacancies occur before the end of a full term. While these interim appointees must eventually run in an election to retain the office, executive appointment, not election, initially places many state court judges on the bench. Thus, states using partisan elections must be seen as states that tend to use the executive appointment method to initially fill judicial positions.

Private Practice (109)

Practice of law by attorneys who are neither employed by a government agency or a private industry or association. Attorneys in private practice may operate out of a one-person office, be part of a large firm with 50 or more attorneys, or something in between. Nearly 70 percent of attorneys in the United States are involved in some form of private practice. The remaining 30 percent divide into two groups of roughly equal size. The first group includes attorneys who practice law for government agencies such as the Department of Justice. This category includes those attorneys who serve as judges in American courts. The second group consists of attorneys who serve as "in-house" counsel for a business or association and have no other clients. A small additional group of attorneys do not practice law, but rather perform various management functions in business, teach in law schools, or hold political office. Attorneys in private practice generally charge clients on an hourly basis for services performed, while attorneys who work for the government or private industry are salaried. The trend in recent years has been away from the solo practice of law. Rather, attorneys are currently more likely to enter into arrangements with at least one other attorney. Such arrangements not only allow for a broadening of expertise, but lowers office operating costs. Large law firms have also become more common. Nearly fifteen percent of attorneys in private practice are affiliated with firms of at least 20 attorneys. *See also* AMERICAN BAR ASSOCIATION, 79; LEGAL PROFESSION, 99.

Significance   A number of attorneys in private practice attempt to maintain a general practice. That is, they try to handle a range of legal problems for their clients. The trend is away from the general practice, however, to a more specialized or focused private practice. It is this trend that is decreasing the number of attorneys who practice law alone. The cooperative approach facilitates specialization. Among the larger legal specialties are corporate law, tax law, and criminal law. The corporate practitioner acts as an adviser to business clients in an attempt to keep them from legal difficulty. Tax attorneys focus on minimizing the tax liability of their clients. Few corporate or tax attorneys are courtroom practitioners, and only a small proportion of those in private practice do trial work. A large group of trial attorneys, of course, are engaged in defending persons accused of crimes. Additional specializations found among private practitioners include civil rights, energy and environment, international business, labor-management relations, personal injury, and domestic relations.

Prosecuting Attorney   **(110)**
Attorney who represents the state in prosecuting those accused of criminal conduct. In some jurisdictions, the prosecuting attorney is

called the district attorney or the state's attorney. Federal prosecutors are called United States Attorneys. Prosecuting attorneys in the states are usually elected at the county level to terms of four years and are structurally at the center of the criminal process. In most jurisdictions, prosecutors stand between police agencies and the courts. Cases come in from the various law enforcement agencies and are screened by the prosecutors. Only those cases deemed worthy by the prosecuting attorney are placed into the courts. Neither victims nor the police may directly initiate criminal cases in most American jurisdictions. The prosecuting attorney retains control of all cases in which charges are formally lodged. Almost every state has an independently elected prosecuting attorney for each of its counties. The performance of these county prosecutors is not supervised from the state level. In most states, the state attorney general has no control over county prosecutors and often has very limited power to initiate criminal prosecutions. This means that policy decisions of local prosecutors will govern in their respective counties, and there is no mechanism requiring their policies or operating priorities to be uniform. The prosecuting attorney's office also acts as civil counsel for most counties. *See also* COURTROOM WORK GROUP, 87; DEFENSE ATTORNEY, 88; PROSECUTORIAL FUNCTION, 178; STATE ATTORNEY GENERAL, 118.

Significance   The prosecuting attorney may be the most powerful participant in the criminal justice process. The prosecuting attorney possesses substantial discretion from beginning to end of the process, and to a large extent determines who is charged, the substance of plea agreements, and the nature of sentences. The great power of prosecutors stems from their central position in the process. The discretion of the prosecutor bridges every stage of the justice system. To start, the prosecutor's office screens all incoming cases to determine whether to charge and, if so, with what specific offense. Often these charging judgments drive the negotiation process, which yields agreements in upwards of 90 percent of criminal cases. The prosecuting attorney also makes recommendations on pretrial release and sentence that are often followed by the courts. As elected officials, county prosecutors are influenced by their perception of public sentiment, and enforcement priorities are often based on these perceptions. This is especially true if the prosecuting attorney has political ambitions and wishes to use the office as a stepping stone to higher office.

Public Defender (111)
An attorney employed by the government for the purpose of representing indigent criminal defendants. In jurisdictions with a public

defender system, the trial judge appoints a specific person to serve as the public defender. He or she, in turn, recruits assistants to the extent budget limits allow. The public defender is a public agent and the office of the public defender exists as a government department in much the same way as the office of the prosecuting attorney. Some public defender systems could be found prior to 1960, but they spread rapidly following the U.S. Supreme Court decision in *Gideon v. Wainwright* (372 U.S. 335: 1963), which required representation of indigent felony defendants at the state level as a matter of constitutional right. This principle was extended to certain misdemeanors in *Argersinger v. Hamlin* (407 U.S. 25: 1972). Federal law provides public defenders through the Federal Public Defender Organization. Many states have similar programs. The public defender system is used in about a third of all state jurisdictions, but can be found in virtually all large urban jurisdictions. The principal alternative to the public defender approach is an assignment system. Under the assignment system, lawyers are appointed by trial judges on a case-by-case basis, either from a list of all attorneys in the jurisdiction or from a shorter list of attorneys who wish assignment. *See also* ASSISTANCE OF COUNSEL, 126; COURTROOM WORK GROUP, 87; DEFENSE ATTORNEY, 88.

Significance   The public defender system is a reasonably effective means of providing legal representation to indigent criminal defendants. As a salaried attorney with no outside practice, the public defender is generally able to devote greater attention to individual cases than some assigned counsel. While public defenders may be young and inexperienced when they begin, they typically become competent criminal defense attorneys because of their large caseloads and exclusive focus on criminal trial work. Assigned counsel are not always as knowledgeable or experienced in criminal defense. Public defenders are more likely to be aware of local and informal operating practices because of their frequent interaction with the judges and prosecutors of the jurisdiction. This enhances their capacity to represent clients effectively. There is criticism of the public defender approach, however. Some believe that public defenders, as locally paid government staff, come to share the values and objectives of others in the courtroom work group. As a result, it is contended that the public defender is less likely to defend vigorously. Further, public defender offices typically suffer from budget limitations, high caseloads, and marginal support staff. Nonetheless, a number of studies comparing performances of public defenders and privately retained counsel show that there is little difference in terms of case outcomes.

Recess Appointment (112)

Appointment of an official by the chief executive to fill a vacancy while the Senate or state legislature is not in session. At the federal level, recess appointments are authorized under terms of Article II, Section 2, which states that Presidents "shall have the power to fill up all vacancies that may happen during the recess of the Senate, by granting commissions which shall expire at the end of their next session." The Senate may confirm the appointee when it returns. If it does not, the commission expires under terms of the last phrase of the constitutional directive. Similar language in state constitutions provides for recess appointments by governors. The power to make recess appointments allows an executive to act immediately, but it may also create political problems with the legislature. The question is when the executive may act. Must the vacancy actually occur while the legislature is in recess or may an executive simply not act on a vacancy until a recess occurs and then appoint a replacement? The latter position would, in effect, allow an executive to circumvent legislative review. The broader definition has been upheld in court cases. However, Congress has enacted a law that prevents payment of a salary to a recess appointee filling a vacancy that existed while the Senate was in session. *See also* ADVICE AND CONSENT, 78; EXECUTIVE APPOINTMENT, 89.

Significance The recess appointment allows an executive to fill a vacancy while the legislature is not in session. The "appointee" is then "in place" when the legislature returns. This places the burden of disrupting the operations of a court on the legislature if it fails to confirm. At the same time, the legislature will be able to examine interim performance in addition to whatever else it would have considered in its confirmation deliberations. Occasionally, this may be decisive, as in the case of John Rutledge in 1797. George Washington filled a Supreme Court vacancy with the recess appointment of Rutledge. Rutledge subsequently was publicly critical of the Jay Treaty, an agreement ratified by the Senate only days earlier. When the Senate returned from its recess, it failed to confirm Rutledge. Recess appointments are used fairly often, but executives have come to exercise some restraint in using them. Seldom will highly controversial persons or persons previously rejected by the legislature be nominated. The recess appointment is especially important at the state level, where some states do not have full-time legislatures and recesses are frequent and/or lengthy.

Referee   **(113)**
A quasi-judicial officer who can conduct a hearing on a pending matter and report findings to the court. Referees are typically attorneys and are appointed by judges to handle particular matters. Referees have the authority to take testimony and are often used to gather information in complex cases. The report of a referee's findings becomes the basis of a court judgment. A similar function is performed by a person known as a master or special master. The term referee is occasionally used in reference to judicial officers who handle traffic or ordinance violations. Most jurisdictions use magistrates to perform this function instead of referees. *See also* JUDGE, 91; MAGISTRATE, 103.

Significance   The term referee derives from the word "refer." Matters handled by referees are specifically "referred" by a court. Referees relieve the courts from matters of volume and detail. Use of referees also creates a two-stage disposition process where preliminary consideration is given to particular issues that will also be considered by courts. Use of a referee allows courts to focus themselves on the more substantial aspects or "bigger picture" issues of a case.

Selection Process Impacts   **(114)**
Outcomes that stem directly from methods of judicial recruitment. Two kinds of impacts are typically discussed by those advocating one method of judicial selection over another. The first is the quality of the people chosen. Obviously, selection of professionally competent judges is a priority. Does one method of selection produce more "qualified" judges? Advocates of "merit" selection frequently make the quality argument. The few studies on the characteristics of those selected as judges are inconclusive, however. Rather, what these studies show is that there is little difference among selection systems in terms of personal characteristics of those chosen. Differences in such quality measures as educational background and prior judicial experience are negligible across the various selection techniques. The second impact most often discussed is the actual behavior of judges selected by one means as against another. The elective judge is presumably more attentive to public sentiment than a judge who does not need to face election. The idea, of course, is that selection systems create dynamics that must influence behavior. While no clear patterns have emerged from empirical studies, some differential impacts seem to exist at least to a limited degree. Judges selected by means of

partisan election reflect that partisanship on issues which themselves have partisan content, such as legislative districting. Partisan impact is virtually irrelevant on issues that have no connection to partisanship. A clearer sense of differential selection impacts will develop with further study. *See also* EXECUTIVE APPOINTMENT, 89; MISSOURI PLAN, 104; PARTISAN ELECTION, 108.

Significance   The different judicial selection processes have not produced appreciably different consequences or impacts. In large part, this is a result of states using a combination of selection methods rather than just one. In elective states, for example, judicial vacancies that occur before a term is completed are filled by executive appointment. While this interim appointee ultimately must stand for election to retain the judgeship, is that judge in the appointed or elected category? In actual practice, judicial selection is conducted in similar ways in most states because of the overlapping of approaches. What is clear is that regardless of which selection system is used, judges retain their offices to an overwhelming degree; that is, incumbent judges are reappointed or reelected in virtually all cases. This is true even in Missouri Plan states. It is also apparent that whichever selection method is formally adopted, state governors possess more influence than any other process participant. The governor's decisive role in executive appointment states is obvious. In elective states, however, gubernatorial influence is almost as great. Through interim appointments, governors typically fill most judicial vacancies. Virtually all interim appointees retain their judgeships in the elections that follow.

Senate Judiciary Committee   (115)

The Senate committee that reviews all federal judicial nominees. The Senate Judiciary Committee is a standing committee of the Senate with jurisdiction over such matters as constitutional amendments, operations of the federal courts, civil liberties, immigration, and revisions of the U.S. Code. The Senate Judiciary Committee screens nominees for all federal courts. Reviews of candidates for the lower federal courts, especially those for the U.S. District Court, are governed by the practice of senatorial courtesy. This arrangement allows Senate members of the president's party from the state in which the judgeship is located to veto unacceptable candidates. This is done by returning a "blue slip" to the chair of the Judiciary Committee. Return of the blue slip, a blue piece of paper containing the candidate's name, indicates that the home-state senator(s) was not sufficiently involved in, or disapproves of, the nomination. The traditional senatorial courtesy turns Judiciary Committee screening of district court nominees into little more than a formality. Review of Supreme Court nominees is far more extensive. Evaluation of the candidate by the American Bar Association's Committee on the Federal Judiciary and background investigations conducted by the FBI are considered by the Judiciary Committee. In addition, hearings are held, and the nominees and other witnesses are heard. The Senate Judiciary Committee concludes its deliberations with a recommendation to the full Senate. *See also* ADVICE AND CONSENT, 78; SENATORIAL COURTESY, 116.

Significance   The Senate Judiciary Committee performs the Senate screening function for all federal judicial candidates. The committee can do one of several things with a nomination. First, it can conclude the nominee is acceptable and recommend confirmation to the full Senate. Second, it can slow down the confirmation process in hopes that further information or evidence appears. This tactic was used by some members of the committee with the nomination of Judge G. Harrold Carswell to the Supreme Court in 1970. By stretching the process out for several months, opponents of the nominations were able to develop a sufficiently persuasive case to defeat the nomination. If nothing else, delay can test the resolve of the nominating president to stay with a nominee. Third, the committee can conduct highly visible deliberations and pass the nomination on to the full Senate without a recommendation. This allows the debate to continue on the Senate floor. This was the approach taken by the committee with the volatile nomination of Judge Robert H. Bork in 1987. The final option of the committee is to recommend rejection. While the Senate normally will defer to any recommendation, it could vote to confirm a nominee who has not been recommended by the committee. The full Senate is the ultimate authority on judicial confirmation, but it assigns most of the screening work to the Senate Judiciary Committee.

Senatorial Courtesy   (116)
A folkway or informal norm of the Senate governing review of nominees for various federal positions. The practice of senatorial courtesy requires that a president confer with Senate members of his party from the state in which a federal appointment is to be made. Federal positions to which senatorial courtesy applies are U.S. District Court judges, U.S. Attorneys, and a number of executive agency offices. Senatorial courtesy gives home-state senators at least a veto on prospective nominees not to their liking. More often, it provides Senate members with an opportunity to suggest names to the president. The Senate will normally defer to the choices of colleagues. A president

who fails to secure at least the concurrence of a home-state Senate member runs a substantial risk of having the nominee rejected. Rejection of nominees for lower federal courts takes place through a technique known as the "blue slip." When a nomination is formally presented to the Senate, it is printed on a blue slip of paper. If a senator has been sufficiently involved with Justice Department representatives in the choice of the nominee, the blue slip is not returned to the chair of the Senate Judiciary Committee. By not returning the slip, the senator expresses no objection to the nominee. If, on the other hand, the senator disapproves for some reason, the blue slip is returned and the nomination is rejected. *See also* ADVICE AND CONSENT, 78; SENATE JUDICIARY COMMITTEE, 115.

Significance   Senatorial courtesy maximizes the influence of a senator from the president's party in the nomination process used in selecting lower federal court judges as well as other officials in the senator's state. Senatorial courtesy redefines the Senate's reviewing role into one of actual nominator. As a result, many U.S. district judges are likely to be reflections of home-state Senate members instead of the administration. Home state senators not of the president's party have little influence generally. In such instances, the administration is likely to bypass senators of the opposing party and confer with party officials in the state. Exceptions may occur where a senator may be an ideological ally of a president despite party difference. Home-state senators may play a role in the selection of U.S. Court of Appeals judges, but it will be limited because of the multi-state jurisdiction of that court. Senatorial courtesy does not come into play with respect to U.S. Supreme Court nominations.

Solicitor General   **(117)**
Third-ranking official in the U.S. Department of Justice (behind the attorney general and the deputy attorney general). Among the responsibilities of the Solicitor General of the United States, three stand out. The solicitor general must decide which of the cases lost by the federal government at the trial level should be appealed. Second, the solicitor general must determine which cases should be pursued to the Supreme Court level. Whenever a federal agency loses a case before the court of appeals, it must formally request the solicitor general to petition for review. The final judgment on these matter rests with the solicitor general. Third, he or she supervises the preparation of cases that are to be reviewed by the Supreme Court. This includes determination of what the government's legal position ought to be and the preparation of the briefs and other documentation that argues for or

supports that position. In addition, the solicitor general conducts the oral argument before the Supreme Court in the most important of these cases. *See also* ATTORNEY GENERAL OF THE UNITED STATES, 80; JUSTICE DEPARTMENT, 57.

Significance   The Solicitor General of the United States functions as chief counsel for the federal government. The solicitor general has the discretion to select the cases that will be appealed. This means the solicitor general has direct impact on the substance of federal criminal and civil law by choosing which cases to review. Generally the solicitor general is quite selective in petitioning the Supreme Court for review. This restraint has several effects. First, it assigns priority to particular policy issues. Second, it allows the government to advance only its strongest cases. Third, this selective approach heightens the chances of the Court reviewing the cases. While only about five percent of the total number of cases seeking *certiorari* review are granted, the Justice Department succeeds in obtaining review in about 70 percent of the cases it petitions for *certiorari*. Finally, screening by the solicitor general has an impact on the Supreme Court's workload because many cases funnel through the Justice Department.

State Attorney General   (118)
The chief legal officer of state government. The state attorney general serves as legal counsel to the state governor and state agencies. The state attorney general represents the state in legal proceedings when the state is a party to a legal action. State attorneys general may be asked to issue formal opinions on questions of state law. This function is quasi-judicial in character and these opinions have the force of law. They remain in effect until such time as they may be reversed or modified by a court. Attorneys general are elected in forty-three states and appointed by the governor in the remaining seven. The attorney general has modest law enforcement authority. While most states allow the attorney general to initiate criminal actions on motion, the prosecutorial functions in most states are assigned to prosecuting attorneys elected at the county level. Only in Alaska, Delaware, and Rhode Island do state attorneys general have supervisory or coordinating power over criminal prosecutions. Also functioning at the local level are corporation counsel who act as counsel for cities, villages, or townships on noncriminal matters. Larger local units may be able to support a staff position(s) for this function. Smaller units may simply retain a local attorney or law firm to serve as corporation counsel when necessary. *See also* ATTORNEY GENERAL OF THE UNITED STATES, 80; PROSECUTING ATTORNEY, 110.

Significance   The state attorney general supervises the legal business of state government. He or she renders interpretations of state and local law as well as administrative rules. All state officials are obligated to abide by the attorney general's view until those interpretations might be removed or modified through court challenge. In the seven states where the governor appoints the attorney general, the latter serves as part of the governor's administration and is typically in full harmony with the policy directions of the governor. This situation is wholly analogous to the relationship between the president and the attorney general at the federal level. Most states, however, elect the attorney general independently from the governor. Under these circumstances, the governor and attorney general may or may not function well together. This is especially true when there are partisan differences. The position of state attorney general is also a political stepping stone for many. It is an office often held by congressional, gubernatorial, or state judicial aspirants.

State Bar Association   (119)
A professional organization of lawyers established at the state level. State bar associations were an outgrowth of organizations initiated at the local level. Many local organizations such as those in New York City and Chicago were founded in the late 1800s and were primarily designed to eliminate corrupt practices in the courts of those cities. The American Bar Association (ABA) was established soon after, followed closely by associations at the state level. Membership in bar associations at all levels was voluntary at the outset. As a result, membership in the local organizations was limited. A number of attorneys saw the bar associations as essential to improving the legal system and sought to heighten their role. This was made possible by requiring bar association membership under state law. This compulsory membership, akin to a "closed shop" for organized labor, was termed an "integrated" bar. The bar associations of about two-thirds of the states are currently integrated by state statute or by order of state supreme courts. Among the principal concerns of state bar associations are legal education, performance standards for practitioners, and improvement of the legal system. *See also* AMERICAN BAR ASSOCIATION, 79; CODE OF PROFESSIONAL RESPONSIBILITY, 83; MISSOURI PLAN, 104.

Significance   State bar associations are interest groups dedicated to promoting the best interests of attorneys. State bar associations are deeply involved in establishing and maintaining professional standards. State bar associations play a role in setting law school admission standards and conducting bar examinations at the conclusion of law school programs. State bar associations also make inquiries into the general fitness of prospective lawyers prior to their admission to the bar. They also investigate grievances filed against attorneys for alleged conduct incompatible with established standards of professional responsibility. State bar associations also represent the state's legal profession in the political arena. Most bar association political activities focus on judicial selection and organizational issues related to the courts. State bar associations, for example, have been at the forefront of efforts to establish "merit" selection of judges. This approach gives the bar the greatest influence in choosing judges for a state's courts. Failing that, the state bar conducts membership "polls" on candidates for judicial office in election states and publicizes the results. State governors routinely consult with state bar associations prior to making judicial appointments. Bar associations are also active in promoting proposals for court restructuring. Support is most likely where changes elevate professionalism within the courts. In addition, bar associations strongly support legislation that expands legal assistance programs for indigents. Such programs not only further the administration of justice but also directly benefit lawyers.

United States Attorney (120)

Federal executive officer whose principal responsibility is to prosecute violations of federal civil and criminal law. The position of United States Attorney was established by the Judiciary Act of 1789. A U.S. attorney is appointed to a four-year term by the president with Senate confirmation required. Each federal judicial district has one U.S. attorney, who is aided by a number of assistant U.S. attorneys. In addition to prosecuting criminal cases, U.S. attorneys and their assistants defend the interests of the United States in federal district court. U.S. attorneys have considerable discretion in determining which criminal cases to prosecute and which civil cases to settle or pursue to trial. As a result, the U.S. attorney has substantial impact on the docket of the U.S. district courts. *See also* ATTORNEY GENERAL OF THE UNITED STATES, 80; DISCRETION, 140; PROSECUTING ATTORNEY, 110.

Significance A U.S. attorney is usually appointed as a political reward. Virtually all the lawyers appointed to the positions are members of the president's party. While the terms are four years, U.S. attorneys may be reappointed or removed by a president at any time. When presidential administrations change, U.S. attorneys typically resign their positions so the incoming president may appoint a full compliment of new U.S. attorneys. The U.S. attorneys are tightly linked to the attorney general of the United States and the Justice Department. U.S. attorneys function under the general supervision of the attorney general, and all assistant U.S. attorneys are appointed by the attorney general although the U.S. attorney typically forwards the names of his or her preferences for formal ratification. It is through the supervisory function of the attorney general that similar performance objectives are established for all U.S. attorneys. Although federal and state jurisdictions are generally separate, the U.S. attorney provides linkage to state and local law enforcement authorities in those few areas where federal and state criminal law overlaps. Service as a U.S. attorney is often a stepping-stone to a federal judgeship.

4. The Criminal Judicial Process

Criminal courts are the most visible element of the judicial system. While civil cases far outnumber criminal cases, public attention and concern seem focused on the criminal courts. The terms contained in this chapter describe the steps in the criminal process, the types of cases making up the criminal docket, and the principal players in the criminal courts.

Crimes are defined by legislative bodies at both the federal and state levels. Only a very small proportion of criminal cases (something under two percent) are federal, because the federal government has limited police power. Rather, the prosecution of criminal cases is largely a responsibility of state government and its local units. There is consensus that many kinds of conduct should be prohibited, thus the criminal codes of the fifty states closely resemble one another. At the same time, some variation exists since each state may exercise sovereign power. As a result, lawful behavior in one state may be criminal if undertaken in another. Occasionally, state criminal jurisdiction overlaps with federal jurisdiction, in which case both levels may prosecute, although federal-state cooperation occurs with such multiple prosecutions.

Criminal cases can be divided into at least three categories. The most serious criminal cases are felonies. Most states and the federal government define felonies as crimes for which a prison sentence of at least one year could result. Misdemeanors, on the other hand, are less serious but far more numerous. Sanctions for misdemeanors typically cannot exceed a year's detention in local facilities. If traffic offenses are defined as criminal, they are included in the jurisdiction of misdemeanor courts. Some states subdivide misdemeanors into more and less serious classes. Another category of criminal behavior is crime by juveniles. Each state has its own structure for dealing with such cases in a manner distinct from the handling of adult offenders.

An overview of the criminal process prompts two general observations. First, while the criminal process operates within the framework of established rules and procedures, those who function in the process possess substantial discretion. Discretion allows an official to make choices among possible courses of action. As a consequence of discretion, the people who work in the criminal justice process influence the ways the procedures actually work. Second, the personnel who perform functions in the criminal courts interact in an ongoing and frequent fashion. These people—judges, prosecutors, defense counsel, and court support staff—are often referred to as the courtroom workgroup. It is important to recognize that while these officials have different roles to play, the dynamics of frequent interaction tend to produce common or shared goals, with a resulting mutual dependence rather than independence.

The formal procedures for handling federal and state criminal cases tend to be similar because federal constitutional restrictions have been extended to state proceedings. As a result, it is possible to generally represent the path a criminal case will follow. The flow chart for such a "typical" case is presented in Figure 4-1. The formal steps serve as the overarching structural framework, but each is subject to informal influences flowing from the exercise of discretion.

The impact of discretion can readily be seen at the entrance to the criminal process where two pivotal decisions are made: the police decision to arrest and the prosecutorial decision to charge. While the decisions to arrest and charge are subsequently reexamined at later stages of the process, the decisions not to arrest or charge are seldom scrutinized. The police decision not to arrest may, for example, result from the perception that the public does not want full enforcement of certain laws, especially those covering "victimless" conduct. The police may also choose not to arrest someone in exchange for information from that person. Prosecutors may use their charging discretion to terminate a case that has little likelihood of yielding a conviction or that suffers from some evidence defect.

The criminal process is formally triggered by the arrest. A complaint is subsequently filed by the prosecutor if there is sufficient cause to believe a defendant committed a crime. Within hours of arrest, the defendant must appear before a judicial officer and be informed of the charges. Such constitutionally protected rights as assistance of counsel and pretrial release must also be considered at this time. Before a criminal defendant is tried, the state must establish a *prima facie* case before a neutral party, either a judge, magistrate, or grand jury. This step is designed to protect the individual from ar-

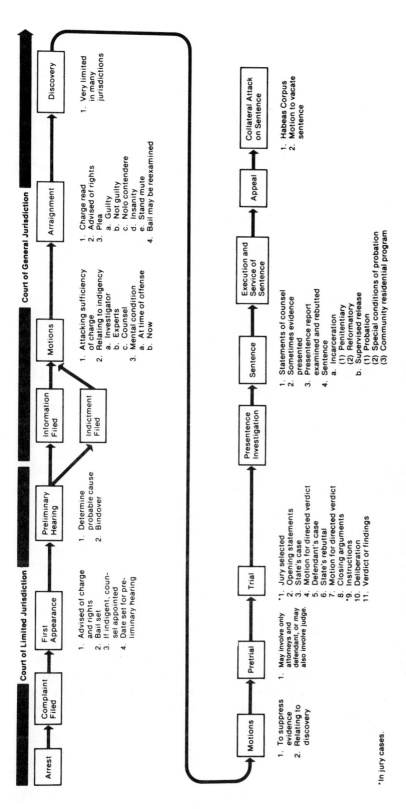

Figure 4-1. Typical Progression of Criminal Felony Litigation

From THE COURTS: FULCRUM OF THE JUSTICE SYSTEM by H. Ted Rubin. Copyright © 1976 by Newbery Award Records, Inc. Reprinted by permission of Random House, Inc.

Court of Limited Jurisdiction

Arrest → Complaint Filed → First Appearance → Preliminary Hearing → Information Filed → Indictment Filed → Motions

Court of General Jurisdiction

Motions → Arraignment → Discovery

First Appearance
1. Advised of charge and rights
2. Bail set
3. If indigent, counsel appointed
4. Date set for preliminary hearing

Preliminary Hearing
1. Determine probable cause
2. Bindover

Motions
1. Attacking sufficiency of charge
2. Relating to indigency
   a. Investigator
   b. Experts
   c. Counsel
3. Mental condition
   a. At time of offense
   b. Now

Arraignment
1. Charge read
2. Advised of rights
3. Plea
   a. Guilty
   b. Not guilty
   c. Nolo contendere
   d. Insanity
   e. Stand mute
4. Bail may be reexamined

Discovery
1. Very limited in many jurisdictions

Motions → Pretrial → Trial → Presentence Investigation → Sentence → Execution and Service of Sentence → Appeal → Collateral Attack on Sentence

Motions
1. To suppress evidence
2. Relating to discovery

Pretrial
1. May involve only attorneys and defendant, or may also involve judge.

Trial
*1. Jury selected
2. Opening statements
3. State's case
4. Motion for directed verdict
5. Defendant's case
6. State's rebuttal
7. Motion for directed verdict
8. Closing arguments
*9. Instructions
10. Deliberation
11. Verdict or findings

Sentence
1. Statements of counsel
2. Sometimes evidence presented
3. Presentence report examined and rebutted
4. Sentence
   a. Incarceration
      (1) Penitentiary
      (2) Reformatory
   b. Supervised release
      (1) Probation
      (2) Special conditions of probation
      (3) Community residential program

Collateral Attack on Sentence
1. Habeas Corpus
2. Motion to vacate sentence

*In jury cases.

bitrary and groundless charges. If the state can establish probable cause to believe the accused committed a crime, he or she then becomes a defendant and is "bound over" or moved along to the trial stage. The decision to bind over may occur at the conclusion of a preliminary hearing, may come in the form of a grand jury indictment, or may result from the information process.

An arraignment typically follows the binding over of a defendant. The arraignment is used to assess the status of a case, review legal options, and obtain a formal response for the record from the defendant. It is at this juncture that plea negotiations often occur in earnest for felony cases. Almost 90 percent of all criminal cases reaching the trial stage are concluded by the defendant pleading guilty. The remainder are tried by judge or jury. In addition to broad constitutional provisions, criminal trials are conducted under intricate procedural and detailed evidentiary rules. The criminal case concludes in one of two ways. The verdict may be to acquit. In that case, the defendant is free to go. A conviction, on the other hand, prompts commencement of the sentencing stage, a step in which the judge's discretion is the ultimate authority. A defendant who stands convicted is entitled to pursue whatever avenues of appeal are available. The question of innocence or guilt, however, cannot be reopened, but any error in the way the case was handled from arrest to conviction can be reviewed and overturned on appeal.

Acquittal (121)

Formal certification that a person is not guilty of a criminal charge. An acquittal is a finding of fact by a jury or a judge that the state has not proven "beyond a reasonable doubt" that the defendant committed the charged offense. A case dismissed before trial on grounds of insufficient evidence may be considered the equivalent of an acquittal. The opposite verdict from acquittal is conviction. *See also* CONVICTION, 134; JURY, 155; VERDICT, 254.

Significance   An acquittal is a verdict of "not guilty," and it formally discharges a person from a criminal charge. An acquittal means that while the prosecution may have been able to sustain charges at a *prima facie* level to obtain bind over for trial, the prosecution was unable to satisfy the more demanding standard of evidence required to convict. An acquittal prohibits the state from retrying a person on the same charge under terms of the double jeopardy protection found in state and federal constitutions.

Affirmative Defense (122)

A response to a criminal accusation that involves more than denial of the charge. An affirmative defense introduces new elements that provide an excuse for the criminal conduct. Among the more common affirmative defenses are insanity, necessity, duress, entrapment, and self defense. Undertaking an affirmative defense does not disturb the prosecutor's obligation to prove the defendant guilty. At the same time, because the affirmative defense brings additional issues to a case, the defendant assumes the burden of proof of those matters contained in the affirmative defense. *See also* ASSISTANCE OF COUNSEL, 126; INSANITY DEFENSE, 154.

Significance   An affirmative defense is a strategy used in hopes of obtaining a not guilty verdict from a jury. An affirmative defense contains some risk because it typically concedes that the defendant was involved in a crime. The affirmative defense of duress or coercion, for example, admits the defendant was present at the crime scene, but that his or her presence was involuntary. Participation under duress raises doubts about the defendant's intent to commit the crime. An affirmative defense is one of the few options available to defense attorneys when they represent clients facing very strong cases.

Alibi Defense (123)

An assertion that a criminal defendant was somewhere else at the time a crime was committed. If an alibi can be established, it conclusively demonstrates that a defendant could not be guilty of the criminal charge. An alibi defense can be asserted by a defendant through his or her own testimony. It is also possible, and probably more credible, to establish an alibi by calling other persons to testify as to the defendant's whereabouts at the time of the crime. *See also* AFFIRMATIVE DEFENSE, 122; CROSS-EXAMINATION, 136; WITNESS, 198.

Significance   Advancing a believable alibi defense can be very effective for a criminal defendant. It is also subject to both federal and state rules of criminal procedure. Federal rules as well as those governing most states require a defendant to give prior notice of an alibi defense. Any witnesses called to support the alibi defense must be disclosed in advance. Disclosure rules are generally intended to make both sides aware of information and allow them to prepare their cases accordingly. The notice of alibi rule gives the prosecutor an opportunity to investigate alibi testimony in advance and prepare for cross-examination of alibi witnesses. Prior disclosure of alibi witnesses may also allow a prosecutor to impeach their testimony by calling other witnesses who might, for example, indicate a long-term friendship between the defendant and the alibi witness. If a long-term friendship could be shown, it might suggest that the alibi witness had motive to lie on behalf of the defendant.

Arraignment (124)

An early step in the criminal process where a defendant is formally charged. The arraignment typically occurs after a defendant is bound over; that is, following an indictment or the filing of an information. At the arraignment, the defendant appears before the trial court, is informed of the charge, and is instructed as to the various responses that can be made. A defendant may plead guilty at the arraignment, but that is unusual when felony charges are involved. More likely, a defendant will enter a not guilty plea or stand mute, in which case a trial is scheduled. In some jurisdictions, an arraignment occurs as the initial step in the criminal process. In such circumstances, a defendant is more fully informed of constitutional protections. Counsel may be appointed if the defendant is indigent, and the question of pretrial release is considered. The defendant is not expected to enter any kind of response at the initial appearance. *See also* CHARGE, 129.

Significance The arraignment is one of the methods used to ensure that criminal defendants are extended due process of law. Charges are specified at the arraignment so that a defendant can begin preparing a defense. Defendants are also apprised of their legal options at the arraignment. Furthermore, it is necessary that an arraignment follows an arrest in a timely fashion. A speedy arraignment shortens the detention period and, as a result, reduces the opportunity for law enforcement officials to inappropriately obtain incriminating statements from a defendant. Indeed, Supreme Court decisions such as *Mallory v. United States* (354 U.S. 449: 1957) have adopted a delay in arraignment rule whereby all incriminating statements obtained as a result of unnecessary delay may not be used at trial. As important as the arraignment is, judges in large municipal courts often arraign a number of defendants at once, a practice that contributes to an "assembly line" or "bureaucratic" image of court operations.

Arrest (125)

The placing of a person under government custody. Arrests deprive people of their liberty because once under arrest, people are no longer free to move about as they please. The objective of arrest is to detain a person for the purpose of bringing criminal charges. An arrest is a seizure and is covered by provisions of the Fourth Amendment. Arrests may be affected with or without a warrant. If a suspect has been named in a formal complaint and arrest is the culmination of an investigative process, a warrant is required. An arrest warrant is issued by a judicial officer authorizing police to detain someone. Such warrants are issued upon a showing of probable cause and specifically name the person to be arrested. *See also* PROBABLE CAUSE, 176; WARRANT, 197.

Significance   Absent some kind of emergency or exigent circumstance, police must obtain a warrant before making an arrest. Lawful arrests can be made without warrants, however. Indeed, this is a common occurrence. There must be probable cause for an officer to arrest without a warrant. Such cause can be provided by an officer's personal observation of a criminal act. Similarly, officers may act upon tips from informants or reports from other law enforcement agencies. The warrant process was designed to minimize arbitrary behavior by law enforcement authorities. If a warrant has been obtained, it is presumed that the police have acted reasonably. If action is taken without a warrant, the adequacy of the police conduct may be a question for judicial consideration. Actions determined to be unlawful taint—and may nullify—everything that comes later.

Assistance of Counsel   **(126)**
A protection of the Sixth Amendment that entitles any accused person to have "assistance of counsel for his defense." The assistance of counsel provision in its early construction was confined to preventing the government from keeping an accused from securing his or her own counsel. There was no expectation that counsel was required or would be provided in the instance of defendant indigency. The Supreme Court has gradually expanded the coverage of the counsel language, however, to require the appointment of defense counsel in all federal and state felony cases and finally in all misdemeanor cases involving the possibility of confinement to jail. An accused must be permitted to consult with an attorney before police interrogation and at all other "critical stages" in the criminal process. The accused may opt not to use the right to counsel, but if he or she does waive this right, it must be both informed and voluntary. It is up to the presiding judge to determine whether a defendant is reasonably requesting waiver. Juvenile delinquency proceedings also require the appoint-

ment of counsel. *See also* CRITICAL STAGE, 135; DEFENSE ATTORNEY, 88; PUBLIC DEFENDER, 111.

Significance   The assistance of counsel doctrine has developed around two basic points. First, the aid by counsel is invaluable to criminal cases, and due process requires the "guiding hand of counsel" for an accused charged with a criminal defense. Justice Black remarked in *Gideon v. Wainwright* (372 U.S. 335: 1963), that lawyers are necessities, not luxuries. Second, a defendant should not be denied assistance of counsel because he or she is indigent. Any person who is charged with a criminal offense and who is not able to afford counsel cannot have a fair trial unless counsel is provided by the state. The right to counsel has also been extended to various critical stages of the criminal process both before and after trial. A critical stage is defined as any step in the criminal process where the advice of counsel may be essential to protecting the rights of an accused person, or where the defendant's overall fate is substantially affected. Currently recognized as critical stages are custodial interrogations, preliminary hearings, arraignments, post-indictment lineups, sentencing, and probation revocation hearings. Assistance of counsel is also a part of the civil trial process. While such assistance is not constitutionally mandated for civil trials, federal appellate courts have held that less strict adherence to evidentiary rules and less formal discovery compliance ought to be applied through trial courts when one of the parties is unrepresented by counsel. In the case of an unrepresented prisoner plaintiff in civil rights actions, counsel is often appointed by the trial judge to ensure fairness.

Attrition   **(127)**
The reduction in the number of cases as they progress through the criminal process. Case attrition is a product of discretion as it is exercised at each step of the process. At each stage, some cases are dropped, others diverted, and some advanced to the next step. Attrition could be represented as liquid moving through a funnel with continually fewer cases remaining to progress all the way through to conviction and sentence. Department of Justice data show that felony case attrition is extremely high. Most attrition occurs at the early stages of the process. Many crimes are not reported, and of those reported, arrests take place in less than 20 percent of the cases. Additional drop-off occurs during prosecutorial review, with many cases either diverted to agencies outside the criminal process and others judged unsuitable for prosecution. Attrition of cases within the courts

is somewhat more limited, particularly where prosecutors screen cases stringently prior to bringing charges. *See also* DISCRETION, 140.

Significance The attrition of criminal cases, especially those at the felony level, is extensive. The point at which attrition occurs varies by jurisdiction and differences in state law. Generally, however, attrition is explained through several factors or variables. Each of these reflect that the criminal process does not operate mechanically. Rather, it is highly subject to the exercise of discretion by those who have official roles. The first factor involves the substantive legal decisions that must be made on each case. A determination must be made as to whether there is sufficient evidence to establish the defendant's guilt. Police, prosecutors, and judges may each apply different standards. Thus cases where police have probable cause to arrest may be rejected by prosecutors or judges at subsequent stages because the case is not sufficient for trial. Another factor is the priority assigned to particular crimes. As prosecutors deal with backlogged court dockets, they may determine, for example, that prosecution for the offense of writing an insufficient funds check has low priority. That is especially true if the victim has civil recourse. Adoption of priorities allows police and prosecutors to direct scarce resources to more serious cases. Finally, attrition is attributable to subjective personal standards of justice pursued by individual members of the courtroom workgroup.

Bind Over (128)

The act of a court after finding there is sufficient evidence to believe that an accused has committed a crime. When a person is arrested and charged, he or she is entitled to an appearance before a judicial officer for a determination of whether there is probable cause to justify sending the case on to the trial stage. This probable cause determination is most often made at a proceeding known as a preliminary hearing or preliminary examination. If the judicial officer finds sufficient evidence to satisfy the probable cause standard, the case is "bound over" for trial. *See also* PRELIMINARY HEARING, 169.

Significance The process leading to bind over is part of the winnowing that is aimed at keeping innocent people from having to undergo the expense and rigors of a trial. The idea is to protect the accused from facing charges that are arbitrarily brought or are otherwise lacking in substance. In states that use grand juries, cases may be bound over for possible indictment. The term *bind over*, then, refers to the passing of the case along to the adjudication stage of the criminal process. If sufficient evidence is not presented, the case is not advanced or bound over. Rather, it is likely (though not necessarily) to be dismissed.

Charge (129)

Formal accusation that a person committed a crime. A charge is the underlying substantive violation reflected in an accusation, and the filing of a charge formally begins the judicial proceedings in the criminal process. The formal charge not only names the accused, but also describes essential elements of the crime in some detail. A charge can be lodged against a person in one of several ways. Charges can be introduced by a prosecuting attorney. In states that do not use grand juries, this usually takes the form of a prosecutor filing an information. Prosecutors may seek indictments from grand juries. Police may also file formal charges. Complaints are charges commonly brought directly by arresting officers. Police also obtain arrest warrants from a judicial officer, although some jurisdictions require the prosecutor to review warrant requests. All of these approaches formally convey an accusation of criminal conduct. *See also* INDICTMENT, 152; INFORMATION, 153; PROSECUTORIAL FUNCTION, 178.

Significance The Sixth Amendment requires that persons be formally notified of criminal charges or accusations against them. Determination of the exact charges is usually done by the prosecuting attorney, although grand juries participate in the accusation process in some jurisdictions. In the former, the prosecutor files an information while in the latter an indictment is sought. Before charges can result in a trial, a judicial officer must determine that there is at least cause to believe the accused committed the crime. A person may be simultaneously charged with more than one offense. It is in this way that prosecutors bring habitual offender charges, for example; at least one for a current violation, and one because the accused has been convicted previously. It is also possible to charge a person with two or more instances of the same offense. Multiple charges are referred to as counts. Thus a person who burglarized nine residences in a neighborhood may be charged with nine counts of the offense of burglary. Charging a person with several counts opens the possibility of negotiating a plea of guilty on one or more of the original counts in exchange for not prosecuting on one or more other counts. The term *charge* is also used to describe the instructions given to a jury by a judge prior to deliberation. The charge conveys the principles and standards a jury is to use in making its decision.

Complaint (130)

A charging method generally reserved for less serious criminal violations. A complaint may also be used in civil cases in which the assertion of a claim is made to initiate the legal action. In criminal cases, a complaint is submitted to a judicial officer and asserts that someone has committed a crime. If sufficient evidence is provided to establish probable cause, an arrest warrant will be issued. *See also* INFORMATION, 153; WARRANT, 197.

Significance A complaint is a document based on the sworn assertions of a victim or an investigating police officer. Complaints are used most often in initiating misdemeanor charges. An information is almost identical, but is generally used to commence felony charges. An information is signed by the prosecuting attorney. The complaint is formal and submitted in writing. The written complaint complies with the Sixth Amendment mandate that a defendant be made aware of the charges in order to allow presentation of a defense.

Compulsory Process (131)

The Sixth Amendment right of an accused person to have witnesses in his or her favor. Compulsory process protects the defendant's right to present a defense that includes witnesses who may not want to appear voluntarily. A defendant may subpoena a party and compel his or her presence. A subpoena is the command of a court requiring a person to appear at a legal proceeding and offer testimony on a particular matter. A subpoena *duces tecum* is a process by which physical items such as papers or records are produced at such a proceeding. *See also* SUBPOENA, 193.

Significance The constitutional right to compulsory process was extended to the states in *Washington v. Texas* (388 U.S. 14: 1967), in which the Supreme Court determined that the right was fundamental. The compulsory process provision has been interpreted more broadly than the right to subpoena witnesses. It has been held to prevent a state from denying access to certain categories of witnesses, such as coparticipants in an alleged crime. Similarly, it prevents a state from creating situations in which the testimony by a witness for the defense is diminished in value by a judicial action or jury instruction. For example, the Supreme Court found a compulsory process violation in *Webb v. Texas* (409 U.S. 95: 1972), a case that involved judicial intimidation of a defense witness. The witness, serving a sentence for a prior conviction, was admonished by the trial judge about the "dangers of perjury," how a perjury conviction would mean substantial supplement of the sentence being served, and how perjury would impair chances of parole. The witness decided not to testify, and Webb argued that his only witness had been coerced into not testifying by the judge. The Supreme Court agreed. It cited the judge's "threatening" remarks as effectively driving the witness from the witness stand, resulting in the impairment of Webb's defense.

Confession (132)

An admission of guilt by a person accused of a crime. A confession is the most extreme form of self-incrimination. Accordingly, if a confession is to be admissible as evidence in a criminal proceeding, it must be freely and voluntarily given. Clearly, physical coercion is an unacceptable means of obtaining a confession. Neither may a confession be induced by promise or deception. Aside from the inhumane character of coercive methods, the confessions obtained by such means are likely to be unreliable. *See also* ASSISTANCE OF COUNSEL, 126; SELF-INCRIMINATION, 185.

Significance   The constitutional protections that apply to confessions are derived largely from the privilege against self-incrimination and the right to assistance of counsel. The traditional approach to confessions focused almost exclusively on physical coercion. Court decisions since the 1960s have stressed more extensively the "inherently coercive" character of custodial interrogation—the questioning of persons who are in police custody. Several conditions must be met before a confession may be used in a criminal prosecution. First, it must meet traditional standards of voluntariness. Second, under terms of such decisions as *Mallory v. United States* (354 U.S. 449: 1957), an arrested person must appear before a judicial officer without "unnecessary delay." This rule insures that an accused is not "worn down" by lengthy questioning. The famous *Miranda* case (*Miranda v. Arizona*, 384 U.S. 436: 1966) added the specific rights for an accused to remain silent and to see an attorney immediately following an arrest. Failure to deliver these warnings or provide counsel to indigents under custodial circumstances renders any confession inadmissible.

Confrontation (133)

The Sixth Amendment entitlement that an accused person must be confronted in court with the witnesses against him or her. The right to confrontation is often thought to be synonymous with the right to cross-examine accusers or adverse witnesses, but cross-examination is only one element in the clause's broader objective of fully exposing evidence to the rigors of close scrutiny. The right to confront requires that witnesses be brought to open court and placed under oath and thereby under the threat of perjury. Their testimony as well as their manner and presence is assessed there. The confrontation right entitles an accused to challenge the evidence against him or her in an attempt to present the best factual defense possible. An accused person is therefore given the opportunity to be present at all proceedings against him or her, and a relatively unrestricted direct examination/cross-examination process can be utilized. The Supreme Court held in *Pointer v. Texas* (380 U.S. 400: 1965) that the right to confrontation is a fundamental right that applies not only in federal cases but to the states as well through the Fourteenth Amendment. *See also* CROSS-EXAMINATION, 136; DIRECT EXAMINATION, 138.

Significance   The right to confrontation protects defendants from anonymous accusers. It permits a defendant to hear testimony and examine the evidence against him or her as fully as possible. Historically, the right to confront has meant that witness and defendant must be present in the courtroom for the trial at least. Though that expectation generally holds, it is not inflexible. A defendant may waive the right to presence and choose not to attend any or all of the proceedings. A defendant's courtroom behavior may also become sufficiently disruptive to justify removal of the defendant from the courtroom as a requisite to continuing. The Supreme Court ruled in *Illinois v. Allen* (391 U.S. 123: 1970) that removal of such defendants was acceptable. The Supreme Court has also said that the right to confront prohibits a state from placing a screen between a defendant and child victims who might testify. The Court said in *Coy v. Iowa* (108 S. Ct. 2798: 1988) that the confrontation protection guarantees the defendant a "face-to-face meeting" with all witnesses.

Conviction   **(134)**
A finding that a person is guilty of a charged crime. A conviction is a formal finding of fact and occurs when the prosecution is able to establish guilt "beyond a reasonable doubt." In the federal courts and in most states, a conviction by jury requires a unanimous decision. The Supreme Court has ruled in such cases as *Apodaca v. Oregon* (406 U.S. 404: 1972) that convictions based on nonunanimous jury decisions are constitutional so long as the margin is no smaller than nine to three. The opposite verdict from a conviction is an acquittal. *See also* ACQUITTAL, 121; JURY, 155; VERDICT, 254.

Significance   A conviction is a legal determination of criminal guilt. A conviction authorizes a court to impose some kind of penalty. The term conviction can also refer to the final judgment in a case that includes sentence. Accordingly, this final judgment or conviction occurs whether it was preceded by a judge or jury's verdict, a defendant pleading guilty, or a defendant pleading no contest.

Critical Stage   (135)

The point in a criminal proceeding at which an accused person is entitled to assistance of counsel. Critical stage assistance is essential to protecting the rights of an accused person and may substantially affect the criminal process as a whole. The Supreme Court has defined a critical stage as one where a defendant is required to take a step that might influence subsequent steps. Similarly, if a defendant has an opportunity to do something that may affect later proceedings, even though it may only be optional, the stage is sufficiently critical to require assistance of counsel. The decisive consideration is whether something may occur at a particular stage that will impact or prejudice adjudication of guilt. For example, if a defendant confesses during interrogation, that act may be difficult to reverse at subsequent stages. Thus it is a "critical stage." *See also* ASSISTANCE OF COUNSEL, 126.

Significance   The trial itself was the only critical stage of the criminal process requiring assistance of counsel until 1963. When the Supreme Court mandated trial assistance for all felonies in *Gideon v. Wainwright* (372 U.S. 335: 1963), it was inevitable that other steps in the criminal process would be reconsidered as well. Soon after the *Gideon* decision, such pretrial stages as custodial interrogations (*Miranda v. Arizona*, 384 U.S. 436: 1966), post-indictment investigations (*Massiah v. United States*, 377 U.S. 201: 1964), preliminary hearings (*White v. Maryland*, 373 U.S. 59: 1963), and post-indictment line-up processes (*United States v. Wade*, 388 U.S. 218: 1967) were determined to be critical stages. Indeed, just prior to *Gideon*, the Court had decided in *Hamilton v. Alabama* (368 U.S. 52: 1961) that counsel assistance was required at arraignments. The critical stage approach has also been extended to such post-trial proceedings as sentencing, probation revocation, and appeals. The formal recognition of so many critical stages reflects the extremely high priority the Supreme Court assigns to assistance of counsel. In effect, all government actions in a criminal case beginning with custodial interrogations and thereafter are deemed critical and require assistance of counsel.

Cross-Examination (136)

A principal feature of the adversary process and a right guaranteed through the confrontation clause of the Sixth Amendment. Cross-examination is a technique by which the credibility of witnesses is attacked. Cross-examination allows an attorney to reveal weaknesses in a witness's testimony, making it possible in some cases to completely discredit the witness. The scope of cross-examination is defined by direct examination since matters probed on cross-examination must have been raised in the direct examination. The right to confront adverse witnesses through cross-examination is a key component in a criminal defendant's need to create reasonable doubt. *See also* CONFRONTATION, 133; DIRECT EXAMINATION, 138; REASONABLE DOUBT, 179.

Significance How the opportunity to cross-examine a witness may impact on a trial can be seen in the fact situation in *Davis v. Alaska* (425 U.S. 308: 1974). In that case, a minor was a key prosecution witness in the criminal trial of an adult. The primary value of his testimony was his identification of the defendant. The young witness also had a juvenile record and was on probation at the time he appeared as a witness. The defense wished to develop both of these facts on cross-examination, but was unable under Alaska law to disclose or refer to either. The idea was to suggest to the jury that the young witness had reason to make the identification—that he was motivated by perceived pressure or undue need to cooperate with authorities. While the Court acknowledged the importance of the state's interest in protecting the youth from disclosure of his record, the Court said this interest was "outweighed" by the defendant's need to probe the "influence of possible bias." The possibility of bias, if pursued on cross-examination, might have substantially lessened the value of the witness' identification. The Court did not permit the restriction on disclosure of the young witness' record. The importance of a comparatively unrestricted opportunity to cross-examine is also evident in the Court's ruling in *Coy v. Iowa* (108 S. Ct. 2798: 1988). Iowa law allowed the use of a screen between a defendant charged with child molestation and the child victims if they testified. While the defendant could see the witnesses and hear their testimony from his side of the screen, the witnesses could not see him. The Court disallowed the practice as a blanket policy. The right to confront and cross-examine requires a "face-to-face meeting" between defendant and witness. A witness may "feel quite differently" during direct or cross-examination when testimony is given while looking at the person who might be harmed by "distorting or mistaking the facts."

Cruel and Unusual Punishment   **(137)**
A criminal penalty prohibited by the Eighth Amendment. Cruel and
unusual punishment standards have been drawn from evolving standards of decency. The status of a particular punishment may change
as society's values change. Currently the Supreme Court has said that
punishments that involve torture or cruelty are prohibited, as are
punishments that are degrading. Neither can a penalty be imposed on
a status or condition. In 1962, the Supreme Court considered
whether a state could impose a 90-day jail sentence for the crime of
narcotics addiction. The Court ruled in *Robinson v. California* (370
U.S. 660) that while a 90-day sentence was not cruel in an abstract
sense, it was cruel given the "crime." The Court regarded Robinson's
addiction as an illness, and said the sentence was analogous to punish-
ing someone for having any other kind of disease. Punishments must
also be "proportional" to the offense. They cannot be excessive. The
proportionality criterion applies to both capital and noncapital cases
when sentences are challenged as cruel and unusual. *See also*
SENTENCE, 186.

Significance   The cruel and unusual punishment doctrine holds
that punishments must "comport with human dignity." The death
penalty, a punishment unique in terms of its severity and irrevocabili-
ty, does not invariably offend the cruel and unusual punishment prohibition. Procedural flaws may make the imposition of the death
penalty impermissible, however. The Court ruled in *Furman v.
Georgia* (408 U.S. 238: 1972) that punishments imposed in an unstructured or arbitrary manner are cruel and unusual as a result. Following
Furman, 37 states modified their capital punishment laws to address
the defects discussed in the decision. The death sentence now may not
be imposed without a two-stage or bifurcated trial and sentencing
process. The sentencer must be provided with sufficient guidance for
making a determination of death. He or she must specify aggravating
circumstances in assessing the gravity of a particular offense, and the
sentencer must consider any and all mitigating circumstances. The
mandatory sentence of death is not permitted because it does not
allow for consideration of mitigating factors. The proportionality
principle has been applied to various capital crimes with the result
that unless a life is taken, the death penalty is an excessive or disproportionate response. The Court has also held that the death penalty
cannot be imposed on persons who were under the age of sixteen at
the time the crime was committed. Existence of a developmental disability, on the other hand, does not necessarily preclude imposition
of the death penalty. The last broadly focused cruel and unusual punishment challenge to the death penalty occurred in 1987 when the

Court reviewed evidence that whites are less likely to receive the death sentence than racial or ethnic minorities. The Court ruled in *McCleskey v. Kemp* (481 U.S. 279: 1987) that sentencing systems did not violate constitutional commands absent a demonstration of discriminatory intent.

Direct Examination (138)

Questioning of a witness by the party on whose behalf the witness is appearing. Direct examination is the first questioning of a witness. It is followed by cross-examination, which is conducted by the opposite party. If the party on whose behalf the witness testifies wishes to ask questions following cross-examination, it may do so on redirect examination. *See also* CROSS-EXAMINATION, 136; WITNESS, 198.

Significance Direct examination allows a party to develop testimony from his or her own witness. The objective of direct examination is to make the strongest case possible through the testimony of one's own witnesses. The questions posed on direct examination also define the scope of the questions that can be asked on cross-examination because cross-examination is limited to those matters addressed on direct examination. Thus, narrow direct examination may keep the other side from obtaining damaging testimony from a party's own witnesses.

Disclosure (139)

Release of information by one side in a legal case to the other side. Disclosure typically involves a prosecutor revealing information to the defense in a criminal case, but defense disclosure occurs in certain situations as well. Disclosure is a kind of discovery. While prosecutorial disclosure is largely informal, it may be mandatory under some circumstances. As a general practice, many prosecuting attorneys routinely share some of their case with defense counsel. Such a practice is often called an "open file" policy and commonly extends to at least making police reports available to the defense. When the prosecutor comes into possession of evidence that might aid the defendant, disclosure is required as a matter of due process. The prosecution must, for example, disclose to the defense that a state witness made inconsistent statements prior to trial. *See also* COURTROOM WORK GROUP, 87; DISCOVERY, 219.

Significance Prosecutorial disclosure occurs for two reasons. First, prosecutors are officers of the court. Considerations of due process require that prosecutors do not knowingly suppress evidence that might clear a criminal defendant. Further, if that evidence is to be of value to the defense and more generally to the judicial process, it must be disclosed in advance of the trial so that, for example, it may be utilized in cross-examination of witnesses. This reasoning sustains mandatory disclosure. Informal disclosure is undertaken for a different reason: it facilitates disposition of cases. When prosecutors share police reports, for example, defense counsel is usually better able to assess the strength of the case against his or her client. When faced with a strong case, defendants often plead guilty. A guilty plea is a conviction for the prosecutor, and prosecutors routinely attempt to "encourage" such pleas by making more information available. In addition to aiding in the disposition of cases, an open file policy reflects those expectations of cooperation consistent with the concept of the courtroom work group. In some jurisdictions, there are disclosure requirements on the defense in criminal cases. Notice of alibi defense is an example. Like mandatory prosecutorial disclosure, such notice is intended to allow the other side an opportunity to prepare for cross-examination.

Discretion (140)
Power possessed by officials to act on the basis of their own judgment. Discretion gives officials choices in making decisions, but the choices are not unbounded. Rather, discretion is generally circumscribed by some rules or principles and cannot be arbitrarily exercised. Discretion stems from many sources. One is that substantive law must be general. No law, including provisions of criminal codes, can anticipate every situation. As a result, it is necessary to determine what the law is trying to accomplish and apply that judgment to specific fact situations. Second, laws establish a wide variety of prohibitions. Often they are too numerous to fully enforce. Sometimes provisions of law conflict or compete with each other. In such circumstances, officials must exercise discretion to set enforcement policy which reflects priorities. Discretion may also be exercised when no guidelines exist. Finally, discretion exists because those who function in the criminal process are supposed to "do justice." This allows personal values to play a substantial role in the operations of the criminal process. *See also* ATTRITION, 127; EQUITY JURISDICTION, 49.

Significance Discretion is at the core of the operation of the criminal justice system. Discretion provides the criminal process with some flexibility and, to some extent, fosters decision making on an individual case base. Processes permitting the exercise of discretion are theoretically used to produce just results. At the same time, they are vulnerable to abuse. Thus it is necessary to create some framework within which the exercise of discretion may be productive but safeguarded as well. Discretion is a central ingredient at all the critical decisional steps of the criminal process. Police, for example, exercise discretion in making arrest decisions. Not all persons who could be arrested are taken into custody. It depends on the circumstances, the legal criteria that apply, and department policy priorities. Thus an officer chasing a fleeing felon through a park will ignore violations of an ordinance that prohibits use of intoxicants there. In other situations, police will not arrest an individual, but rather allow the person to remain free in exchange for information. Prosecutors determine whether or not to bring formal charges, and if so, what charge to bring. A judicial officer then exercises discretion with respect to pretrial release and on the issue of whether the prosecutor can demonstrate probable cause. Determination of sentence is also a step where judges possess substantial discretion. There is no doubt that discretion permeates the criminal process. Many view discretion as essential to obtaining just results. On the other hand, discretion may run counter to the value of equal protection. Substantive and procedural rules have been fashioned to operate as a counterweight to discretion in an effort to retain the positive results of its use while simultaneously diminishing the chances of its misuse.

Diversion (141)

Diversion is the routing of persons into alternative programs or activities rather than formally charging them with crimes. Diversion is one of the most important options available to law enforcement and prosecutors at the screening or charging stage of the criminal process. It is a technique used extensively with both adults and juveniles. Programs that deal with drug problems, for example, may provide a better alternative for an offender than formal prosecution. When a person is diverted, formal prosecution is not necessarily abandoned. Rather, the person is given an opportunity to participate in a particular alternative activity by deferring the prosecution decision. If the alternative program is successfully completed, prosecution will not occur. If, on the other hand, a person does not wish entry into a program or fails to perform satisfactorily once in a program, he or she will likely be prosecuted as though no diversion option existed. Diversion programs are usually quite attractive to the offender because successful completion of the activity eliminates any record of the offense. *See also* CHARGE, 129; PROSECUTORIAL FUNCTION, 178.

Significance   Diversion judgments are made by police, prosecutors, or courts. In the case of police-based or prosecutor-based diversion, the judgment to divert rests with a police agency or the prosecutor. Cases diverted by police or prosecutors neither appear in court nor require prior court approval. Court-based diversion is more extensive and typically involves community agencies outside the court structure as well as some units structurally attached to the courts. Diversion attempts to capitalize on the presence of community alternatives to adjudication, many of which are for substance abuse problems. If diversion is successful, it benefits the offender and saves the judicial system from having to process a particular case. Diversion has been a particularly effective technique for handling juveniles.

Double Jeopardy   (142)

Subjecting an individual to prosecution more than once for the same crime. The provision against double jeopardy precludes the state from repeatedly putting a citizen through the ordeal of prosecution for a particular offense and the possibility of conviction on the charge. The ban on double jeopardy was extended to the states by the Warren Court in *Benton v. Maryland* (395 U.S. 784: 1969). The double jeopardy clause of the Fifth Amendment is seen by the Court as representing a "fundamental ideal in our constitutional heritage." The clause does not prevent both federal and state levels of government from prosecuting persons for the same criminal act on the basis of dual sovereignty. Bank robbery, for example, is both a federal and a state crime if the bank has federal insurance coverage. Successive prosecutions at the state and local levels are precluded because local units of government are subordinate instrumentalities of the state. Dual sovereignty does not exist within a state. In a jury trial, jeopardy commences when the jury is sworn. In a nonjury trial, jeopardy begins when the first witness takes the stand. Cases dismissed prior to the beginning or "attachment" of jeopardy may be reinstated. The double jeopardy clause does not apply to cases where a defendant successfully appeals following a conviction and has the conviction set aside on grounds other than evidence insufficiency. Reprosecution in such situations is limited to a charge no greater than the equivalent of the original conviction that prompted the appeal. A sentence may be more severe following successful reprosecution without violating the clause if multiple punishments have been imposed. *See also* CHARGE, 129; PROSECUTORIAL FUNCTION, 178.

Significance   A double jeopardy determination is frequently made difficult by what constitutes sameness. Sameness is usually resolved by precluding prosecutions for two offenses where the same evidence is required to prove guilt. A "same transaction" test, which views offenses in terms of similar actions by the defendant, may also be used. Neither approach clearly delineates sameness, however. The doctrine of collateral estoppel is held to be part of the double jeopardy protection and provides some assistance in solving the sameness problem. The doctrine forbids reprosecution in cases where a key fact issue present in the second case was resolved in favor of the accused in the first case. Another double jeopardy problem is created by the declaration of a mistrial after jeopardy has attached. If the defendant makes the mistrial motion, ordinarily there is no double jeopardy issue. But if the prosecution makes the motion, or if the judge grants a mistrial without a motion, an ambiguous situation is created. In the latter two situations, jeopardy may be double on a reprosecution unless the trial was "manifestly necessitated."

Entrapment (143)

Intentional action by a government official that induces a person into committing a criminal act. Entrapment is an affirmative defense that excuses a person from responsibility for crimes prompted by governmental deception or persuasion. An entrapment defense is possible where a case can be made that government so aggressively sought evidence against a person that it actually prompted illegal conduct. In an entrapment situation, the government agent originates the plan for committing the crime and either persuades or encourages another to participate or falsely creates the perception that the act is not criminal. An accused who wishes to assert a defense of entrapment must show that except for the action of government, he or she would not have committed the crime. *See also* AFFIRMATIVE DEFENSE, 122.

Significance   Entrapment constitutes governmental conduct so offensive that it is a denial of due process. Accordingly, prosecution based on evidence from such crimes is prohibited. The entrapment defense often comes from "sting" operations where law enforcement agents go undercover and arrange purchases of contraband, commonly narcotics, from persons against whom they are trying to develop a case. Under such circumstances, it is difficult for an accused to show that criminal conduct was not otherwise intended. Thus, the entrapment defense is seldom successful.

Evidence (144)

Material presented as proof at a trial. Evidence provides the basis upon which a fact dispute is resolved. Evidence generally takes the form of witness testimony or physical objects such as documents and records. Parties to a dispute are entitled to submit evidence that will support their respective positions before the trier of fact. Submissions or evidence are governed by rules enforced by the court. Evidence that fails to meet evidentiary standards is not placed before the fact-finder. *See also* RULES OF EVIDENCE, 183.

Significance   Evidence is offered to support a claim or allegation. There are three broad types or classes of evidence. The first is direct evidence, which comes in the form of witness testimony. If a witness actually saw an event or heard something relating to a particular dispute, he or she may convey that information to the court. The party calling the witness elicits some information through a series of questions called direct examination. The opposing party is then able to respond through cross-examination. Second, there is indirect or circumstantial evidence, which is not based on direct knowledge, but rather deductions that are drawn from other facts. Circumstantial evidence speaks indirectly to the dispute. Third, there is real or demonstrative evidence. This class of evidence consists of objects that themselves relate to the fact question before the court. A gun with fingerprints or financial records are examples of real evidence.

Exclusionary Rule   (145)
A court-fashioned rule of evidence that in criminal trial prohibits the use of items gained from an unconstitutional search or seizure. The exclusionary rule was designed to give effect to the Fourth Amendment prohibition against unreasonable searches and seizures. The rule is highly controversial and is not explicitly required by the Fourth Amendment. Until 1914, common law provided that evidence obtained in violation of the Fourth Amendment could still be used in a criminal trial. *Weeks v. United States* (232 U.S. 383: 1914) broke from the tradition and established the exclusionary rule in federal cases. The Supreme Court said that without the rule, the Fourth Amendment is of no value and "might as well be stricken from the Constitution." The Court refrained, however, from taking a parallel step for state criminal trials. In *Wolf v. Colorado* (338 U.S. 25: 1949), the Court chose to leave the states free to choose whether the rule would operate in their courts. In 1949 the Court did not see the rule as essential enough that it must be extended to the states. *Mapp v. Ohio* (367 U.S. 643: 1961) overruled *Wolf* and established the rule for state trials. Since *Mapp*, the Court has had occasion to consider the exclusionary rule quite often. While the Court has chosen to re-

tain the rule, dissatisfaction with it is apparent. Two patterns are revealed in the Court's recent handling of the rule. First, the rule will not be extended beyond the trial setting. The Burger Court rejected extension of it to grand jury proceedings in *United States v. Calandra* (414 U.S. 338: 1974). The Court then allowed illegally obtained evidence to be used in a civil tax proceeding in *United States v. Janis* (429 U.S. 874: 1976). Second, the Court is willing to limit the coverage of the rule. It allowed otherwise inadmissible evidence to be used in impeaching a defendant's trial testimony in *Oregon v. Hass* (420 U.S. 714: 1975), and it limited *habeas corpus* access to the federal courts in state search cases in *Stone v. Powell* (428 U.S. 465: 1976). *See also* PRETRIAL MOTION, 173; RULES OF EVIDENCE, 183.

Significance   The exclusionary rule is justified in many ways. It is seen by many as an indispensable doctrine for making operational the personal protections guaranteed by the Fourth Amendment. The rule creates disincentives for police misconduct in the search context by making the products of such searches inadmissible. Others argue that the exclusionary rule protects the integrity of the courts by keeping the judicial process free of illegally seized evidence. Criticisms of the rule are numerous and substantial, however. Many regard it as excessive because it goes beyond Fourth Amendment provisions. The costs of the rule are seen as too high because it often results in criminal conduct going unpunished. Further, it tends to defeat the best test of evidence, which is its reliability. The rule frequently allows suppression of reliable evidence because the means of obtaining it were flawed. In sum, critics of the exclusionary rule argue that instead of sanctioning police officers, the rule rewards criminal defendants. The rule is clearly threatened as political pressures mount to modify it. The exclusionary rule survives because its detractors have not been able to find an adequate alternative. However, in the British legal system, for example, illegally obtained evidence can be introduced in a case with police miconduct subject to administrative discipline.

Felony   (146)
A classification that covers the most serious kind of crime. Felonies can be penalized by imprisonment for a year or more. A felony is different from petty crimes, which are called misdemeanors. Conviction for certain felonies may bring the possibility of the death sentence. Most felonies also involve civil disabilities such as loss of voting rights or certain licensure privileges. Felonies are defined by legislatures. They vary somewhat from state to state, although such differences typically involve only internal gradations of criminal conduct. For ex-

ample, some states distinguish between Class A and Class B felonies with sentences that vary by class. Nonetheless, all felonies are serious offenses and include murder, criminal sexual conduct, arson, and a number of assaultive offenses as well as those committed with a weapon. *See also* MISDEMEANOR, 160.

Significance   A felony represents the most severe criminal behavior. Accordingly, felonies are processed by the major trial courts of a state. This is usually the state's court of general jurisdiction. Federal felonies are handled by the United States district court. Those charged with felonies are entitled to a wide range of procedural protections. If a felony involves the possibility of the death sentence, the Eighth Amendment requires a two-stage process that considers an intricate array of possibly aggravating and mitigating factors. Misdemeanors, on the other hand, are usually handled more summarily because the issues are usually less complex, and the range of penalties is certainly more restricted.

Fine   (147)

A monetary punishment levied by a court on a person convicted of a crime. A fine is generally used as an exclusive penalty for less serious offenses and ordinance violations, but may often be used, in addition to imprisonment, for more serious crimes. A fine is also often coupled with the sanction of probation. *See also* RESTITUTION, 182; SENTENCE, 186.

Significance   The fine is the oldest form of criminal sanction and remains the most frequently used. Fines do punish, but they do so without adding to the number of incarcerated persons, an important by-product in a time of great overcrowding in detention facilities. Fines are the punishment of choice for those who advocate alternatives to imprisonment for convicted offenders. Fines also generate substantial revenue for state and local governments. Most estimates place this amount in excess of $1 billion each year. Refusal to pay a fine may result in imprisonment. The Supreme Court ruled, however, in *Williams v. Illinois* (399 U.S. 925: 1970) that imprisonment of an indigent person for failure to pay a fine violates standards of due process and equal protection. A variation on the basic concept of the fine is forfeiture. Forfeiture involves the seizure of property and other assets of those engaged in criminal conduct. Typically, forfeiture judgments are sought against those in organized crime activities. Recently, drug traffickers have been the principal target of forfeiture processes. The Comprehensive Forfeiture Act, enacted by Congress in 1984, contains the current federal law on forfeiture. Most states have similar forfeiture statutes. The rationale for the forfeiture of assets is that law breakers ought not to profit from their criminal behavior. A person subjected to forfeiture may also be punished by imprisonment and/or fine upon conviction.

Grand Jury   (148)
An investigative body that makes accusations rather than determines guilt. The grand jury evaluates information generated on its own or brought to it by a prosecutor. If the grand jury determines that probable cause exists, it returns an indictment against an individual. The indictment signifies that the grand jury feels a trial on specific charges is reasonable. In English law the grand jury had the function of protecting persons from being tried arbitrarily. An American grand jury typically ranges from 12 to 23 persons with selection occurring under guidelines that require neutral and nondiscriminatory processes. These guidelines have been carefully defined by the Supreme Court in such cases as *Alexander v. Louisiana* (405 U.S. 625: 1972). Grand juries operate in secret to protect persons they may not indict. Witnesses appear before grand juries under subpoena. Failure to provide information desired by a grand jury may result in a witness being cited for contempt, as in *Branzburg v. Hayes* (408 U.S. 665: 1972). Upon hearing all testimony relating to a particular person, the grand jury determines by a simple majority vote whether to indict. While grand juries may function through their own initiative, they are usually guided and sometimes dominated by a prosecutor. The latter determines which witnesses will appear and which evidence will be developed. The prosecutor has virtually complete discretion in grand jury proceedings through control of relevant information. Grand juries usually indict persons whom prosecutors want to be indicted. A person need not appear before a grand jury to be indicted. Witnesses who do appear usually are not permitted counsel at the proceeding itself, although out-of-room consultation during the proceeding is often permitted. A witness must be advised of his or her rights against self-information, but this warning may be quite general under *United States v. Washington* (431 U.S. 181: 1977). The Fifth Amendment requires grand juries in the American federal system. The requirement has never been extended to the states, however. In *Hurtado v. California* (110 U.S. 516: 1884), the Supreme Court held that California's use of the information process, instead of the grand jury, did not deny due process. *Hurtado* gave the states the opportunity to determine their own procedure for bringing criminal charges. Thirty-two states have elected to use the grand jury, at least for some portion of

their criminal proceedings. Only eight states use it for all cases. Decisions subsequent to *Hurtado* have enhanced the investigative powers of grand juries. An alternative accusatorial process to grand jury indictment is the information. This procedure allows a prosecutor to submit charges directly to a judge. *See also* INDICTMENT, 152; INFORMATION, 153.

Significance   The grand jury function is completely different from the guilt adjudication function. Grand jury proceedings have therefore been freed from the rigorous procedural and evidentiary standards used at trial. Such decisions as *Costello v. United States* (350 U.S. 359: 1953) stress the need for informality for grand juries. The relaxation of procedural constraints was intended to maximize the opportunity for a grand jury to consider as much evidence as possible before making its decision to charge. Flexibility designed to enhance the investigative power of grand juries has some costs, however. Procedural protections of witnesses are less extensive than at the trial stage, and a heightened potential for misconduct exists relative to contempt and immunity practices. Michigan permits a one-person grand jury. This person is always a trial judge, and he or she functions in the same manner as a grand jury composed of laypeople.

Hearsay   (149)
A statement by a witness repeating the words of another person rather than testifying on the basis of direct knowledge. Hearsay testimony is not based on what a witness sees, hears, or otherwise senses himself or herself. Rather, hearsay repeats what someone else saw or heard. If someone testified that "my supervisor told me that she saw John Doe leave work early," that would be an example of hearsay. Hearsay is indirect evidence and, as a result, is generally inadmissible as a matter of evidentiary rule in courts. The reason for the hearsay rule is that such testimony cannot be subjected to such tests of truthfulness and reliability as cross-examination. *See also* CROSS-EXAMINATION, 136; RULES OF EVIDENCE, 183.

Significance   Hearsay is second-hand or indirect evidence. It is evidence from a witness based not on what the witness heard or saw personally. Rather, hearsay testimony merely repeats what a witness heard from someone else. Rules of evidence barring hearsay are designed to ensure that testimony coming before a court is reliable. Assertions that occur in open court and survive cross-examination by the opposing party are regarded as credible, and the hearsay rule protects this method of screening evidence. There are exceptions to the hearsay rule, but before a court allows hearsay, it must be convinced of both the reliability of hearsay testimony and the compelling need to use it. In some cases, for example, declarations of dying persons may be represented in court as truthfully uttered. Similarly, hearsay may be allowed when a defendant is charged with criminal conspiracy. Courts generally permit greater use of hearsay in civil actions.

Immunity (150)

A means of securing testimony in a judicial or legislative proceeding by satisfying the privilege against self-incrimination. Immunity prevents a person from involuntarily becoming a witness against himself or herself. The government can compel a person to disclose incriminating evidence, but when a witness is granted immunity, he or she cannot be prosecuted based upon the compelled testimony. Immunity was first considered by the Supreme Court in *Counselman v. Hitchcock* (142 U.S. 547: 1892). In that case, the Court held that the federal immunity statute was defective in that it left a witness vulnerable to prosecution based on evidence derived from compelled testimony. Four years later, in *Brown v. Walker* (161 U.S. 591: 1896), the Court was asked to determine whether immunity could shield a witness beyond prevention of actual prosecution. The Court decided that disgrace or impairment of reputation, which were possible consequences of involuntary testimony, were outside the coverage of the self-incrimination privilege. They need not be addressed when granting immunity. The matter of personal disgrace arose again in the mid-twentieth century during the investigations into political subversion and national security. In *Ullmann v. United States* (350 U.S. 422: 1956), the Court upheld provisions of the Immunity Act of 1954, which authorized immunity for testimony in national security cases. Both the *Ullmann* and *Brown* decisions held that self-incrimination protects only from the danger of prosecution, not the danger of disgrace or other costs stemming from it. *See also* PROSECUTING ATTORNEY, 110; SELF-INCRIMINATION, 185.

Significance   Immunity is typically used to obtain evidence from one person leading to the conviction of another. It allows information to develop that is not readily available through other investigative techniques. Given the frequent use of immunity, a critical question revolves around how extensive it must be. It must extend to direct use of the testimony itself, known as *use immunity,* but it frequently includes more. *Counselman* held that a witness must be protected from prosecution based on evidence derived from compelled testimony, known as *derived use immunity.* Even derived use immunity is limited, however. It does not prevent prosecution of a witness for a crime about which he or she may have involuntarily testified as long as the evidence used in the prosecution was developed wholly apart from the witness' testimony. *Transactional immunity* is the most inclusive form of immunity. It prevents prosecution for any matter or transaction about which the witness testifies. In *Kastigar v. United States* (406 U.S. 441: 1972), the Court determined that derivative use immunity satisfied the prohibition against self-incrimination and that transactional immunity "affords the witness considerably broader protection than does the Fifth Amendment privilege." Derived use immunity is coextensive with the protection to which a person is entitled under the Fifth Amendment. *Kastigar* did require, however, that if a witness is subsequently charged, the prosecution must bear the burden of demonstrating that the evidence is independent of the witness' compelled testimony. Grants of immunity also apply across jurisdictions. When the Supreme Court made the self-incrimination protection applicable to the states in *Malloy v. Hogan* (378 U.S. 1: 1964), it also looked at federal-state reciprocity on grants of immunity. In *Murphy v. Waterfront Commission of New York* (378 U.S. 52: 1964), it ruled that a witness granted immunity to testify at a state or federal proceeding could not be prosecuted at the other level based on the compelled testimony.

Imprisonment (151)
Sanction of confinement imposed on a person found guilty of a crime. Terms of imprisonment are defined by legislative bodies, which establish minimum and maximum sentences for an offense. Judges then chose from the statutory range when imposing sentence on a particular offender. Sentences may be either determinate or indeterminate. Determinate or fixed sentences require a judge to specify a definite term from the range. If the range for an offense runs from five to ten years, the judge fixes the sentence at, for example, six years. Indeterminate sentences, on the other hand, are those where a judge sets a minimum and maximum from the range. How long a person actually serves beyond the minimum is indefinite. The decision as to actual length is made by correctional authorities, most often parole boards. If an offender is convicted of more than one offense or count, sentences may be imposed for each. These sentences may be concurrent or run simultaneously. If the offender must serve consecutive sentences, they are served one after the other. Terms of imprisonment may be supplemented on the basis of recidivist or habitual offender statutes. Such laws require additional periods of incarceration for offenders with previous convictions. The length of recidivist supplements increases with prior convictions. In virtually every im-

prisonment situation, prisoners may earn time off their sentences by behaving satisfactorily. Such early release consideration is called "good time." It acts as an incentive for good behavior, and is generally recognized as an essential ingredient for maintaining order in prisons. *See also* PROBATION, 177; SENTENCE, 186.

Significance Imprisonment is a criminal sanction generally reserved for serious offenders. An exception, of course, is the local jail terms for certain misdemeanors. Detention in county jails for a misdemeanor cannot exceed one year in length. This misdemeanor maximum sentence is imposed infrequently because local facilities are typically filled to capacity with people awaiting felony trials and those awaiting transfer to state prison facilities to begin more lengthy sentences for felony convictions. Increasing use of imprisonment, especially for fixed or determinate periods, reflects a movement toward the view that sentences are supposed to punish rather than rehabilitate. Long term incarceration also keeps those who have been convicted of violent or assaultive crimes physically segregated from the public. Implementation of punishment or segregative sentencing objectives requires a capacity to house many prisoners, however, leading to costly expansion in prison facilities in recent years.

Indictment (152)

A formal accusation brought by a grand jury. If a grand jury decides by a majority vote to return a "true bill," an indictment is issued after consideration of evidence presented by a prosecutor. A true bill represents a grand jury finding that the prosecutor has established probable cause that a person has committed a crime. The true bill also reflects the grand jury's finding that it is reasonable to make a person stand trial on a criminal charge. The true bill is itself an accusation. Grand jury decisions to indict need not be unanimous. Indeed, most of the states that use grand juries require a two-thirds or three-quarters majority to return an indictment. If a grand jury does not indict at the request of a prosecutor, the case can generally be reintroduced before another grand jury. *See also* GRAND JURY, 148; INFORMATION, 153.

Significance The indictment is a means of protecting individuals from arbitrary or unjust prosecution. It is part of the complex winnowing process aimed at preventing individuals from having to undergo the stress and expense of trial unless substantial evidence of wrongdoing exists. Indictment reflects the grand jury's accusatorial function. Grand juries are also used as a means of information gathering. Under terms of the Fifth Amendment, a grand jury indictment is required in the prosecution of federal offenses, at least for serious crimes. In addition, thirty-two states use grand juries for at least some of their criminal cases. While the grand jury system remains in many states, it tends to be inefficient and expensive. The alternative to indictment is the information, a preliminary hearing process where a prosecutor directly petitions a court to bring criminal charges.

Information (153)

An accusation made by a prosecuting attorney before a court. The information is offered under oath and supports the charges with at least probable cause level evidence. The information is used in almost every state for misdemeanors, but more than half the states have also substituted the information for grand jury indictment even for serious crimes. An information is almost identical to a complaint except it is signed by the prosecutor instead of a police officer or the victim. The federal government, though required to use grand juries for serious crimes by provision of the Fifth Amendment, has begun using the information for less serious crimes. *See also* COMPLAINT, 130; INDICTMENT, 152; PRELIMINARY HEARING, 169.

Significance   The information is designed to determine if sufficient evidence exists to bind a defendant over for trial. The information places final determination of whether probable cause exists in the hands of a judicial officer rather than a grand jury. The Supreme Court ruled in *Hurtado v. California* (110 U.S. 516: 1884) that states could use the information without violating the Fourteenth Amendment. The *Hurtado* ruling still stands. Indeed, the pattern has been that most states have substituted the information for grand jury proceedings for some, if not all, criminal offenses. While protecting the accused from being taken to trial arbitrarily, the information is also much more cost-efficient than the grand jury.

Insanity Defense (154)

Assertion that mental disease excuses a criminal act. The insanity defense is built on the concept of criminal intent or *mens rea*, the "guilty mind." Persons who are mentally ill, under terms of this defense, cannot be held accountable for their behavior because they have no criminal intent. While this proposition may be generally reasonable, there is no real consensus on how mentally ill a person must be to be excused from criminal responsibility. This lack of consensus is reflected in the several different standards or criteria used in the fifty states.

A number of states use the old (mid-nineteenth century) English standard, the *M'Naghten* rule. This test is also referred to as the "right and wrong" standard. Under this standard, a person is legally mentally ill if he or she does not understand the nature of the criminal act or know the act to be wrong. Other states use a modified form of the *M'Naghten* standard, which integrates the notion of the irresistible impulse. That is, while the person may have known an action was wrong, the mental illness prevented the persons from controlling his or her conduct. Still other states use the American Law Institute standard. Under this test, a person is criminally responsible if the mental illness prevents him or her from possessing "substantial capacity" to "appreciate the criminality" of an action or to control behavior to the "requirements of the law." Separate from the insanity issue is the matter of competency to stand trial. Competence does not relate to guilt, but rather to the capacity of a defendant to consult with counsel effectively and understand the meaning of the proceedings in which he or she is involved. When the competence of an individual is in doubt, a formal hearing is held to determine competency to stand trial. *See also* AFFIRMATIVE DEFENSE, 122; *MENS REA*, 159.

Significance   The insanity defense is an affirmative defense in that it introduces a new fact issue to a criminal proceeding. The defense not only requires the state to prove guilt, if a not guilty plea is entered, but also offers evidence as to mental illness that eliminates culpability even if the criminal act can be proven. Like other affirmative defenses, the burden of proof in an insanity defense resides with the defendant. The defense has always been somewhat controversial, but the controversy heated substantially with the acquittal of John Hinckley on charges stemming from the attempt on President Ronald Reagan's life. The insanity defense, however, is not frequently asserted. Many states have established an option for juries in insanity defense cases to find a defendant guilty but mentally ill. This verdict requires that the person be placed in a mental health facility to undergo treatment. The person remains institutionalized until recovery is deemed sufficient to transfer the person to some kind of correctional facility.

Jury   (155)

A specific number of citizens called to render a judgment on various issues of fact in a legal proceeding. A jury functions in its most common forms as a grand jury or as a petit, or trial, jury. The grand jury hears evidence and determines whether a person must stand trial on a criminal charge. A petit jury makes an actual determination of guilt or innocence in a criminal trial or resolves disputes in civil cases. Article IV of the U.S. Constitution mandates jury trials in all federal criminal cases. The right is repeated in the Sixth Amendment, which entitles an accused to "a public trial, by an impartial jury." The Seventh Amendment preserves the right of jury trials in civil cases where the amount in controversy exceeds $20. In 1968, the Supreme Court extended the jury trial provision in criminal cases involving "serious" crimes to the states in *Duncan v. Louisiana* (391 U.S. 145). The Court said trial by jury is "fundamental to the American scheme of justice." Selection of jurors must conform to constitutional and statutory guidelines. Juries must be selected in ways that do not systematically exclude any segment of the population, although no particular jury needs to reflect proportionately a community's population. The *venire* or jury pool from which a particular jury is to be drawn is created by random selection from a master list of registered voters or licensed drivers within the jurisdiction. Once the *venire* has been established, a *voir dire* examination is conducted to determine if the potential jurors are impartial. Jurors whose responses to questions during *voir dire* are not acceptable are excused for cause. Following *voir dire,* counsel for either party may exclude jurors through a peremptory challenge. Juries are typically composed of twelve people, but states are permitted to use juries of as few as six people in criminal or civil cases. Federal civil juries may be smaller than twelve people, but in criminal proceedings juries must consist of twelve citizens. State juries need not resolve fact issues by unanimous decision even in criminal cases. Decisions by juries divided by as much as nine to three are constitutionally permissible in state criminal cases. Unanimity is required if the jury is as small as six and is required in all federal criminal jury decisions. *See also* GRAND JURY, 148; MASTER JURY LIST, 158; VENIRE, 194; VERDICT, 254; *VOIR DIRE,* 196.

Significance   A jury trial is guaranteed to all defendants in federal criminal cases by the Sixth Amendment. The jury system, like many other elements of the U.S. legal process, was inherited from England. The expectation that selected citizens should participate in making judgments about other citizens is deeply ingrained in the legal traditions of both countries. Indeed, the utilization of the jury is seen by many as imperative to the proper functioning of the adversary system. Yet the quality of jury performance is frequently questioned. The options the Supreme Court has permitted states regarding jury size and unanimity will prompt further questions. Nonetheless, the jury fosters citizen involvement in the justice system, and, specific case deviations notwithstanding, it brings a common sense element into the legal process. A defendant in a criminal case need not exercise the right to trial by jury. Upwards of 90 percent of all criminal defendants waive jury trial and plead guilty to some charge in lieu of trial, or agree to have both questions of fact and law decided by the presiding judge.

Juvenile Process (156)

Steps followed to adjudicate charges of criminal conduct by minors. The juvenile process is located in juvenile courts, which are created by statute in each of the fifty states. Jurisdiction of juvenile courts is derived directly from a child's status as a minor. Juvenile status is commonly defined as age eighteen or younger, and the juvenile courts have jurisdiction over minors who commit conventional criminal acts, those kinds of crimes such as assault or robbery that have exact counterparts for adults. Criminal conduct for a juvenile is called delinquency. Juvenile courts also have jurisdiction over status offenses, acts that stem directly from juvenile status and for which adults are not prosecuted. Truancy is an example of a status offense. While the processes may vary slightly across the states, there is a similar pattern to the juvenile process in most states. The process usually begins with an arrest. Law enforcement authorities who arrest juveniles may decide not to refer the case at all or divert a juvenile to some other agency. If, on the other hand, the case is formally referred, it is done through the filing of a delinquency petition. Juvenile authorities then conduct an intake interview, which roughly corresponds to a preliminary examination in the adult process. This review may or may not be extensive, but its objective is to determine whether the case ought to remain in the process, be diverted to an agency outside the juvenile court structure, or be dismissed altogether. If the case is continued for adjudication, at least two other questions may be considered. Normally juveniles are released to the custody of their parents pending adjudication. Some juveniles, however, may need to be detained during this period. Detention can only occur following a formal hearing. Second, some cases may be transferred to adult court. These are cases where the offense is serious and the juvenile probably has an extensive record of delinquency. In order for a case to be transferred, the juvenile court must waive its jurisdiction over the case. Such a decision can only be made after a formal waiver hearing. The cases that remain in juvenile court move to an adjudication hearing, a stage where evidence is taken on the delinquency allegation. The adjudication hearing is quite formalized, but is somewhat less adversarial in character than an adult trial. If the adjudication hearing produces a finding of delinquency, a final hearing must be held to determine appropriate disposition of the case. *See also* DIVERSION, 141; JUVENILE COURT, 58; STATUS OFFENSE, 190.

Significance The establishment of a separate court process for juveniles occurred around 1900. The objective was to implement the *parens patriae* concept that the state has a special quasi-parental role with minors. It was contended that with separate juvenile processes, minors could be dealt with in a way different from adults. The approach of juvenile courts was to be paternalistic and nonadversarial. Prior to the 1960s, the influence of *parens patriae* led to a highly informal juvenile process. While this informality was generally benevolent, juveniles possessed virtually none of the constitutional protections available to adults. Assistance of counsel, for example, was not required and evidentiary rules were substantially relaxed. This situation changed rather dramatically in the mid-1960s as the Warren Court imposed a number of legal requirements on juvenile proceedings. Three Court decisions form the foundation for these changes. The first was *Kent v. United States* (383 U.S. 541: 1966), which involved the waiver of jurisdiction by a juvenile court to allow transfer of a juvenile's case to adult court. The juvenile judge had transferred the case without making any findings in a formal proceeding and had not offered any reasons in support of the transfer decision. The Supreme Court imposed several specific procedural requirements on the transfer process including a hearing, representation by counsel, and access to all records and reports on the juvenile that might be germane to the transfer. *Kent* was limited to a relatively small number of cases involving waiver to adult courts. Nonetheless, it clearly conveyed the Court's growing concern for the fundamental fairness of juvenile proceedings. A more comprehensive pronouncement was to come in *In re Gault* (387 U.S. 1: 1967). The Court recognized that juvenile and adult proceedings had been intentionally different up to that point in time, but said that the differences could not remain at the cost of basic constitutional protections. Although juveniles benefitted from the informal process, the Court sought to add some procedural protections. "Under our Constitution," said the Court, "the condition of being a boy does not justify a kangaroo court." The holding in *Gault* required that delinquency proceedings that may lead to detention must provide juveniles with access to counsel, with appointed counsel in the instance of indigency, adequate notification of charges with a right to confront witnesses, and the privilege against self-incrimination. The Court reiterated views first expressed in *Kent* that proceedings "must measure up to the essentials of due process and fair treatment." The third case of this group was *In re Winship* (397 U.S. 358: 1970). In *Winship* the Court considered whether juvenile courts could continue to use the civil standard of preponderance of evidence to determine delinquency. Using the old civil standard as provided by state law, Winship was found guilty of robbery. The Court determined that

152

proving guilt beyond a reasonable doubt was an essential element of due process. The informality that marked juvenile processes before *Kent* and *Gault* was clearly a thing of the past after *Winship*. After *Gault*, juvenile processes have continued to become more formalized.

Lineup   (157)

A process by which a suspect in a crime is presented with others to a witness. The purpose of a lineup is to obtain identification of a suspect. A lineup requires the lining up of a number of people generally resembling one another for observation by a witness. If a lineup is properly conducted, a witness who identifies a suspect may testify to that effect at trial. A lineup differs from a showup, which is a one-to-one confrontation between suspect and witness. A showup is used as an alternative to a lineup when a situation makes the lineup impossible. A showup is, however, subject to the same due process standards as the lineup.

Significance   Identification procedures such as lineups are admissible in criminal cases so long as they meet basic considerations of due process. In assessing identifications, the Court used the totality of circumstances doctrine with the reliability of the identification being the key consideration. Identifications cannot be made under circumstances that are suggestive or point to a particular suspect. Lineups, for example, with only one person dressed in the manner described by the witness or only one person approximating the physical description provided by the witness are categorically prohibited. The Supreme Court also struck down a lineup identification in *Foster v. California* (394 U.S. 440: 1969) because Foster was the only person who appeared in a second lineup after appearing in the first. The Court characterized the process as one that made "identifications virtually inevitable." The standards used in assessing the reliability of identifications were set out in *Neil v. Biggers* (409 U.S. 188: 1972). Reliability rests upon the opportunity of the witness to observe the criminal at the time of the offense, the attentiveness of the witness at that time, the accuracy of the witness' description of the suspect, and the witness' level of certainty at the time of confrontation with the suspect. Without sufficient reliability, identification testimony may not be used. The Court has also determined that post-indictment confrontations are a sufficiently critical stage in the criminal process that a suspect is entitled to assistance of counsel.

Master Jury List   (158)

Representative list of citizens from which the trial jury selection process begins. Juries are supposed to reflect a cross-section of the community, and the master jury list provides the source from which a representative sample of citizens may be drawn for service on specific cases. The procedure developed to select master jury lists must yield a representative sample. Under provision of the Federal Jury Selection and Service Act of 1968, the procedure must not exclude anyone from the possibility of jury service on the basis of race, gender, national origin, or economic status. The most common source for gathering names for the master jury list (or jury wheel) are lists of registered voters. While registered voter lists are not without some bias, they are usually current and computerized. Some jurisdictions operate from lists of licensed drivers or those billed for utilities like water service. Many jurisdictions have used computers to merge two or more different kinds of lists to maximize representation of the master jury list. *See also* JURY, 155; PEREMPTORY CHALLENGE, 167; *VENIRE*, 194.

Significance   Master jury lists must reflect a cross-section of a community. Master lists can be challenged if they fail to represent blacks, Hispanics, or women solely on the basis of race, national origin, or gender. The first Supreme Court ruling on racial discrimination in creating a master list came in *Norris v. Alabama* (294 U.S. 587: 1935). This decision came on appeal of the infamous Scottsboro trial, and the Court categorically prohibited systematic exclusion of persons from jury service on the basis of race. The *Norris* holding, however, did not require that any particular jury must reflect the racial, socio-economic, or gender composition of the community. Only since the mid-1970s has the Court ruled out jury selection methods that seriously underrepresent, as distinct from systematically excluding, particular groups. In *Taylor v. Louisiana* (419 U.S. 522: 1975), for example, the Court invalidated a selection method that required additional qualifying steps for women, thus substantially reducing their numbers from the master list. In *Batson v. Kentucky* (476 U.S. 79: 1986), the Court examined more subtle discrimination through the use of peremptory challenges. Where a *prima facie* case of intentional discrimination can be established, *Batson* shifts the burden of proof to the state to offer a neutral explanation for striking black jurors.

Mens Rea (159)

Latin term that refers to a "guilty mind." *Mens rea* is that subjective condition or element of a crime involving intent. *Mens rea* is one of the two elements that together constitute a crime. The other element is the criminal act itself or the *actus reus*. In any criminal prosecution, the state must demonstrate beyond a reasonable doubt that an accused not only performed a criminal act, but knowingly and intentionally did so. Certain affirmative defenses such as entrapment or insanity attempt to mitigate the existence of *mens rea* or the guilty mind. *See also* AFFIRMATIVE DEFENSE, 122; INSANITY DEFENSE, 154.

Significance   *Mens rea* is the more difficult dimension of criminal conduct to demonstrate because it is based on a state of mind. Nonetheless, criminal intent is often the determining element in the American approach to defining and classifying crimes. American criminal codes contain numerous categories of offenses each of which is generally based on the same behavior or *actus reus.* These crimes are differentiated on the basis of intent, with varying degrees of punishment accorded upon conviction. Several crimes involve taking of a victim's life, for example. First degree murder requires proof of premeditation. Second degree murder or voluntary manslaughter are different in terms of such premeditation. These offenses are more impulsive and the same degree of criminal intent as first degree murder is lacking. Involuntary manslaughter is the product of recklessness and may not involve any real criminal intent. Criminal codes mandate a showing of general criminal intent for most crimes. This general level of intent requires only that defendants be aware that their actions are wrong. Each class of within-category crimes requires different proofs to convict and involves quite different sentencing ranges. Some crimes require the existence of specific intent. For example, to convict a person of assault with intent to rape, a prosecutor must show intent not only to perform an assaultive act, but the specific intent to engage in some sexual act by force.

Misdemeanor   (160)
A misdemeanor is a relatively minor criminal offense. Misdemeanors are generally punished by fine, but can involve detention at a county jail for up to one year. Misdemeanors are defined by each state and will vary somewhat. Some states choose to create gradations of misdemeanors and categorize them into classes such as Class A and Class B. Misdemeanors are typically such offenses as moving traffic violations, disorderly conduct, petty theft, or shoplifting. Misdemeanors are quite different from felonies, which are the more serious category of criminal behavior. Simply put, the consequences of a misdemeanor are limited as measured by injury or economic loss suffered by the victim. *See also* FELONY, 146.

Significance   Misdemeanors are the most common criminal offense, and misdemeanor cases place a great demand on judicial dockets. Jurisdiction over misdemeanors is usually assigned to courts of limited jurisdiction such as local district or municipal courts. Because of the high volume of misdemeanors, many are handled summarily. This means that there is seldom a trial and often cases are concluded at first appearance with the payment of a fine. It is the court with misdemeanor jurisdiction that is in the mind of those critical of the "mass production" approach to criminal justice. In reality, the more formalized criminal proceedings are reserved for those accused of felonies rather than misdemeanors.

Mistrial (161)

A trial ended before it arrives at a conclusion. A mistrial occurs in the wake of an extraordinary situation. A mistrial may be declared, for example, because one or more of the jurors cannot continue. More often, a mistrial occurs because of a prejudicial error that cannot be corrected. A prosecutor, for example, may refer to the existence of inadmissible evidence. The remark may produce such prejudice toward the defendant that its impact cannot be repaired by instructions to the jury to disregard it. As a result, a judge may determine that the trial cannot continue. A mistrial also occurs because of a hung jury. Such a jury is one whose members cannot produce a verdict because they are hopelessly deadlocked. When a unanimous vote is required, refusal by only one juror to agree with the others on a decision results in a hung jury. *See also* DOUBLE JEOPARDY, 142; JURY, 155.

Significance   A mistrial does not produce a resolution to a dispute. To the contrary, a mistrial represents the failure of the process to return a judgment. Under the double jeopardy concept, a mistrial may prevent retrial of an accused. Trials terminated at the initiative of the defendant or with the accused's consent may be retried, however. Similarly, if a proceeding is stopped for reasons of "manifest necessity," reprosecution may occur. Death of a juror or illness of the trial judge constitute manifest necessity. Under the manifest necessity doctrine, trial courts must balance the accused's interest in concluding the trial with the societal interest of successfully prosecuting the accused. This balance is not done by means of a mechanical test, but by assessing the "totality of circumstances" that emerge at the trial.

Nolle Prosequi (162)

A prosecutorial decision not to continue a criminal case. *Nolle prosequi*, often referred to as "nolle" or "nol pros," is a formal entry on the record dismissing a charge against a defendant. *See also* AT-

TRITION, 127; CHARGE, 129; PLEA BARGAINING, 168; PROSECUTORIAL FUNCTION, 178.

Significance   The *nolle prosequi* is a key option for prosecutors as they exercise control over the charging process. Prosecutors must screen cases before they come into the process and determine whether there exists cause to charge. Prosecutors may initially seek charges only to later dismiss some of these cases through the *nolle prosequi.* Often dismissal of one charge produces a decision by a defendant to plead guilty to another. Thus, the *nolle* is important in the plea negotiating process. The pattern in the United States is that once charges are initiated against an accused, cases are statistically more likely to be terminated through the *nolle* than by actions of judges or juries. In some states, a court must agree to the prosecutor's motion to dismiss.

Nolo Contendere   (163)
The equivalent of a plea of guilty to a criminal charge. The *nolo contendere* plea literally means "I will not contest it." The *nolo contendere* or "no contest" plea has value to a criminal defendant only under particular circumstances. While the plea leaves the defendant convicted of the criminal charge, the plea cannot be used against the defendant in a parallel civil action based on the same conduct as the prosecution. *See also* PLEA BARGAINING, 168.

Significance   The *nolo contendere* plea is the functional equivalent of an admission of criminal guilt, but more accurately is a response that the defendant will neither put forth a defense nor formally admit guilt. It is a strategic option in those cases where the criminal defendant might also have civil liability. Corporations prosecuted for antitrust violations often use the no contest plea to limit potential damage from a collateral civil action. Like a guilty plea, a no contest plea is accepted at the discretion of the court.

Opening Statement   (164)
Outline of arguments an attorney plans to present to a jury during a trial. The opening statement characterizes the case and previews the evidence that will be submitted during the trial. Opposite from the opening statement is the closing statement or summation. The summation is intended to review the evidence presented. Both opening and closing statements allow counsel an opportunity to suggest a favorable interpretation of evidence. These statements are optional,

but the closing statement is seldom waived. It is rendered before a judge instructs or charges the jury. *See also* ASSISTANCE OF COUNSEL, 126.

Significance   An opening statement is not evidence in itself. The value of the opening statement is that it introduces the issues in the case to the jury. The opening statement is designed to enable the jurors to better understand the evidence that will be presented. In addition, the opening statement may also prompt the jurors to anticipate particular evidence and incline them to view that evidence favorably. The opening statement sets the stage, and each attorney tries to establish some basis for advantage through these remarks.

Pardon   (165)
The power to grant exemption from criminal penalty. The power to pardon is discussed in Article II, Section 2, of the U.S. Constitution. It conveys to the president "power to grant reprieves and pardons for offenses against the United States, except in cases of impeachment." A similar power exists for governors at the state level. A pardon may be used in cases of individuals or groups. In the latter case, the pardon may be called amnesty. A pardon not only exempts persons from penalties such as imprisonment or fine, but also restores any civil rights that may have been lost with criminal conduct. The only limitation on the federal pardon power is that it may not reverse the outcome of an impeachment process. A pardon or the granting of clemency has the legal effect of removing a conviction altogether. Executives also possess the authority to commute sentences and grant reprieves. The commutation of a sentence does not remove the conviction but mitigates the penalty. Commutation occurs most frequently when a prisoner has a life sentence without the possibility of parole. The sentence may be commuted to life, a sentence which carries at least the potential for parole consideration. A reprieve, on the other hand, does not disturb either a conviction or a sentence, but delays implementation of the sentence. A governor may issue a reprieve in a capital punishment situation to allow further appeals. A reprieve has the same effect as a court-ordered stay from carrying out a sentence. Unless something intervenes, neither reprieves nor stays are permanent. *See also* SENTENCE, 186.

Significance   The power to pardon may completely or partially nullify the effects of a criminal conviction. When the president grants a full or complete pardon, it "blots out" the conviction so that it is as though no offense had ever been committed. A president may also grant a partial or "conditional" pardon. In the case of *Schick v. Reed* (419 U.S. 256: 1974), the Court upheld a presidential order reducing a death penalty murder conviction to a life sentence with the condition that parole could never be obtained. As seen in *Ex parte Grossman* (267 U.S. 87: 1925), the pardon power may extend to judicial contempt situations. Executive review of sentences is wholly discretionary. Some states, however, require petitions to be filed with and reviewed by clemency boards or committees.

Parole (166)

Release of a prisoner prior to the end of a criminal sentence. The release of a prisoner on parole is conditional. The person is supervised during the release period by a parole officer. Failure to conform to the conditions of parole results in its revocation and the person is returned to prison. Revocation of parole requires a formal hearing to determine if the conditions of parole have been violated. A parolee is entitled to representation by counsel at such a hearing. Parole is administered by parole or correctional boards at the state level. When Congress adopted fixed sentences in 1984, the federal parole system was essentially eliminated. Federal prisoners may, however, gain early release through a process of awarding "good time," days off sentences for good behavior. Parole obtained at the discretion of the parole board is generally earned by appropriate conduct and a probability that the convict will behave properly if released. *See also* PROBATION, 177; SENTENCE, 186.

Significance Parole serves two principal functions. First, it can facilitate offender rehabilitation. Release into a supervised situation theoretically enhances the probabilities of successful reintegration into society. Second, early release programs such as parole is a necessary component of administering prisons. Early release provides incentive for prisoners to behave, a key to maintaining order in penal institutions. Parole can also be used as a device to reduce facility overcrowding. At the same time, many states have turned away from indeterminate sentences in a belief that fixed sentences are more effective deterrents. This has led to a decline in the use of parole systems. Parole is distinguished from probation in that the former is an executive action taken after a period of incarceration while probation is an actual sentence imposed by a judge, which does not include physical detention.

Peremptory Challenge (167)

Summary removal of a juror from sitting on a case. Peremptory challenges or "strikes" may be made by either party to a case. When a party strikes a juror, no reason is required for doing so. The number of peremptory challenges is normally limited by law and varies with the seriousness of a charge. For example, some jurisdictions permit only three or five peremptory challenges in less serious cases, but allow as many as fifty challenges in capital cases. The peremptory challenge differs from the removal of a juror for "cause" in that no specific reason for believing a juror to be less than impartial need be offered. *See also* JURY, 155; *VOIR DIRE*, 196.

Significance Peremptory challenges allow the parties to a lawsuit to influence the composition of a jury about to hear their case. This is done to make sure that the jury is impartial, but also for strategic reasons. The peremptory challenge allows the prosecutor, for example, to remove a young juror from the trial of a college student charged with marijuana possession. Such a removal is not based on direct evidence the juror may not be impartial, but on intuition or information gleaned from such sources as public records or opinion polls. Occasionally lawyers, as they prepare for jury selection, use consultants who advise them of local population attitudes and characteristics. The use of peremptory challenges may be influenced by such advice. While both sides are generally free to strike whomever they wish within the legal limits, a peremptory challenge may not be used to exclude persons based on race, gender, or national origin. As a long-standing policy, jury selection techniques cannot "systematically exclude" persons from jury service because of race. Nonetheless, demonstrating that peremptory challenges were racially motivated remained difficult to show. In *Batson v. Kentucky* (476 U.S. 79: 1986), the Supreme Court required prosecutors to demonstrate a nonracial reason for striking black jurors if a defendant could establish a *prima facie* case of intentional discrimination.

Plea Bargaining (168)

A process whereby the prosecutor and the accused negotiate through his or her attorney a mutually acceptable settlement in a criminal case. The practice of plea bargaining is extensive in the United States. Approximately ninety percent of all criminal cases, both federal and state, are resolved by plea bargain or plea agreement. Plea agreements usually focus on one of the key variables: charge, counts, or sentence. A defendant may agree to plea in exchange for a reduction in the charge. A person originally charged with the felony of larceny, for example, may plead guilty to the reduced charge of shoplifting, a misdemeanor. The shoplift plea is a criminal conviction, but the consequences are far less severe. So, too, are career opportunities for the person with only a misdemeanor as opposed to a felony conviction. Similarly, a defendant may plead guilty to one or more offenses in exchange for the prosecution dismissing other charges or counts. Like the charge bargain, pleading after the dismissal of at least one other count limits a defendant's sentence exposure. Third, an agreement may be reached on the sentence itself. Since judges retain final authority over sentences, prosecutors cannot formally bind them through a plea agreement. Prosecutors may agree, however, to make particular sentence recommendations to the judge. If a defendant pleads guilty because the prosecutor agrees to recommend probation, the defendant is entitled to withdraw the plea if the judge determines that he or she cannot impose that sentence. All proposed plea bargains must be accepted by the court before they take effect. If a judge refuses to accept the plea, the case is docketed for trial. *See also* JURY, 155.

Significance   Plea bargaining is a practice that sparks some controversy. Nonetheless, benefits accrue to both prosecution and the accused to produce a "mutuality of advantage" sufficient to support the high plea rate. For the prosecutor, the plea produces a conviction without expending scarce prosecutorial resources, and a good "track record" of convictions if he or she decides to seek higher elective office. For the defendant, risk is replaced by some level of control and certainty. Like other negotiated settlements, the plea agreement "hedges bets" on both sides. The Supreme Court has reviewed the practice in a number of cases, and rejected the contention that it is unconstitutional. On the contrary, in *Santobello v. New York* (404 U.S. 257: 1971), the Court spoke of plea bargaining as "an essential component of the administration of justice," and a practice to be encouraged if it is properly conducted. Plea bargaining moves cases through the courts, relieving docket pressure that could not be handled through any other means. It is desirable because it produces prompt and largely final dispositions without lengthy pretrial confinement, diminishes the chances of additional criminal conduct by those on pretrial release, and enhances rehabilitative prospects. The procedures by which pleas are made are carefully prescribed. The Federal Rules of Criminal Procedure set forth the steps by which pleas are to be entered in federal courts. The Supreme Court has also set standards. The Court said in *Boykin v. Alabama* (395 U.S. 238: 1969), for example, that no plea can be taken without a trial judge inquiring into the voluntariness of the plea. If the plea is determined freely and offered intelligently, all elements of the settlement agreement must be honored. Nonetheless, there are those who are highly critical of plea bargaining because it enlarges the discretion of the prosecutor and heightens the possibility of abusive conduct. Because plea negotiations do not take place in court, judges cannot monitor these cases as they can those that are tried. Finally, plea bargaining is criticized by those who argue that it allows defendants to avoid more serious punishment.

Preliminary Hearing (169)

A proceeding conducted by a judicial officer of a lower court to determine whether an accused person should be bound over to a higher court for trial. A preliminary hearing, sometimes called a preliminary examination, is the first time a case is formally reviewed by an official outside the executive or enforcement branch of government. The purpose of a preliminary hearing is to determine whether the prosecutor can establish probable cause to believe that an accused committed a particular crime. This is also called establishing a *prima facie* case against the accused. A preliminary hearing is a step in the process that occurs only if the defendant wants it. If it is not waived, it follows the filing of an information by the prosecutor. Both the prosecution and defendant are able to call witnesses and introduce whatever other evidence they wish. Cross-examination of witnesses called by the other side is permissible. Otherwise, many of the rules of evidence that apply to trials do not apply to preliminary hearings. Unlike grand jury proceedings, preliminary hearings are open to the public and the defendant has a right to be present and represented by counsel. If a case against a defendant is dismissed at this stage, it may be reinstated by the prosecution at a later date without violating the double jeopardy protection. *See also* BIND OVER, 128; INFORMATION, 153.

Significance The preliminary hearing is designed to protect the defendant from baseless accusation. While in theory this function seems straightforward, it is quite complex in practice. Indeed, several patterns have developed, depending on the jurisdiction. In some jurisdictions, the preliminary hearing actually screens weak cases. In such jurisdictions, many examinations are conducted and a comparatively high proportion of dismissals result. On the other hand, in jurisdictions where prosecutors perform stringent screening themselves, preliminary hearings tend to be mere formalities and dismissals infrequent. In these jurisdictions, preliminary hearings are often waived. Preliminary hearings also provide defense counsel with an opportunity for discovery. Requiring the prosecution to put forward at least a portion of its case, defense counsel can sometimes better assess the strength of the case against the accused. Often prosecutors adopt an "open file" policy whereby they share at least police reports with defense counsel in all cases. This practice provides the defense with more information than could probably be obtained through a preliminary examination. It also saves prosecutorial resources in that an attorney need not invest half a day participating in a preliminary hearing. As a result, preliminary hearings are seldom utilized in such jurisdictions.

Presentence Investigation (170)

Information gathering about a convicted offender to be used by a judge in determining sentence. In many jurisdictions, presentence investigations are required by statute or mandated by court rules. Even where such investigations are not required, they are conducted at the discretion of sentencing judges. Presentence investigations are done by probation officers and take place during the period between conviction and sentencing, a period typically running from 10 to 20 working days. The investigation includes consideration of the offense, information provided by the defendant, record of previous offenses, psychological evidence if pertinent, and a general social history. Information on these matters is drawn from the police report and interviews with appropriate people. *See also* SENTENCE, 186.

Significance   The presentence investigation and report provides important information for a sentencing judge. This report is particularly important in those cases that are concluded by plea agreement as opposed to trial because the sentencing judge has virtually no other exposure to the defendant before sentencing. In most jurisdictions, the presentence report also includes a sentencing recommendation by the investigator. While judges are not required to adopt these recommendations, they generally do so. The investigator's recommendation tends to be based, at least in part, on notions of the "typical" sentences for particular offenses and defendant characteristics. Actual sentencing data may be used to determine a "usual" sentence. As a result, sentences based on such recommendations tend to be similar.

Presentment (171)

A criminal accusation made by a grand jury acting on its own initiative. A presentment takes the form of a bill of indictment, but it is individually signed by all grand jury members voting to return it. *See also* GRAND JURY, 148; INDICTMENT, 152.

Significance   Grand juries possess broad investigative powers. They have the authority to compel appearance of witnesses and the production of records. Normally a grand jury considers only those matters brought before it by a prosecutor. A grand jury may, however, investigate on its own when a prosecutor fails or chooses not to pursue certain lines of inquiry. This may occur when a grand jury is examining the possibility of misconduct by government officials. In such cases, the grand jury may return a presentment that requires a prosecutor to pursue those accusations it deems appropriate. In other words, a presentment is an instruction from a grand jury that an indictment be prepared.

Pretrial Detention (172)

Holding an accused in custody prior to adjudication of guilt. Pretrial detention may result from the inability of the accused to meet release conditions. For example, an accused may not be able to secure the money necessary to be released on bond. Pretrial detention may also occur because a judicial officer determines that the accused presents too great a risk of fleeing from the jurisdiction. It may also be determined that an accused represents a substantial threat to the security of a community. In such cases, an accused may be detained pending trial to prevent him or her from engaging in additional criminal conduct. Denial of release on this basis is called preventive detention. The decision to detain an accused before trial is a judicial determination usually made at the arraignment. Although this judgment may be altered later, it typically remains intact throughout the pretrial period. *See also* ARRAIGNMENT, 124; PRETRIAL RELEASE, 175.

Significance   Pretrial detention is not compatible with the presumption of innocence. Further, some persons are detained before trial only because they do not have the economic resources to meet release conditions. There are other negative consequences to detention as opposed to release. Aside from the matter of freedom, detained persons cannot maintain family contact as easily nor can they retain jobs. The latter often makes probation less probable if they are eventually convicted. Persons detained before trial also consume much of the available space in local detention facilities. Nonetheless, there are many who advocate pretrial detention as a way of combating crime. The Supreme Court has held preventive detention to be constitutional in two important cases. In *Salerno v. United States* (481 U.S. 739: 1987), the Court upheld provisions of the Bail Reform Act of 1984, saying that detention following a hearing does not constitute punishment. Rather, the Court saw the method as a legitimate response to the problem of crimes committed by those already on some form of release. Preventive detention for juveniles was also upheld by the Court in *Schall v. Martin* (467 U.S. 253: 1984).

Pretrial Motion   (173)

A formal request for a trial judge to rule on a particular question. Motions can be filed at virtually any time, and may involve a wide range of matters. Most commonly in criminal proceedings, motions focus on evidence issues and are filed before a trial commences. Such pretrial motions usually attempt to have evidence suppressed. Searches, custodial interrogations, and such identification processes as lineups are most likely to be targeted in a pretrial motion as somehow defective. These motions are also called suppression motions. *See also* EXCLUSIONARY RULE, 145.

Significance   Once a motion is filed, a hearing is held to determine whether the motion is to be granted or not. If evidence is challenged, the burden generally rests with the defendant to establish a legal violation, although the state retains the burden with respect to *Miranda* issues. The judge's ruling on the motion carries over to the trial. If evidence is found to have been unlawfully obtained, the evidence is not allowed at trial; it is suppressed or excluded. On the other hand, if the judge rules the evidence was reasonably obtained, it may be admitted at trial and used against the defendant. Most pretrial motions, especially those seeking to suppress evidence, are unsuccessful. This is true because there is seldom any evidence other than the word of the police against the word of the accused. The police tend to prevail in these situations. In addition, if there is a serious problem with evidence and it is obvious the evidence will be suppressed on motion, the prosecutor has the option of not bringing a charge in the case because it is so irreparably flawed.

Pretrial Publicity   (174)

Information about a particular case disseminated through the media. The basic problem with pretrial publicity in criminal cases is that it may impair a defendant's right to an impartial jury. If publicity is pervasive enough, it may lead citizens toward at least tentative judgments about guilt or innocence. In such cases, the publicity is said to be prejudicial. Given the current reach of the media, especially the broadcast media, virtually an entire community can be influenced by information untested by accepted rules of procedure and evidence. The famous case involving Dr. Sam Sheppard portrays prejudicial consequences at their worst. *See also* VOIR DIRE, 196.

Significance   Containing prejudicial publicity is difficult because the media is protected from most restrictions by the First Amendment. Trial judges, for example, cannot restrain the media from reporting information about a crime or a defendant except under the most extreme circumstances. Nonetheless, there are other measures that can be taken to ensure the defendant's right to a fair trial. Trials may be delayed until publicity has subsided, or the venue (location) of a trial may be changed to a place where prospective jurors have not been exposed to media coverage of the case. Key to determining if either of these options is necessary is the *voir dire* process. If impartial jurors cannot be found, delay or change of venue may be ordered. The Supreme Court has ruled in *Murphy v. Florida* (421 U.S. 794: 1975) that prospective jurors need not be "totally ignorant" of a case. They need only be able to "reach a verdict based on the evidence presented in the court." Once a jury is selected, it can usually be insulated from prejudicial publicity effectively, although this, too, may be difficult with a lengthy trial. The difficulty in restricting media conduct has prompted the industry itself to fashion principles of conduct for criminal case coverage.

Pretrial Release   **(175)**
Practice of allowing an accused to remain free pending trial. Pretrial release is consistent with the presumption of innocence. The alternative to pretrial release is detention in a local detention facility until guilt or innocence is adjudicated. Pretrial release may take one of several forms. A common means is the posting of bail. A person released on bail pays an amount of cash (or the equivalent in property) to the court as a guarantee that he or she will appear at all subsequent proceedings up to and including the trial. If all appearance obligations are met, the cash or property bond will be returned. If an accused does not have sufficient cash or property, someone else may cover the required amount. A third party hired to do so for a fee is a bail bondsman. The amount of cash or property it will take to secure release is determined by a judicial officer. The principal considerations involve seriousness of the charged offense, prior criminal record of the accused, and the probability of additional criminal conduct if the accused is released. While most states create a general right to bail, people accused of certain crimes may be categorically denied pretrial release. The U.S. Constitution only prohibits "excessive" bail. Excess has been held to mean the imposition of pretrial release conditions

beyond what is necessary to ensure subsequent appearance. *See also* PRETRIAL DETENTION, 172; RELEASE ON RECOGNIZANCE, 181.

Significance   Pretrial release allows an accused to retain his or her freedom prior to adjudication of charges. Several benefits result from obtaining release. It has been shown statistically that those people released before trial obtain more favorable outcomes in their cases than those who are detained. This is especially true if the person is convicted because probation is a more likely sentence for an offender who has been able to maintain employment during the pretrial period. A person on release is also able to maintain family contacts and possibly able to assist counsel more effectively in preparing a defense. In addition to the presumption of innocence rationale, pretrial release also reduces the number of people who must be housed in already overcrowded detention facilities. The critical objective of the pretrial release process is to ensure subsequent appearance by the accused. This view directly conflicts with that which says that the bail process ought to be used to safeguard community security. What we have in the United States is something of a compromise between the two positions. The pretrial release system has been substantially reformed since the 1960s with particular attention directed toward the economic inequities of bail. The reforms have essentially three forms. First, a number of jurisdictions permit officers to issue citations to minor violators instead of taking them into custody. Second, many jurisdictions permit people to obtain release by making a deposit, usually ten percent, against the bail amount. This reduces the amount of cash needed and also allows defendants to get around the nonreturnable fees charged by bail bondsmen. Third, those accused may be released on their own recognizance. Instead of posting money or property, an accused may be released because there are sufficient family or work-related factors to minimize the likelihood of flight. Release on recognizance tends to be limited to those charged with nonassaultive offenses.

Probable Cause   (176)

Standard of evidence used to assess various governmental actions in criminal matters. Probable cause is a level of evidence required to convince a judicial officer to issue an arrest or search warrant or bind a case over for trial. The level of evidence needed for probable cause is not as substantial as that required to prove guilt. Probable cause relates to reasonable inferences rather than technical judgments based on rigid requirements. In *Draper v. United States* (385 U.S. 307: 1959), the Supreme Court spoke of "probabilities that focused closely enough on a person or location to allow a neutral magistrate to authorize an arrest or search." The standard established in *Draper* holds that probable cause exists when trustworthy information known to authorities is sufficient to encourage a person of reasonable caution to believe that an offense has been or is being committed. *See also* BIND OVER, 128; REASONABLE DOUBT, 179; WARRANT, 197.

Significance   Probable cause is a standard that governs police and prosecutors. In order to obtain a warrant to arrest or search, police officers must have at least enough evidence to demonstrate the probable involvement of a person in criminal conduct. The standard can be met by providing evidence such as direct observation of a criminal act by an officer, indirect observation through informants, physical evidence, or witness accounts of criminal behavior. Police are permitted to act in the absence of a warrant, but must establish that probable cause existed at the time the action was taken. The probable cause standard also applies to prosecutorial charging decisions. Prosecutors must have at least probable cause to formally charge. The sufficiency of evidence is assessed by a judicial officer in response to an information filed by a prosecutor or presented at a preliminary hearing. The probable cause burden on the prosecution is sometimes called making a *prima facie* case. *Prima facie* means "at first sight," and refers to a claim that may be sufficient without further support. If the prosecutor establishes probable cause, a criminal case is bound over for trial. In order to prove guilt at trial, the prosecutor must meet the more demanding standard of beyond a reasonable doubt. Failure to establish probable cause at a preliminary hearing or by information results in dismissal of charges without trial.

Probation   (177)
A criminal sentence that allows a person to return to the community under supervised release. Probation is an alternative to imprisonment and is applied to almost two-thirds of sentenced offenders in the United States. Control is maintained over the offender by an agent of the court called a probation officer. Judges are permitted substantial latitude in placing offenders on probation. Legislatures typically make probation the minimum sentence for most offenses, although probation for certain violent crimes is often prohibited. Probation is a conditional sentence. It is often used in conjunction with other sanctions such as fines, restitution, community service, or treatment for chemical dependency. Other conditions, such as maintaining employment or frequent contact with probation officers, are attached as well. If any of the conditions of probation are not met, it may be revoked

by the sentencing judge. Prior to revocation, hearings must be held to establish that conditions of probation have been violated. A probationer is entitled to assistance of counsel as a matter of right at such hearings. If probation is revoked, the offender is typically sentenced to a term of imprisonment. *See also* IMPRISONMENT, 151; SENTENCE, 186.

Significance   The principal contemporary rationale for probation as a criminal sanction is the belief that many offenders should not be sent to prison. For the young or first offender and those convicted of nonassaultive crimes, prisons may constitute an overly harsh punishment. It is also true that for many offenders, supervised release provides greater likelihood of rehabilitation. This has been particularly true of the youthful offender. Indeed, there is evidence to suggest that sending young and/or first offenders to prison only heightens their inclination to engage in criminal behavior. Furthermore, less experienced offenders often learn how to become more proficient criminals by interacting with repeat offenders or those convicted of violent crimes. Probation also lessens the demand on already limited space in corrections facilities. Probation allows corrections officials to reserve detention facilities for the more serious offenders, those for whom rehabilitation is no longer a realistic probability. Finally, detention of offenders is substantially more costly than supervised probation. Supervised release is certainly not failsafe, however. Indeed, public opinion reflects dissatisfaction with probation when a person on probation commits another crime.

Prosecutorial Function   (178)
Representation of the interests of the victim and the community in the criminal justice process. The breadth of the prosecutorial function is extensive. Unlike other participants in the criminal process, the prosecutor or district attorney is connected to each of the various stages. The prosecutor has the choice of whether to initiate prosecution. This is a fundamental gatekeeping task. If the decision is made to enter a case into the court, the prosecutor determines which specific charge or charges will be lodged against the defendant. The prosecutor then guides cases through the various steps of the judicial process. It is the prosecutor, for example, who is responsible for establishing a *prima facie* level case to have a defendant bound over for trial. Once this happens, the prosecutor is responsible for presenting the state's case at trial. More likely, the prosecutor will engage in negotiations with the defendant in an effort to settle the case. In pursuing plea agreements, the prosecution retains much leverage since the

prosecutor can redefine or dismiss particular charges, which constitute the principal variables in plea negotiations. Whether or not sentencing is part of the bargaining process or not, prosecutors also offer sentence recommendations to the court. The prosecutor participates in the appellate process as well. When a defendant appeals, he or she is usually trying to have a conviction set aside. The prosecutor attempts to defend the challenged conviction as properly obtained. Thus, from the time a person is arrested until the case is concluded, the prosecutor possesses wide discretion that can have a direct impact on the outcome of the case and on general criminal justice policy. *See also* CHARGE, 129; DISCRETION, 140; PLEA BARGAINING, 168; PROSECUTING ATTORNEY, 110.

Significance   The prosecutorial function spans the full length of the criminal justice process. As a result, the prosecutor interacts with each of the participants in the criminal process more extensively than any of the others. Except at the federal level, the prosecutorial function is decentralized in the United States. Federal prosecutors, called United States Attorneys, are all part of an overarching agency, the Department of Justice. Their activities are extensively coordinated through the supervisory authority of the Attorney General of the United States. No parallel structure exists at the state level. Indeed, state attorneys general possess little or no supervising authority over prosecuting attorneys. Rather, prosecuting attorneys are independently elected, usually at the county level. Thus, accountability exists only through the local electoral process. Prosecutorial decisions that lead to prosecution are checked by judges in preliminary hearings or by grand juries. On the other hand, prosecutors have virtually unlimited discretion over those cases for which charges are not commenced. The prosecutor is at the center of the criminal process and plays a decisive role in setting enforcement policies within a jurisdiction. These policies may be explicit and take the form of case screening or plea bargaining guidelines. Often, however, these policies are implicit or indirect. Such policies are established by patterned behavior in certain kinds of cases. A particular prosecutor, for example, may not charge in an insufficient funds case if restitution for a bad check is made. Such a pattern clearly conveys a policy position even though it has not been formalized.

Reasonable Doubt   (179)
A standard of evidence used in determining guilt in criminal cases. The standard requires the prosecution to prove to a fact-finder (judge or jury) that the accused committed the crime charged. If reasonable

doubt remains, the accused must be found not guilty. Reasonable doubt is not imagined doubt or doubt the fact-finder creates to avoid finding someone guilty. Reasonable doubt is that level of uncertainty that would cause a prudent person to withhold action in a matter of importance to him or her. Indeed, fact-finders in criminal cases must be satisfied "beyond" a reasonable doubt, which means that they are fully convinced by the facts presented that the accused is guilty. Reasonable doubt is created by the defense in a number of ways. One, of course, is through the cross-examination of prosecution witnesses. *See also* CROSS-EXAMINATION, 136; STANDARDS OF PROOF, 188.

Significance   The reasonable doubt standard is used as part of the approach that presumes the accused to be not guilty. This presumption requires the State to demonstrate a compelling case against the defendant. The reasonable doubt standard was used for decades as part of the common law tradition, but was held to be a requirement of due process by the Supreme Court in the case *In re Winship* (397 U.S. 358: 1970). *Winship* specifically examined the question of the reasonable doubt standard in juvenile delinquency proceedings, but the decision in the case clearly established the standard of proof needed for both adult and juvenile cases. The reasonable doubt standard is not used in the adjudication of civil issues. Rather, the less demanding standard of "preponderance of evidence" is sufficient in civil proceedings.

Recidivist   (180)

A repeat criminal offender. The recidivist is the habitual offender who makes a career of criminal conduct. A high proportion of the prison population are recidivists who commit new crimes after having already been convicted, and possibly imprisoned, for earlier offenses. *See also* SENTENCE, 186.

Significance   The large number of recidivists reflects the failure of corrections processes to effectively deal with criminal behavior. The phenomenon of recidivism has prompted two related sentencing policies. First, most states have formally adopted recidivist or habitual offender laws that supplement the sentences of repeat offenders. A second felony, for example, often results in a sentence that exceeds by 50 percent the maximum sentence for the first offense. A third offense, in turn, may result in a doubling of the length of the prison sentence. In many jurisdictions, conviction for a third or fourth felony produces a mandatory life sentence under terms of the recidivist sentencing laws. The objective is clearly not rehabilitation, but segregation of the offender from society. A second policy is less formal, but no less operational. Many judges see prisons as places where repeat offenders become more accomplished criminals. Thus, prisons are not the place for first offenders who are likely to become habitual offenders because of prison socialization. It is largely for this reason that first offenders are placed on probation or given short sentences in local jails rather than state prisons.

Release on Recognizance (181)

A method by which people awaiting criminal prosecution are released. Release on recognizance, also known as ROR, is an alternative to pretrial detention and does not require the accused to post bail in order to obtain release. A determination as to whether a person is released on personal recognizance is made by the trial court. Often, release is based on nothing more than the accused's written promise to appear at all remaining legal proceedings. In deciding whether to permit ROR, a judge or magistrate must consider the nature and circumstances of the charged offense as well as assess the likelihood of flight. Such factors as family relationships, employment, previous criminal record, length of residency in the community, and general character are relevant to such a determination. Release on recognizance is wholly within the discretion of the court and special conditions such as release to the custody of another may be attached. Those charged with violent felonies are usually categorically ineligible for ROR. *See also* PRETRIAL DETENTION, 172; PRETRIAL RELEASE, 175.

Significance Release on recognizance was developed in large measure to reduce the inequities of pretrial release based on financial resources. Indeed, ROR and the deposit system are among pretrial release "reforms" instituted since the early 1960s to take the harsh economic edge off the pretrial release process. ROR is not only effective in providing greater equity of access to pretrial release, but also in assuring that defendants appear when required. The first extensive examination of ROR came in the Manhattan Bail Project conducted in New York City in the early 1960s, and it became immediately apparent that personal ties to the community provide sufficient incentives for a person to return to court. Subsequent studies continue to show that ROR lowers "bail jumping" among those who qualify for ROR.

Restitution (182)

Repayment to a victim of losses suffered at the hands of a criminal offender. The idea of restitution is that no person ought to be enriched by misconduct against another. While restitution has been a component of the American justice system from the beginning, it has gained visibility through its recent endorsement by the American Bar Association and the National Advisory Commission on Criminal Justice Standards. Most states have statutory law authorizing restitution, and it has become a frequently used condition of probation. *See also* PROBATION, 177; SENTENCE, 186.

Significance   An objective of restitution is to restore losses suffered by a victim. Often, the offender does not have the resources to make restitution. In such cases, the offender may have to perform some service for the victim. As an alternative, the offender may have to perform some specified kind of community service. In a few states, some measure of restitution from a public fund has been attempted. Aside from the victim-related aspects, restitution also has some rehabilitative value and, for that reason, remains a viable criminal sanction. It is a comparatively mild sanction, however. Accordingly, its use is typically confined to property offenses. It has also become a primary element in the sanctioning of juvenile delinquents.

Rules of Evidence (183)

Standards that govern the presentation of evidence at a trial. The rules of evidence are designed to facilitate the truth-seeking function of the adversary process. Rules of evidence come largely from decisions of appellate courts, but are also established by statute. The rules generally focus on the admissibility of particular evidence. Trial judges make determinations about admissibility of evidence in individual cases based on the general principles contained in the rules. *See also* EVIDENCE, 144; EXCLUSIONARY RULE, 145; HEARSAY, 149.

Significance   The primary objective in setting rules of evidence is that trials produce judgments based on truthful evidence. The basic theme of the rules is the truthfulness or reliability of evidence. Hearsay evidence is not permitted, for example, because it is indirect or second hand. Information represented second hand is generally regarded as unreliable because the source cannot be subjected to tests of truthfulness, principally cross-examination. Evidence must also be directly related to the issue before the court. That a person was expelled from a school for cheating would not be germane to a person's criminal trial. Some reliable evidence may also be inadmissible if it was obtained illegally. If law enforcement officers improperly elicit an incriminating statement from a person under arrest or improperly seize evidence from someone, it may be inadmissible under the exclusionary rule. The objective of the exclusionary rule is to deter governmental misconduct even at the cost of not allowing reliable evidence to be considered at a trial. Challenge of the admissibility of particular evidence in criminal proceedings comes in the form of a pretrial suppression motion. If a jury hears any evidence it should not, the judge will instruct the jurors to disregard it. If the evidence is too prejudicial, and the instruction to disregard will not sufficiently repair the problem, a mistrial can be declared.

Search and Seizure (184)

Action of government officials whereby people or places are examined in an effort to locate and confiscate evidence of a crime. Government power to search and seize is part of its greater authority to exercise police power and enforce the law. The power to search is vulnerable to abuse, however, so the Fourth Amendment was added to the U.S. Constitution to help ensure that government searches and seizures be reasonable. The principal mechanism in protecting against unreasonable searches is the warrant process. Government agents must be able to show that there is cause to believe that evidence of a crime will be found by a search of a particular person or place. If a judicial officer can be convinced that probable cause exists, a warrant authorizing a search of specified persons or places will be issued. In a wide range of circumstances, it is virtually impossible for officers to obtain a warrant before acting. Items seized without a warrant may still be used so long as the search that produced them was reasonable. Before such evidence can be admitted at trial, a judge must be satisfied that cause to act existed in the absence of a warrant. Searches, particularly those made at the time of arrest, are a principal means of obtaining evidence against those accused of criminal behavior. *See also* EXCLUSIONARY RULE, 145; WARRANT, 197.

Significance When government searches and seizes evidence, it has invaded personal privacy. While the government enforcement function is clearly legitimate, it must be balanced against the individual liberty interest in privacy. It is for this reason that the provisions of the Fourth Amendment were added to the Constitution. The framers of the Bill of Rights had direct experience with arbitrary searches conducted under general warrants known as writs of assistance, and they wished to safeguard against the invasions of privacy resulting from them. The reach of the Fourth Amendment was extended substantially in 1949 when the Supreme Court ruled in *Wolf v. Colorado* (338 U.S. 25) that the reasonable search language applied to the states as well as the federal government. Judicial enforcement of the Fourth Amendment has come largely through a device known as the exclusionary rule. The rule, based on common law, prohibits the use of evidence obtained by means of an illegal or unreasonable search and seizure. The rule was first applied to federal proceedings by the Court's ruling in *Weeks v. United States* (232 U.S. 383: 1914). The rule was later extended to state criminal cases in the landmark decision, *Mapp v. Ohio* (367 U.S. 643: 1961). Evidence obtained from a suspect search or seizure is challenged by a defendant in a pretrial suppression motion, which asks the judge to disallow the evidence.

Self-Incrimination (185)

Testimony offered by a person that may lead to his or her conviction. The privilege against self-incrimination is designed to keep the burden of proof on the prosecution. The Bill of Rights speaks to the matter of self-incrimination in the Fifth Amendment, which says that no person "shall be compelled in any criminal case to be a witness against himself." This provision was initially applied only to persons on trial. The concept has been extended, however, to include statements made prior to trial that may have the effect of implicating a person in a crime. The privilege also applies to testimony from witnesses appearing before legislative committees or executive agencies. No unfavorable inference may be drawn from a person's exercise of the privilege. If, for example, a defendant chooses not to testify on his or her own behalf at trial, neither the judge or prosecutor may suggest that anything pertaining to guilt be read into that decision. Indeed, a defendant is entitled to request a specific jury instruction admonishing the jury to draw no inference from refusal to speak with police after arrest or to testify at trial. *See also* CONFESSION, 132; IMMUNITY, 150.

Significance   The privilege against self-incrimination was fully recognized in Great Britain by the early eighteenth century and was established in common law by the time the U.S. Constitution was written. As the Supreme Court said in *Murphy v. Waterfront Commission of New York* (378 U.S. 52: 1964), the self-incrimination clause reflects "many of our fundamental values and most noble aspirations." Those values and aspirations include "our unwillingness to subject those suspected of crime to the cruel trilemma of self-accusation, perjury or contempt." The privilege against self-incrimination represents a society's preference for an accusatorial rather than an inquisitorial system of criminal justice. It extends only to criminal prosecutions, however, and does not prevent compelled testimony that may damage a witness's reputation or create adverse economic or social consequences. The Supreme Court resisted early attempts to make the self-incrimination privilege applicable to the states through the Fourteenth Amendment. In *Twining v. New Jersey* (211 U.S. 78: 1908), the Court concluded that the privilege did not rank "among the fundamental and inalienable rights of mankind," but rather it constituted a "wise and beneficent rule of evidence." The Court said it may be a "just and useful principle of law," but it need not be required at the state level. The Warren Court reversed *Twining* in *Malloy v. Hogan* (378 U.S. 1: 1964). It declared "the *Twining* view of the privilege has been eroded," and that it was incongruous to have different standards dependent upon whether the right was asserted in a state or a federal court. The contemporary significance of the self-incrimination protection was underlined not only by the Warren Court's decision to apply the privilege to the states but by the Court's decision to extend the privilege to pretrial situations such as custodial interrogations. It did so in *Miranda v. Arizona* (384 U.S. 436: 1966). *Miranda* required that all detained people be advised of their constitutional rights prior to interrogation. Voluntary confessions are not prohibited by *Miranda*. Statements taken without following *Miranda* guidelines may be used, nonetheless, to impeach a defendant's trial testimony. The privilege against self-incrimination has been confined to communicative or testimonial evidence. Accordingly, it prohibits comment on a defendant's refusal to testify, but the prohibition does not extend to such defendant-derived evidence as blood samples or to involuntary identification procedures such as lineups. Self-incrimination may be satisfied by granting immunity to a witness, thereby protecting the witness from having compelled testimony used in a subsequent prosecution against him or her.

Sentence (186)

A sanction or punishment imposed on a person convicted of a crime. Sentences fall into two broad categories, custodial and noncustodial. The former involves imprisonment for at least one year or confinement in a local detention facility for up to a year. Noncustodial sentences take such forms as fine, probation, community service, or restitution. Judges may impose combinations of these sentences. Probation is often accompanied by a fine or restitution. A noncustodial sentence may also be coupled with a custodial sentence. Some offenders, for example, commence a period of probation following completion of a term of detention. Sentences are imposed on those convicted of crimes for a variety of reasons, but sentences generally connect to one of four basic justifications. First, sentences can be seen as treatment that eventually rehabilitates the offender. The rehabilitation rationale is based on the assumption that criminal conduct has social or psychological causes and that certain kinds of programs can modify the offender's behavior. Probation and the use of indeterminate sentencing are based on the rehabilitation theory. A second theory suggests that sentences are supposed to deter others from criminal conduct. The deterrence theory stems from the utilitarian notions of Jeremy Bentham, and it argues that people will be discouraged from engaging in crime if they observe others being punished for that conduct. In other words, people will behave because they wish to avoid the consequences associated with conviction. A third view is that sentences are to incapacitate offenders. Sentences take criminals off the streets and segregate them from society. Incapacitation is not so much punishment for past offenses but prevention of future crimes by confining those who have committed crimes before. Extending confinement for recidivists or repeat offenders in based on the incapacitation rationale. Finally, there is the punishment rationale. The idea is that the offender has earned the consequences with his or her criminal conduct. This justification is often called the retributive rationale. It embraces the idea of "pay back;" the victim and to some extent society at large have suffered from the offender's crime, and the offender should be made to suffer as well. Capital punishment is a sentence often defended largely on retribution grounds. *See also* FINE, 147; IMPRISONMENT, 151; PRESENTENCE INVESTIGATION, 170; PROBATION, 177.

Significance   Criminal sentences are imposed by judges. Sentencing options are set forth in statutes by legislatures. This is usually done by specifying a minimum and a maximum sentence for the offense. A judge is free to choose from within that range. Sentencing, at least for felony level offenses, occurs at a proceeding separate from that which establishes guilt. It follows a presentence investigation, which examines the specifics of the offense and relevant background characteristics of the defendant. A probation officer completes the investigation and submits a report to the sentencing judge. The report usually contains a recommendation on sentence, although the judge retains final authority on sentencing. Consistency of sentence has been one of the more troublesome criminal justice problems. A number of techniques have been developed to address the problem of sentence disparity. Among the more popular is the use of sentencing guidelines. While not mandatory, guidelines provide "suggested" sentences when various factors indicate offenses and offenders are similar. The guidelines are set out in a grid configuration with point values assigned for a number of variables. The idea is to require sentencing judges to consider comparable factors across cases and arrive at a sentence judgment in a more objective manner. The guidelines serve to limit judicial sentencing discretion, and tend to make sentences more uniform.

Speedy Trial (187)

A Sixth Amendment safeguard that entitles a criminal defendant to a timely and public trial. Speedy trial is intended to keep an accused from protected pretrial detention, and it protects against the diminution of a criminal defendant's ability to offer a defense. Speedy trial also ensures that the prosecutor's case will not erode because of delay, thus forming a two-edged constitutional sword. The speedy trial protection begins at the time a person is formally accused unless pre-charging delays aimed at gaining prosecutorial advantage occur. The speedy trial provision of the federal Constitution was made applicable to the states through the Fourteenth Amendment in *Klopfer v. North Carolina* (386 U.S. 213: 1967).

Significance   Speedy trial challenges that would establish fixed time limits for trials or would depend on formal demand by the accused for a speedy trial have been rejected by the Supreme Court. Rather, the Court developed a balancing test for speedy trials in *Barker v. Wingo* (407 U.S. 514: 1972). The four components are: (1) length of delay; (2) sufficiency of reasons for the delay; (3) assertion of the right by the accused; and (4) injury or prejudice suffered by the accused through pretrial incarceration, anxiety, and/or impairment of the ability to present a defense. In addition to these guidelines established by the Court, both federal and state legislation exists to govern the speed by which a criminal case progresses through the courts. The Speedy Trial Act of 1974, for example, establishes a 30-day period from arrest to indictment in federal cases. Trial must then occur within 70 days of indictment. Delays caused, for example, by hearings on motions or competency examinations are excluded from speedy trial calculations. The objective of the federal statute is first to protect the integrity of a prosecutable case, and secondarily the defendant's interest. State laws, on the other hand, tend to be aimed first at protecting the accused from excessive delay. Defense-initiated requests for postponements are not considered delays covered by speedy trial protection. Generally, speedy trial statutes are only marginally successful in moving criminal cases through the justice system. No effective enforcement mechanisms exist, so specified time periods become goals rather than formal requirements.

Stand Mute (188)

A response of silence by an accused at an arraignment. When an accused stands mute, the court enters a plea of not guilty and the case is docketed for trial. *See also* ARRAIGNMENT, 124.

Significance An accused stands mute rather than respond with a plea of guilty or not guilty. This typically occurs at the arraignment, which is the first point in the criminal process where an accused is formally asked to enter a plea. An accused who stands mute is exercising his or her self-incrimination protections. Standing mute is the functional equivalent of pleading not guilty.

Standards of Proof (189)

Level of persuasion that must be met by evidence offered in a legal dispute. Standards of proof vary depending on the nature of the dispute. Standards of proof define the burden that must be carried to demonstrate affirmatively a fact at issue in a case. In a criminal case, the trier of fact must be satisfied or persuaded beyond a reasonable doubt. Proof beyond a reasonable doubt is conclusive enough to remove all reasonable uncertainty. Occasionally the term moral certainty is used for reasonable doubt. No proceeding utilizes a more stringent standard than reasonable doubt; absolute certainty is not required for resolving any class of dispute. In most civil matters, a party is required only to meet the preponderance of evidence standard. This requires that one party offer evidence that is more persuasive or convincing than the other party. Put another way, the standard demands proof that convinces the fact-finder that one party's representation of "fact" is more plausible than the other party's. A level of evidence located between preponderance and reasonable doubt is reflected in the "clear and convincing" standard. Clear and convincing establishes a firm belief in the mind of the fact-finder. This standard is applied to certain classes of civil cases. *See also* PREPONDERANCE OF EVIDENCE, 240; REASONABLE DOUBT, 179.

Significance Standards of proof define the level of certainty needed to prevail in particular kinds of fact disputes. The standards address the issue of burden of proof. Burden of proof, in turn, defines the obligation of a party to create sufficient belief in the mind of the fact-finder to resolve the dispute legally. The standards of proof define how extensive the burden of proof will be. The burden of proof is substantially greater in a criminal case than a civil case because only in the former must one party, the prosecution, convince the trier of fact beyond a reasonable doubt.

Status Offense (190)

A kind of violation or offense that is defined by the character or condition of the offender. Vagrancy, for example, is a status crime. A vagrant is a person who has no visible means of support. Status crimes or offenses are most commonly used in connection with juvenile status. There are a number of things juveniles may do for which they can be placed under the authority of the juvenile court that have no adult counterpart. Such offenses as running away, truancy, or curfew violation are examples of status offenses. They derive from the offender's status as a minor. Status offenses are handled exclusively through state law and are elements of state juvenile codes. *See also* JUVENILE PROCESS, 156.

Significance Historically, status offenses have been used as indicators of potential delinquency or special needs. They have commonly triggered some form of state intervention. The idea of creating offense categories separate from delinquency conduct was to insulate the status offender from the consequences of actually being labelled a delinquent. In the late 1960s, many states tried to underscore the line of separation between status offenses and delinquency by revising and renaming particular classes of offense categories. Most states chose to call these categories Children or Minors in Need of Supervision. Notwithstanding the attempts at distinguishing, the lines remain blurred and the practical effects may be of only marginal difference. Often, juveniles in either category may be taken into custody by law enforcement authorities, will likely appear in the same juvenile courts, and may come under supervision of the same treatment personnel. The issue of status offenses is complicated, and it continues to trouble state legislatures. Indeed, a number of states are actively entertaining the elimination of status offense categories from the jurisdiction of juvenile courts. Other changes of a less extensive kind are also under consideration.

Statute of Limitations (191)

A law that establishes a time period within which legal action must commence. Statutes of limitation are legislative enactments and the operative time limits vary across jurisdictions and by the issue involved. Statutes of limitation typically set limits of three, five, or seven years. These limits apply to almost every kind of legal action, criminal or civil. In criminal cases, a statute of limitation is viewed as an act of "grace" whereby the state relinquishes its right to prosecute. Serious crimes such as murder are excepted from statutes of limitation and prosecution may be initiated at anytime. *See also* SPEEDY TRIAL, 187.

Significance Statutes of limitation require that legal actions be commenced in a timely fashion. Statutes of limitation apply to criminal prosecutions (with some exceptions), civil litigation, and the enforcement of legal rights. Several policy objectives are served by statutes of limitation. The first is that at some point in time a person need no longer be concerned about the commencement of legal action against him or her. Second, there is a view that legal claims are eventually forfeited. In other words, persons ought not be able to put legal claims "on hold" for an unreasonable period of time. Finally, disputes ought to be adjudicated using evidence that is as "fresh" as possible. The reliability of fact-finding diminishes as evidence gets "stale," and a time limit encourages timely commencement of legal actions.

Stay (192)

A formal stopping of a judicial proceeding or some other process. A stay is put into effect by an order from a court. The stay holds the status quo until some specified action occurs. Stays differ from recesses and continuances, which are simply short or long-term adjournments of proceedings. A recess is like an intermission, and proceedings resume at a specified time. Resumption of proceedings stopped by a stay is typically contingent on the completion of some other action. *See also* INJUNCTION, 226.

Significance A stay resembles an injunction in that it may suspend particular actions. The stay permits consideration of some issue that might not be otherwise possible. Stays are often obtained in capital punishment cases to delay executions long enough to permit additional appeals. If an appeal is unsuccessful, the stay is dissolved and the punishment is implemented. When a court issues a stay, it makes no ruling on the merits of, for example, an additional appeals issue. Stays may also be obtained to delay the execution of orders in various civil actions.

Subpoena (193)

An order that commands a person to appear at a particular time and place to offer testimony. Subpoenas are most likely to be issued by courts and grand juries, but may also come from legislative bodies or independent commissions. A subpoena *duces tecum* is a command to someone holding or controlling records or documents that compels the production of those items at a particular proceeding such as a trial. Failure to comply with a subpoena may subject a person to punishment for contempt. The right of a criminal defendant to use the subpoena or compulsory process is protected by the Sixth Amendment. This means an accused can compel the appearance in court of even the most unwilling witness. *See also* COMPULSORY PROCESS, 131; GRAND JURY, 148.

Significance The power to subpoena is essential to the functioning of a number of public institutions. Testimony and certain records may be pivotal components of trial court fact-finding. Similarly, the capacity to compel the appearance of witnesses allows grand juries to perform their investigative role. An agency must have legal authority over a particular subject matter in order to issue a subpoena. In addition, the information to be provided by the witness must be relevant to the agency's inquiry. A subpoenaed person must appear under threat of contempt, but does retain the constitutional protection against self-incrimination. In other words, a witness cannot be compelled to disclose information that may result in his or her prosecution. If the testimony from such a witness is important enough, the witness may receive immunity from prosecution. Under a grant of immunity, the witness need no longer fear criminal prosecution and can be compelled to disclose what would have been incriminating testimony absent the immunity.

Venire (194)

A list of persons summoned to serve as jurors for a particular district and period of time. The *venire* will provide the pool from which each trial jury will be chosen. Jury selection is a three-stage process with the selection of a *venire* from a master jury list being the middle step. Compilation of the master list and screening the jury pool for bias precede and succeed, respectively, creation of the *venire*. A *venire* must be randomly drawn from the master list. Prospective jurors making up the *venire* may be selected for service on a particular case for a period of time known as a term. Court officials know how many jury trials are scheduled during the term, and a *venire* large enough to provide jurors for all trials is created. Persons are then randomly drawn from the *venire* to provide jurors for a specific trial. Jurors not chosen remain in the *venire* and are available for trials of other cases scheduled during the term. *See also* JURY, 155; MASTER JURY LIST, 158; *VOIR DIRE*, 196.

Significance   Those making up the *venire* are called to appear by summons. Everyone receiving a summons may not serve as a juror, however. Jurors must, for example, be residents of the locality in which the court summoning them has jurisdiction. Pre-screening normally occurs on such criteria as residency, citizenship, and age, and some prospective jurors will be excused because they do not meet these qualifying requirements. Other jurors will be excused because they are exempted by law. These exemptions are usually occupational categories such as teachers and medical personnel. These exemptions were initially established in a time when members of the *venire* could be selected to sit on more than one case during a term. This extended obligation created problems in certain professions, hence the exemption. Most jurisdictions currently require service for only one case, however. This limit minimizes the time any juror must serve and has prompted removal of most occupationally defined exemptions.

Venue   (195)
The geographical area or district in which a court may hear a case. Venue refers to the location of a trial. Venue differs from jurisdiction in that the latter defines the authority of a court to hear a matter while the former defines only the place that judicial power may be exercised. Venue is typically established by the location of the act that is the subject of the judicial proceeding. A criminal prosecution, for example, takes place in the district in which the alleged crime was committed. *See also* JURISDICTION, 56; PRETRIAL PUBLICITY, 174.

Significance   Defendants in criminal cases or civil actions are not entitled to the venue of their choice, but can generally expect the case to be heard before the courts and jurors from the immediate area. Indeed, the Sixth Amendment requires that federal criminal prosecutions are to be conducted in the district in which the crime was committed. On balance, this allows legal proceedings to reflect local values. Occasionally a defendant's interests may be adversely influenced by prejudicial pretrial publicity. Such publicity may preclude selection of an impartial jury. If a judge determines during the *voir dire* examination of prospective jurors that a case cannot be fairly tried in a particular community, the location or venue of the trial may be changed to a location where publicity has not been so pervasive.

Voir Dire (196)

Process by which prospective jurors are examined to determine both competence and impartiality. The term *voir dire* is French and translates "to speak the truth." The *voir dire* process is conducted by the presiding judge, counsel, or both. Members of the *venire* are typically questioned about possible acquaintance with the parties, prior personal experience with the same kinds of issues as are involved in the case, or any other matter that may have a bearing on the prospective juror's capacity to judge the case fairly. Exposure to potentially prejudicial pretrial publicity is measured during *voir dire*. If a juror is unable to judge the case fairly, he or she may be challenged for cause. If the judge sustains the challenge, the juror is replaced. A juror may also be replaced by means of a peremptory challenge. In such cases, jurors may be excluded by either side without having to offer an explanation. *See also* JURY, 155; MASTER JURY LIST, 158; PEREMPTORY CHALLENGE, 167; *VENIRE*, 194.

Significance The supervision of *voir dire* rests exclusively with the trial judge. The judge possesses the discretion to determine how far-ranging *voir dire* may be in a given case. In *Ristaino v. Ross* (424 U.S. 589: 1976), the Burger Court ruled that a trial judge could properly deny the opportunity to probe the racial prejudice of prospective jurors absent a showing that such prejudice was a factor of consequence in the case. Beyond determination of their qualification, *voir dire* allows attorneys to "educate" jurors with respect to how they might evaluate evidence. Defense attorneys frequently use *voir dire* to reiterate the presumption of innocence and that the state carries the full burden of proof. Such an approach may impact on juror attitudes and ultimately the conclusions they drawn from the evidence. While *voir dire* does not usually take more than an hour or two, the process can be inordinately long in celebrated cases.

Warrant (197)

An order issued by a court authorizing the arrest of a person or the search of a specified location. The warrant requirement in criminal cases is found in the Fourth Amendment following the assertion of the people's right to be secure against unreasonable governmental intrusions. A warrant must be obtained from an appropriate authority, usually a judge or magistrate. A request for a warrant must establish probable cause that the person to be arrested is linked to a criminal act or that the location to be searched likely contains particular seizable items. The warrant must describe in detail the people to be arrested or the items sought in a search. Slightly different from the arrest warrant is the bench warrant. A bench warrant is issued by a court and authorizes the seizure of a person. The bench warrant is most commonly used when a person fails to appear in response to a subpoena or when a person's presence is required in a civil contempt situation. *See also* ARREST, 125; PROBABLE CAUSE, 176; SEARCH AND SEIZURE, 184.

Significance   A warrant authorizes an official governmental intrusion into personal security. Arrests or searches may be made without warrant if exigent circumstances exist. Such circumstances make it impossible or impracticable to obtain a warrant in advance of an action. Exigent circumstance exceptions to the warrant requirement are necessitated by situational demands, but also reflect that Fourth Amendment protections are not absolute. Use of exigent circumstance exceptions does place the burden of justification on law enforcement officers. Exigent circumstance searches include searches of automobiles, for example. The exigency or emergency is created by the unforeseen need to search and the fleeting opportunity to accomplish the search because of the vehicle's mobility. A stop-and-frisk encounter is also an exigent circumstance. In *Michigan v. Tyler* (436 U.S. 499: 1978), the Supreme Court also permitted a warrantless search of a fire scene under the exigent-circumstance exception. The Court held that a burning building "clearly presents an exigency of sufficient proportions" to permit a reasonable warrantless entry. It would defy reason to require a warrant before entering a burning building. Once on the premises to fight the fire, police and fire officials are entitled under the "plain view" doctrine to gather visible evidence. A hot pursuit chase may also create sufficient exigency to allow a warrant exception. The exigent-circumstance principle takes cognizance of the impossibility of completing the warrant process in certain situations where making a search or an arrest may be demanded.

Witness   **(198)**
A person who offers testimony or presents evidence to a court or investigative body. Witnesses are generally divided into two categories. The first is the lay witness. This is a person who has direct or personal knowledge of facts at issue in the case. Lay witnesses may only testify as to what they perceived through such basic senses as sight. A person who was present in a bank at the time of a robbery may be able to offer testimony describing the incident and possibly identifying the offenders. Visual observations are most common, but the other senses may be utilized as well. Identification of a person by the sound of his or her voice, for example, may be made by a witness. Lay witnesses

185

may not offer opinion. The other kind of witness is the expert. Unlike the lay witness, the expert witness may offer opinions based on his or her expertise in an effort to assist the jury. In order for a witness to qualify as an expert, he or she must possess expertise not found in the common person. Further, the witness must have qualifications that establish him or her as a bona fide expert. The trial judge determines whether a person qualifies as an expert witness. *See also* COMPULSORY PROCESS, 131; CONFRONTATION, 133; EVIDENCE, 144.

Significance Obtaining evidence from witnesses is a principal component of the adversary system. The parties to legal actions are entitled to examine their own witnesses in an effort to establish facts supporting their positions. Parties are also entitled to challenge the testimony presented by witnesses called by the other side through cross-examination. Indeed, in criminal cases the right to confront adverse witnesses is protected by the Sixth Amendment. In addition, the Sixth Amendment guarantees a criminal defendant the right to compel the appearance of a witness. This right entitles an accused to use the subpoena power of courts and other government support in obtaining favorable witnesses.

5. The Civil Judicial Process

Civil actions comprise the greatest volume of legal business confronting the court system. Although most civil cases are not as intriguing as their criminal counterparts, the outcomes of civil cases are likely to have profound consequences on the interests of the parties. Civil actions cover a broad span of matters ranging from extremely complex litigation to matters as straightforward as small claims. This chapter will examine the kinds of cases that appear on civil dockets and the legal processes dedicated to resolution of civil disputes.

Civil cases differ in several key respects from criminal cases. First, there is no governmental party that plays a role comparable to that of a prosecutor. As a result, the plaintiff or initiating party in a civil case exercises substantial control over a case. If the plaintiff wishes to drop a case or settle, he or she is able to do so. As a representative of society at large, a prosecutor has the authority to proceed with a criminal case even if the victim or complaining party changes his or her mind. Second, criminal cases are more stringently governed by constitutional and other legal safeguards. Defendants in criminal actions, for example, are legally entitled to assistance of counsel. If a criminal defendant is indigent, the court is required to provide counsel. Civil litigants are essentially responsible for their own lawyers. Speedy trial and other requirements of due process tend to ensure that criminal cases are not unduly delayed. It is not unusual for delays in excess of two or three years to exist for civil dockets, especially in urban courts. Thus, litigants in civil cases are more susceptible to the inequities stemming from resource differences between parties. Third, different standards apply to decision making for the two categories of cases. A jury must be convinced "beyond a reasonable doubt" that a defendant committed a crime before it can convict.

Civil cases may be decided in favor of the party carrying a "preponderance of evidence," a less demanding standard than used in criminal cases.

There are several kinds of matters confronting the civil courts. The largest category are cases aimed at recovery of debts. What the litigant seeks is the payment of what is legally due. For example, a person buys a house for a contracted amount and is obligated to make mortgage payments on a monthly basis. If the person falls behind in the payments, the financing agency may bring suit to either enlist the court's assistance in recovering past due payments or recover control of the property by foreclosure. The situations under which debt recovery issues might arise are virtually infinite. A more complex kind of civil action is one where damages are involved. The compensation sought in this kind of case is often more difficult to gauge because it may involve, for example, some kind of physical disability and what constitutes adequate compensation for the loss.

A third category of civil case are those that involve people's status or their relationships to one another. The most common of these cases are domestic relations or divorce actions. In addition to focusing on the marital relationship of the spouses, this kind of case often involves the matter of child custody and support. Adoption of children and the involuntary commitment of people to institutions are other examples of this category of civil case. Finally, there are public policy cases in the civil courts. These cases focus on a particular matter of substance or procedure arising out of governmental policy or practice. Application procedures or eligibility criteria for public assistance, for example, might be challenged as arbitrary or discriminatory by a person unsuccessfully seeking access to such a program. This category does not produce large numbers of cases, but their policy consequences make them disproportionately significant.

Special mention needs to be made of the matter of congestion and backlog found in civil courts. Congestion exists because new filings have outpaced the courts' capacity to dispose of cases. This has been true for many years. The problem is compounded because there is no agent, such as a prosecutor, to act as a screen on new cases. The victim of a crime cannot pursue the case without going through the prosecutor while a civil litigant can file any kind of case directly with the appropriate court. In addition, as the rules governing both civil and criminal cases have become more extensive, the time it takes for the fact-finding processes of trials has lengthened. Finally, some litigants benefit from delay, so delay in moving a case forward to conclusion will be strategically pursued.

The consequences of delay are many and generally undesirable, but three stand out. Delay necessarily erodes the quality of fact-finding. Witnesses forget or become unavailable, and the court becomes less able to accurately judge fact disputes. Delay also prompts certain behaviors that would not exist otherwise. Courts tend to become dependent on civil case settlements as a way of moving the caseload. Indeed, the courts often strongly encourage settlement. To the extent a court feels a sense of urgency about disposing of cases, the role of the court has been redefined. Finally, delay affects parties to civil actions differentially. The litigant seeking damages in a serious personal injury case may not be able to withstand a lengthy delay and settles the case for a fraction of the amount sought when the case was originally filed. The defendant in our example is typically an insurance company, a party whose interests are enhanced by delay and the pressures to settle that stem from delay.

The civil process is governed by rules and procedures established largely through statute. While these processes are relatively formalized, civil litigants do not bring with them the constitutional protections that apply to criminal defendants. A schematic of the basic civil process is presented in Figure 5-1. While a number of discrete steps are shown, the process can be divided into four principal stages. The first is commencement of the suit. The plaintiff files a complaint, jurisdiction is established over the defendant through a service or notification process, and the defendant files some kind of answer. Next, there is a lengthy pretrial period during which discovery of evidence occurs. Discovery can take several forms and is the heart of the civil process in many respects. Other pretrial procedures exist, including conferences scheduled by civil courts between the parties. The objective is to ready a case for trial, but judges use the conference to move the parties to settlement if possible. It has also become common for alternate means of conflict resolution to be sought, such as mediation and arbitration. In some jurisdictions, these processes must be attempted before a case can be tried. By the time the third or trial stage is reached, much time has elapsed and an overwhelming majority of civil cases have been resolved by settlement. A trial occurs when fact-finding by a third party—a judge or jury—is still required to conclude the case. The final stage has to do with relief or remedy. It is the function of civil courts, once a judgment has been rendered, to enforce that judgment in some way such that a successful civil plaintiff has his or her injury remedied to the fullest extent possible. As with criminal cases, there are avenues of appeal that may be pursued by parties to civil actions.

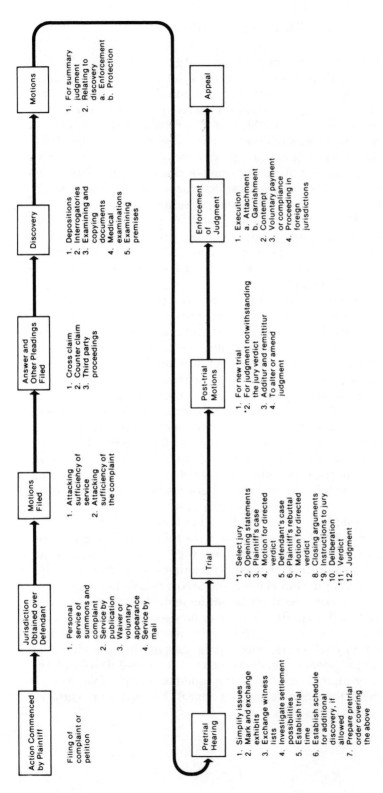

Figure 5-1. Typical Progression of Civil Litigation

From THE COURTS: FULCRUM OF THE JUSTICE SYSTEM by H. Ted Rubin. Copyright © 1976 by Newbery Award Records, Inc. Reprinted by permission of Random House, Inc.

Access to Courts **(199)**
The availability of the judicial process to respond to cases. A person's access to court is governed by several factors. The first, of course, is jurisdiction. Jurisdiction defines a court's power to act. Access can only occur where a court possesses proper authority to hear a controversy. Second, courts cannot be accessed unless justiciability requirements are met. That is, courts can withhold power from those situations where standing does not exist or where the issue is more appropriately addressed by another governmental branch. Third, organizational structure and caseload directly affect access. The structure of a court system establishes entry points. Some structures facilitate access while others do not. For example, if a court system has only a single general jurisdiction court at the trial level, access may be limited. Similarly, if case volume is heavy and the court system has too few judges, cases will accumulate. Docket backlog delays and possibly discourages access. *See also* DELAY, 215; JURISDICTION, 56; JUSTICIABLE ISSUE, 231; STANDING, 246.

Significance The factors that influence access to courts are technical, structural, and environmental. The technical factors establish threshold conditions. Besides jurisdiction and justiciability issues, access can be formally restricted by statute or court decision. For example, the abstention doctrine directs federal courts not to assume jurisdiction over a case being tried in state courts unless an extraordinary federal question is involved. Similarly, federal class actions were limited by the court in *Eisen v. Carlisle & Jacquelin* (417 U.S. 156: 1974) to those situations where direct injury to individual class members exists. Structural factors also govern access. Legislatures that establish state court systems can encourage access by creating sufficient points of entry or judges of sufficient numbers to allow adequate response to case demand. For example, states that designate a particular court to handle small claims as a separate docket issue facilitate access for these matters. Finally, access is a function of such environmental factors as backlog. Even if the technical criteria are met, parties are discouraged from commencing civil cases if it is likely that they must wait in excess of three years to reach trial.

Advisory Opinion **(200)**
A response by a judge or court to a legal question posed outside a bona fide case or controversy. Advisory opinions are typically requested by a legislative body or other governmental official. An advisory opinion is a reply to an abstract or hypothetical question. It

indicates how the court would respond to the issue should actual litigation take place. It has no binding effect unless it is legally accepted by the requesting body. *See also* CASE OR CONTROVERSY, 6; DECLARATORY JUDGMENT, 265; LEGISLATIVE COURT, 59.

Significance   An advisory opinion may not be rendered by a federal constitutional court (one created under provisions of Article III) because of the constitutional mandate limiting jurisdiction of federal courts to actual cases or controversies. The limitation is designed to preserve separation of powers and keep the judiciary from certain political entanglements that might adversely affect the judicial branch. The Supreme Court spoke to the issue of advisory opinions in *Muskrat v. United States* (219 U.S. 346: 1911). This case involved a congressional act that altered distribution of Indian property. Because the law diminished the lands and monies to which certain tribes were entitled, its validity was in doubt. Congress included a specific provision in the law authorizing Muskrat and others to file a test case. The law even went so far as to provide for reimbursement of all costs associated with the litigation. The Court ruled that because the parties were not truly adverse in this situation, the test case really presented an advisory or hypothetical question. Accordingly, the Court ruled that the federal courts did not have jurisdiction to rule on the matter. Legislative courts, those created under authority granted by Article I, may render advisory opinions. A number of states also allow the rendering of advisory opinions in order to clarify state legislation without the necessity of burdensome litigation. Advisory opinions differ from declaratory judgments in that the latter involves an actual controversy.

Affidavit   (201)
A written statement of facts. An affidavit contains a voluntarily offered representation of information. An affidavit is generally used to establish or confirm a point of fact. The person who makes an affidavit is called an affiant. The affiant offers information while under oath or must otherwise affirm the truthfulness of the information in the affidavit. *See also* DISCOVERY, 219; WARRANT, 197.

Significance   An affidavit has a variety of uses in the legal process. Affidavits may be used, for example, to itemize losses in a civil action. Affidavits are also used to indicate that proper notice of a hearing has been made to all parties. An affidavit is commonly used as a means of discovery and is essentially like a deposition. An affidavit is also used for such other reasons as certifying the giving or receiving of a hearing notice or service of a summons. Affidavits may also be offered in response to an action by a plaintiff as in the case of a motion for summary judgment.

Alternative Dispute Resolution   (202)

Settlement of civil disputes by means other than trial. The move to alternative dispute resolution (ADR) was prompted by a number of factors, but largely the time, expense, and complexity associated with trials. Several techniques of dispute resolution are currently used; most have existed for some time. What has changed is that courts are now endorsing use of these alternatives and, in some cases, even ordering parties to avail themselves of one of these methods before accessing the judicial process. The most common techniques are mediation and arbitration. Mediation is generally nonadversarial and uses a third party to aid parties in seeking a voluntary settlement. Mediation does not involve fact-finding as such. Rather, reconciliation of differences is the objective. Arbitration, on the other hand, uses a third party, possibly a panel of three or more people, to hear arguments and render a judgment. If the arbitrator's decision is not satisfactory to the parties, the dispute may then be tried. Another ADR technique involves assignment of a judge to examine settlement positions of parties in an effort to facilitate agreement. The settlement judge is a regular judge assigned to a case upon request of the parties. Another method of resolution is the use of minitrials. Here parties meet with a judge in conference and exchange summaries of their respective positions. Such hearings tend to be quite abbreviated; they can usually be concluded in a day. Decisions based on these hearings follow shortly thereafter. *See also* ACCESS TO COURTS, 199; ARBITRATION, 4; MEDIATION, 25.

Significance   The various techniques of alternative dispute resolution are attractive to disputants. The current emphasis on ADR, however, is largely a response to the incapacity of the civil courts to keep current dockets. Civil litigation is often complex and expensive. It is also the case that civil courts are badly backlogged. Many civil disputes must wait in excess of three years from filing to trial. As a result, many attorneys and businesses who are frequently involved in legal disputes have supported use of alternate ways to settle disputes because they are faster and less expensive. The courts have also embraced ADR. Trial courts at all levels frequently order its use, especially mediation or arbitration, before a case can be docketed for trial. Thus, ADR has been extensively assimilated into to existing judicial structure. Furthermore, a large number of ADR programs have been created legislatively, which reinforces the present trend toward institutionalizing ADR.

Answer (203)

A pleading submitted by a civil defendant as a formal written response to a plaintiff's complaint. The answer may simply admit or deny the assertions of the plaintiff. An admission eliminates the need to engage in fact-finding. A denial, on the other hand, focuses the fact issue(s) that must be resolved at trial. Among the things an answer may claim is a defense that asserts certain facts that prevent the plaintiff from winning a judgment as a matter of law. *See also* COUNTER CLAIM, 209; PLEADING, 239.

Significance Answers are governed by rules of civil procedure. They are generally required to assert all the defenses that will be offered, although supplemental answers are permitted. A supplemental answer is filed to amend a previously submitted answer by correction, addition, or clarification. The answer should contain discussion of any counter claim the defendant might have against the plaintiff. A response to a counter claim might come in the form of a reply, a special and defensive pleading that reacts specifically to the counter claim and the new dimension that adds to a civil action.

Challenge (204)

The questioning of the legality of governmental actions. A challenge is undertaken when a person or group wishes to object or take exception to something. A particular public policy may be challenged, for example. The challenge may come in a case already before the courts, or a specific test case may be initiated in order to create an opportunity to challenge the policy. A group of construction contractors, for example, may choose to challenge a legislative policy that sets aside a portion of public construction contracts for minority contractors. Similarly, a practice may be challenged. For example, a local court clerk might only add newly registered voters to the roster of eligible jurors once a year. The annual updating may not be the result of formally adopted policy, but rather administrative convenience. The effect of the practice, however, is to keep 18-year olds, among others, off juries for at least a year. On a more particular level, it is possible to challenge the participation of a specific judge in a specific case. It may be felt, for example, that a judge has a personal interest in a case. A challenge may be filed as to whether the judge is qualified to sit on the case. In similar fashion, particular jurors may be challenged for cause if it is believed that they could not render an impartial judgment in a particular case. *See also* INTEREST GROUPS IN COURT, 272; TAXPAYER SUIT, 251; TEST CASE, 252.

Significance   The civil courts are frequently used to challenge particular governmental policies or actions. Interest groups are particularly instrumental in focusing challenges to certain public policies or practices. While these cases are not as numerous as debt recovery or domestic relations cases, they are disproportionately important because they contain a public dimension not present in other civil actions. Illustrations of legal challenges are virtually infinite, but several examples will highlight the category. The Jehovah's Witnesses have been successful at challenging a number of policies such as the requirement that a license be obtained before engaging in door-to-door solicitations. The Witnesses challenged this and other policies they felt impinged on their religious practices. Similarly, a state "moment of silence" law was struck down by the Supreme Court in *Wallace v. Jaffree* (472 U.S. 38: 1985). Discriminatory practices are also frequently the basis of legal challenge. The Supreme Court overturned the trespass conviction of a number of individuals in the "sit-in" case of *Peterson v. Greenville* (373 U.S. 244: 1963). The convictions stemmed from enforcement of a local ordinance requiring segregated meal service at restaurants. The racially discriminatory use of peremptory strikes by prosecutors was prohibited by the Supreme Court in *Batson v. Kentucky* (476 U.S. 79: 1986). For every case decided by the Supreme Court, there are countless challenges that do not progress beyond the civil trial courts. Challenges to land-use restrictions or zoning ordinances are quite common. Challenges to possibly overbroad local responses to the current drug problem have also reached the civil courts.

Class Action   **(205)**
A suit brought by several people on behalf of a larger group whose members have the same legal interest. A class action is indicated when a group is so large that individual suits are impractical. Group suits have been used frequently in recent years and are often the means by which civil rights, consumer, and environmental questions are litigated. A class action is sometimes called a representative action. It can be brought in either federal or state court. It must be certified by a trial court at the outset, and all class members must be made aware of the suit and given the opportunity to exclude themselves. Certification involves a determination that the asserted class actually exists and

that the people bringing the action are members of the class. *See also* ACCESS TO COURTS, 199; JUSTICIABLE ISSUE, 231; MOOTNESS, 234.

Significance   A class action provides economy and efficiency in the adjudication of an issue. It allows a suit to continue even when some initial class members no longer have standing. The class action is thus an effective device to prevent a suit from becoming moot. It also measurably reduces the possibility of conflicting judgments resulting from numerous individual suits. Class actions overcome the requirement that a plaintiff in a suit must have a direct interest beyond that of the public good. The courts have thus been able to respond to substantial social questions in which the plaintiff was not the only one injured. Several limitations apply to a class action, however. In *Zahn v. International Paper Company* (414 U.S. 291: 1973), the Supreme Court held that, in order to use federal diversity jurisdiction for class actions, each member of the class must have suffered an injury amounting to at least $10,000 in value. The Court also said in *Eisen v. Carlisle & Jacqueline* (417 U.S. 156: 1974) that the initiators of a class action must notify, at their own expense, all members of the class. The impact of these decisions has been to reduce the number of large consumer and environmental suits. The more numerous smaller class actions have not been adversely affected.

Contempt of Court   (206)

Any act that obstructs the administration of justice by a court or that brings disrespect on a court or its authority. Contempt may be direct in that it occurs in the presence of the court and constitutes a direct affront to the court's authority. Contempt may be indirect in that the behavior that demonstrates contempt may occur outside of the courtroom. While some due process protections apply to contempt, it is generally a summary order through which penalties of fine or imprisonment may be directly imposed by the court. It is necessary to distinguish between criminal and civil contempt. Criminal contempt is an act of obstruction or disrespect typically occurring in the courtroom. A party who acts in an abusive manner in court is in criminal contempt. He or she may receive a fine and/or imprisonment for up to six months may be summarily imposed. Civil contempt results from failure to comply with an order of a court. Civil contempt is designed to coerce compliance with an order to protect the interests of the party on whose behalf the order or judgment was issued. Civil contempt ends when the desired conduct or compliance occurs. A legislative contempt power also exists. It may be used if a disturbance is created within a legislative chamber or if people subpoenaed to appear before legislative committees refuse to testify. Congressional contempt is not summarily imposed, however. It is handled through the standard criminal process with trial occurring in a federal district court if an indictment has been secured from a grand jury.

Significance   The contempt power provides courts with leverage to maintain courtroom decorum appropriate for judicial proceedings. Contempt enables a court to punish disruptive or disrespectful conduct, and it serves as a deterrent to such conduct. The Supreme Court ruled in *Illinois v. Allen* (397 U.S. 337: 1970) that, in addition to contempt, it is "constitutionally permissible" to bind, gag, or even remove from the courtroom a particularly obstreperous defendant. The contempt power also permits courts to compel compliance with a court order, backing up the authority of all such orders. Contempt constitutes an exception to the mandated right to trial and right to trial by jury. Due process requires that formal hearings take place in cases where contempt sentences might be lengthy. Indeed, extensive jail sentences can occur only after a trial on the contempt charge. In addition, such cases cannot be tried by the judge pursuing the contempt sanction.

Contingent Fee   (207)

Charges by an attorney for legal services that are dependent on a successful outcome in a civil case. Under the contingent or contingency fee approach, an attorney handles a case involving a money claim without prepayment for services by the client. If the action is successful, the attorney receives a percentage of the recovered money as the fee for services rendered. A contingent fee of one-third of the recovered amount is typical. If, on the other hand, the client does not recover any money through the legal action, the attorney on contingent fee will receive no fee. Use of a contingent fee does not preclude an attorney from charging a fixed fee as well. It is unethical for attorneys to represent criminal defendants on a contingent fee basis. *See also* PRO BONO PUBLICO, 242.

Significance   The contingent fee is a device whereby people may be able to avail themselves of legal representation. Litigation is expensive, and few plaintiffs could sustain such costs in advance. While the contingent fee approach is not possible for all kinds of legal problems, it is the method used in upwards of 70 percent of cases that assert money claims. Without the contingent fee system, many people would be unable to pursue relief in personal injury or negligence cases. At the same time, some are critical of the contingent fee approach. The principal concern is that the hope or expectation of large judgments prompts attorneys to litigate in cases that might be settled out of court. As a consequence, some states have limited the amount that can be gained in contingent fees for certain kinds of cases.

Continuance (208)

Postponement of a court action to a later date. A continuance is essentially the same as an adjournment. The continuance is formally entered on the record as reflecting the adjournment. The term *continuance* derives from this entry on the record, which is done in an effort to link the separated proceedings or make them part of a single, continuous process. A continuance differs from a recess, which is only a short-term interruption of proceedings. *See also* STAY, 192.

Significance A continuance may be sought for a variety of reasons. A key witness may be hospitalized, for example, and not be available to appear on the scheduled date. If the information to be provided by the witness is critical to resolving the fact dispute, the proceeding will be delayed until the witness can appear. A continuance may be sought for less legitimate reasons, however. A court has the authority not to continue a case if the judge believes the request is aimed at gaining unfair advantage. In any event, continuing cases contributes to delayed disposition of cases and backlogged dockets.

Counter Claim (209)

Demand made by a defendant against the plaintiff in a civil action. A counter claim is a response to a claim. Instead of seeking to defend or deny the plaintiff's claim, the defendant files a counter claim or action against the plaintiff. The counter claim is a method designed to contest the plaintiff's complaint by the filing of an independent cause of action. A compulsory counter claim is one stemming from the same fact situation as the plaintiff's initial claim. A permissive counter claim does not arise out of the original incident or transaction. *See also* ANSWER, 203; CROSS CLAIM, 210.

Significance A counter claim allows a defendant to do more than merely defend against a legal action. The counter claim permits a defendant to set forth a claim of his or her own that might entitle the defendant to reduce or offset what might be owed the plaintiff. In the most successful scenario, the defendant would actually win the case on the counter claim. Where a mandatory counter claim is pursued, a trial would proceed in much the same way as it would in the absence of a counter claim. If the counter claim stems from a totally separate fact situation, a separate case is required. As a result, restrictions exist on permissive counter claims. A counter claim is a particular response to a civil action. A plaintiff might, for example, sue to obtain the full purchase price of some item from a buyer, the defendant. The defendant could either attempt to defend not paying the full price or file a counter claim alleging, for example, that the purchase was made on the basis of false representation.

Cross Claim (210)

A secondary claim filed by parties on the same side of a legal action. A cross claim is brought by a co-plaintiff or co-defendant. This claim is separate from the overarching claim against the party on the opposing side of the main litigation. A cross claim must directly relate to a substantial issue contained in the original and larger action or a counter claim based on it. *See also* COMPLAINT, 130; COUNTER CLAIM, 209.

Significance A cross claim turns a legal action into essentially a three-sided suit. It allows a co-defendant to assert a claim against another co-defendant in an effort to place part or all of the liability on the second defendant. For example, if an airline files an action against a contractor and one of its sub-contractors because of a defect in a plane it purchased, the contractor may wish to file a cross claim against the sub-contractor in an effort to demonstrate full responsibility resides with the sub-contractor. Both the contractor and sub-contractor are defendants to the initial action, but within that suit, they are contesting through a cross claim. A cross claim differs from a counter claim. In the former, claims are litigated by parties on the same side of the principal lawsuit, while the latter is litigated between the parties contesting the original litigation. A cross claim may also be called a cross complaint.

Damages (211)

Compensation to a person for injury suffered. *Damage* (singular) refers to loss or injury to a person by accident or the negligence of another. *Damages* (plural) refers to the money it will take to repair that damage. Damage may take the form of personal injury in an automobile accident or injury done to one's property or reputation. Damages for injury would, at minimum, cover incurred costs such as hospital bills. Damages, however, include an additional and more imprecise dimension: compensation for "pain and suffering" or for injury to reputation or community standing. The latter involve the exercise of a court's equity power. *See also* DEBT RECOVERY, 212; EQUITY JURISDICTION, 49; LIABILITY, 232; TORT, 38.

Significance   Actions to recover damages are covered by tort law. This kind of action requires the establishment of liability. That is, the plaintiff must show that he or she was actually injured by an action (or inaction) of the defendant. If this can be shown, it is then necessary to define the extent of compensation required. Included, of course, will be the documented losses that stem directly from the injury. In addition, there might be compensation for mental and emotional distress. Personal injury and wrongful death cases often contain this element, for example. There are several categories of damage. First is actual damages, which are those losses that can be proven or documented. A plaintiff who prevails in a civil suit is legally entitled to compensation for actual damages. Nominal damages, on the other hand, may be awarded when a plaintiff's injury is recognized but where substantial compensation for the loss is either not warranted or indeterminable. Punitive damages are occasionally awarded to punish the defendant for misconduct that is seen as intended and malicious.

Debt Recovery   (212)
Collection of monies owed, usually under terms of a contract. Debt recovery cases span a wide array of situations, but typically stem from disputes between businesses or businesses and individuals. The disputes are commonly over obligations set forth in voluntarily entered agreements or contracts. Debt recovery situations are often settled without litigation, but this category produces extensive litigation nonetheless. Most often, these cases involve contracts through which products or services are conveyed or by which money is loaned by one party to another. In most of these situations, the plaintiff has not received payment as provided in the contract and is seeking some kind of judicial remedy. Also included in this category of debt recovery are those actions seeking payment of claims under terms of insurance contracts. A related category of cases involves bankruptcy where legal protection is sought by those owing money. Here the legal interests of the borrower are balanced against the creditor's interest in recovering some of the debt. *See also* DEFAULT JUDGMENT, 214.

Significance   Some debt recovery actions are relatively simple, while others are complex. Commercial law actions involving two or more businesses may be quite involved. Individual credit situations are more numerous and quite straightforward. For example, an individual contracts to buy or rent a house or car. If the person fails to make the contracted payments, the creditor seeks relief. The courts have several options in these cases. A foreclosure or eviction proceeding can eventually return property to the seller or creditor. This allows the seller to recover by conveying the property to someone who will make the payments. Creditors can repossess items such as cars by a similar process. Courts have additional options as well. A court may order the garnishment of a debtor's wages. This allows the court to obtain a portion of the debtor's earnings before the debtor is paid. The proceeds of the garnishment are then paid to the party who obtained the order to garnish. A lien or claim against a debtor's property may be issued instead as a way to secure resources to repay a debt. Plaintiffs almost always prevail in debt recovery cases because the defendant has normally failed to abide by explicit provisions of a contract. Indeed, in most debt recovery situations, defendants fail to even appear, and plaintiffs then are granted default judgments.

Decree (213)

A court judgment issued in the exercise of its equity power. A decree is based on a fact judgment of a court and directs what must happen to give effect to a decision. The purpose of a decree is to enable a court to fashion relief that is uniquely suited to the case. The decree allows the court not only to render a judgment on behalf of one of the parties, but also to govern execution of the remedy in an attempt to achieve the most just outcome. *See also* EQUITY JURISDICTION, 49; JUDGMENT, 230; ORDER, 236.

Significance Like orders, decrees are either final or interlocutory. A final decree resolves all questions raised in a case. Once a final decree is entered, no further judicial action is required. An interlocutory decree is of an interim character. It does not resolve a dispute but rather addresses a matter that needs attention in preparation for arriving at a final decree. There are several types of specialized decrees, including the consent decree. A consent decree is based on an agreement between the parties. The agreement is obtained under the auspices of the court, but is not the product of full adjudication of the facts.

Default Judgment (214)

Court decision rendered in a civil proceeding where the defendant fails to respond. A default judgment comes after a proceeding for which the defendant has been notified, but chooses not to appear. *See also* EX PARTE, 224; JUDGMENT, 230.

Significance   A default is an omission of action. It is a failure to do something, and it produces a forfeiture or loss of legal rights. Failure to appear at a proceeding to respond to a plaintiff's action may bring a judgment against the defendant without his or her position being heard by the court. Default judgments are often issued in small claims cases when defendants do not appear. While only one party participates, this is not the same as an *ex parte* proceeding, which is designed to hear only one side in a dispute. Indeed, certain *ex parte* proceedings may take place without the opposite party even being notified.

Delay   **(215)**
Lengthening of the time for cases to proceed to trial. Delay is an acute problem in American trial courts. Litigants in virtually every federal and state court experience delay before trial, especially with civil cases. Delays in excess of three years for many categories of civil dispute are not uncommon. The delay experienced in criminal cases is comparatively slight because the Sixth Amendment mandates speedy trials for criminal defendants. Federal and state speedy trial statutes typically specify processing time of 120 days or less from formal charging to trial. One of the causes of delay in civil dockets, however, is that criminal cases consume a disproportionate amount of trial time in order to comply with these speedy trial requirements. This, of course, necessarily delays the progress of civil cases. A second cause of civil case delay is the rapid escalation in the volume of new cases filed. Many civil courts have experienced increases of several hundred percent since 1950. This rate of growth far exceeds increases in population and the number of new courts added to a judicial system. Furthermore, these civil filings are unscreened. Unlike a criminal case, which can only enter the courts after review and consent by the prosecuting attorney, any civil plaintiff may directly file a complaint. Without screening, cases of varying quality compete for scarce court time. Another factor contributing to civil case delay is that some jurisdictions are not managed well enough to improve the number of case dispositions. Similarly, the U.S. legal system has been slow to move to other methods of revolving disputes. *See also* ACCESS TO COURTS, 199; ALTERNATIVE DISPUTE RESOLUTION, 202; SPEEDY TRIAL, 187.

Significance   The delays encountered in civil courts have several consequences. Delays can lead to at least a partial breakdown of the adversary process. The regular participants in the process such as judges, prosecutors, and legal counsel come to pursue the common objective of settling disputes without trial. The behavior of the courtroom work group tends to become influenced, if not governed by, the pressing need to dispose of cases. Second, a trial delayed for two or three years cannot engage in the same quality of fact-finding as a case tried within six months. Among other things, witnesses cannot recall information as well. As a result, proceedings that depend on such testimony may be diminished in quality. Third, some parties whose trials are delayed are not as able as others to withstand the delay. A plaintiff in a personal injury action, for example, will often not be able to wait three years, as a defendant insurance company can. One positive consequence of backlogged dockets is that alternative methods of dispute resolution are being sought more often. The choice of going to such an approach as mediation resides with the parties, but courts are beginning to require mediation in certain types of cases as a prerequisite to trial. Disputes resolved by alternative methods are concluded more quickly. Furthermore, disputes resolved this way do not wind up on court dockets, which in turn contributes to lessening the delay experienced by those litigants who require trial.

Demurrer (216)

A way of challenging the legal sufficiency of the other party's case. A demurrer is a formal contention by a party to a lawsuit that asserts that even if the other side's representation of the facts is accurate, it is legally insufficient to sustain the case. When a person demurs, he or she does not legally admit the other party's position is right. Rather, the challenge focuses on whether there is a legal remedy that can be provided if the other side's fact position is true. *See also* DIRECTED VERDICT, 218; DISMISS, 220.

Significance A demurrer is used to dispute the legal adequacy of a pleading or other evidence offered by the opposing party. The demurrer allows a defendant to assert that the effect of an argument or unit of evidence, whether true or not, is insufficient to prevail if the case is tried. Presentation of a demurrer has been largely replaced in contemporary practice by motions to dismiss or motions for directed verdicts.

Deposition (217)

The principal approach to discovery in civil cases. A deposition involves the taking of a statement from a witness who is under oath. The statement is given by the witness in response to a question from an attorney. Both sides to a case are present during a deposition, and cross-examination can occur. Responses are recorded and transcribed for later use. For example, a deposition may be produced and admitted by the court as evidence as though the person actually testified in court. In taking a deposition, one party asks oral questions of the other party or his or her witnesses. A witness who is deposed is called a deponent. The deposition is not conducted in a courtroom, but usually in the office of one of the attorneys. The deposition process may also require a witness to produce particular documents or records. *See also* DISCOVERY, 219; INTERROGATORIES, 228.

Significance A deposition is the most common form of discovery. Because counsel for both parties are present and may examine witnesses, interviews are often thorough and lengthy. A complete transcript is made of a deposition. Depositions frequently yield information that allows an attorney to obtain an acceptable settlement or more fully prepare for trial. Because it may be excessively drawn out, expensive, and contribute to delays in court proceedings, the deposition process is subject to frequent criticism. Some states have revised their rules of civil procedures to impose limits on depositions.

Directed Verdict (218)

Decision by a jury made under binding instruction from the trial judge. A directed verdict reflects the failure of a party to present enough evidence to win a lawsuit. A directed verdict is sought on motion by a party to a civil action. The motion asserts that one party must win because the other party has failed to establish either a *prima facie* case or establish a particular defense. If the judge grants the motion, the jury is not allowed to actually deliberate the matter. Rather, the judge instructs the jury that there is only one possible verdict as a matter of law. The jury is bound by this instruction. In a criminal case, the defendant can seek a directed verdict of acquittal. The defendant's right to jury adjudication of guilt prohibits a directed verdict for conviction. *See also* DEMURRER, 216; DISMISS, 220; SUMMARY JUDGMENT, 248.

Significance Motions for a directed verdict are seldom successful because they are both preemptive and conclusive. That is, they end a case by removing the issues from a jury's consideration. Granting a motion for a directed verdict is essentially the same as granting a motion to dismiss a case before the trial begins. The only difference is when in the process the case is terminated. In the instance of the directed verdict, the case concludes during trial, most often at the point the plaintiff has rested his or her case.

Discovery (219)

A procedure used before civil trials that allows one party to obtain information about a case from the opposing party. Discovery assists litigants in civil suits prepare for trial. Evidence is basically gathered in three ways during discovery. The first is by deposition, where counsel for one party interviews the other party and the witnesses for the opposing side. A second method is through interrogatories, a technique by which one party poses questions to the other party for detailed written response. Finally, a party may obtain documents and records in the possession of the other side. While a judge does not directly supervise discovery, it is conducted under court auspices and judicial remedies are available if compliance with discovery initiatives does not otherwise occur. *See also* DEPOSITION, 217; INTERROGATORIES, 228.

Significance   Civil dockets are often badly backlogged, and there is frequently a waiting period in excess of two years before a trial date can be obtained. Discovery occurs during this period and is intended to better prepare the opposing parties for trial. In practice, discovery often leads to settlements. As information is exchanged, litigants reassess their chances at trial. This, in turn, may prompt a litigant to modify a position or even drop the lawsuit. Discovery is not without problems. Parties may use the processes of discovery to wear down opponents through excessive requests. If the discovery process is drawn out unnecessarily, it produces delay and excessive cost. Some states have amended their rules of civil procedure to regulate discovery processes. Upon completion of discovery, most courts schedule pretrial conferences where judges and the parties meet to prepare for trial as well as explore settlement possibilities.

Dismiss (220)

Discharge of a case without further consideration. A dismissal is an order that cancels a lawsuit. It can be granted at any point in the process. A case is dismissed by a court in response to a motion requesting such action. A case may be dismissed for a variety of reasons, but typically dismissal stems from some kind of legal deficiency. A court can grant a motion to dismiss in civil or criminal cases. Granting a motion to dismiss in a criminal case terminates the charges. In some criminal cases, the motion to dismiss charges is requested by the prosecutor as part of a plea agreement. *See also* DIRECTED VERDICT, 218; SUMMARY JUDGMENT, 248.

Significance   In most cases, dismissal occurs without consideration of the merits of an action. As a result, the dismissal does not prohibit the action from being reinitiated. This is called dismissal without prejudice. Dismissal with prejudice, on the other hand, is a judgment by a court on the merits of the case, and it is final. In other words, dismissal with prejudice bars bringing a subsequent action on the same matter.

Docket   **(221)**
A record of court activities. A docket contains a summary of all court proceedings and the actions taken there. The term docket is also used to refer to the calendar of cases awaiting trial. This is called a trial docket. An appearance docket contains a summary of the decisions made at each step of an action. A civil docket is a record of all pending cases. *See also* DELAY, 215; SPEEDY TRIAL, 187.

Significance   Dockets reflect the volume of activity in courts. The demand on American trial courts is extensive and substantial backlog exists. Trial dockets for criminal cases are generally current because the Constitution as well as federal and state speedy trial statutes provide that those accused of crimes are entitled to prompt trials. Criminal cases, especially at the felony level, will probably be cleared within six months of charges being formally brought. Civil cases, on the other hand, typically experience extensive delay. Speedy trial requirements do not apply to civil cases. In addition, the great bulk of cases fall in the civil category. Thus, it is not unusual for civil trial dockets to run three to four years behind.

Domestic Relations   **(222)**
An area of the law that involves family matters. Domestic relations issues affect many people and place substantial volume demands on civil courts. While family law covers both conditions for entering and terminating a marriage, it is the latter that produces those situations that require court intervention. Indeed, divorce cases often represent the largest single category of civil cases. Most states have attempted to lessen the adversarial character of divorce cases by moving to no-fault divorce. Rather than having to establish legal grounds for a divorce, the no-fault approach merely requires both parties to ac-

knowledge the marriage is no longer viable. The no-fault approach, however, has not made other divorce-related issues, such as child custody, levels of child support, and access or visitation matters easier to resolve. On the contrary, disagreements over these matters frequently require extensive involvement of courts and administrative agencies established to support the courts in divorce cases. Once the issues are resolved, the courts retain jurisdiction to ensure that provisions of orders are fulfilled. Courts with jurisdiction over domestic relations matters also deal with paternity actions. In these cases, a claim is made that a man fathered an illegitimate child. If paternity is established, issues such as support are then addressed.

Significance   Domestic relations cases touch issues at the center of many people's lives. Domestic relations may involve pleasant matters, such as the legal adoption of a child. Generally, however, courts with jurisdiction over domestic relations encounter distressed people looking to terminate the marital relationship or issues associated with that action. Normally, such matters are handled through a hearing process that does not involve a jury. In many jurisdictions, some form of mediation is undertaken before formal hearings, especially if minor children are involved. Once an order or decree is entered, courts retain supervisory authority over the case to ensure full compliance. Most states have established extensive bureaucracies designed to monitor timely payment of child support and the other conditions of the court's judgment. If a party subsequently requests a change in one or more of the terms of custody, support, or visitation, the court normally will not act without a recommendation from a representative of this supporting bureaucracy.

Estate Cases   (223)
Disputes over the succession of real and personal property. An estate, in a broad sense, is property owned by a person. This property may be real or personal. Real property is land and anything like a building on it. Personal property, on the other hand, includes items that can be moved or carried. Civil disputes arise over property in a number of ways, but one of the most common is when someone dies. The question is what becomes of the estate of the deceased. This issue is addressed by the law of succession. Generally, a person will be allowed to convey an estate in any way he or she wishes. This is normally done under terms of a will. Even with a will, however, challenges may arise surrounding the competence of the deceased to convey the estate in the manner chosen. Close relatives who have been disinherited are the most likely to contest a will. Conflicts are far more likely when a

person dies without a will, or *intestate*. In these situations, the estate is distributed to heirs under terms of state succession law. If succession is contested, probate proceedings resemble the fact-finding found in other civil trials. Otherwise, estate matters are handled in a largely administrative, almost clerical fashion by probate courts. *See also* PROBATE COURT, 63.

Significance   Probate courts, which proceed under terms of state law, are designed to ensure the proper succession of estates. Residence of the deceased and the location of any real property determine which state law applies. Estate cases are more straightforward if a will distributes property or if an executor of the estate is designated by the deceased. Even in the presence of a will, a probate court is responsible for attending to any claims from creditors of the deceased prior to distributing any assets. Often the stakes in estate cases are substantial, which in turn elevates the protential for conflict. Protecting the estates of living persons also falls under the jurisdiction of most state probate courts. It may be that a person is unable to handle his or her own financial affairs. In such situations, most probate courts are empowered to appoint legal guardians or conservators. A guardian may or may not be a relative. The guardian has legal power to make judgments concerning the care of another as well as oversee that person's estate. A conservator may be appointed for a shorter period of time to handle financial matters. Courts maintain supervision over guardianships and conservatorships and require periodic reports on the status of the person's affairs.

Ex Parte   (224)

Latin for "by one party." *Ex parte* refers to a kind of legal proceeding initiated for the benefit of only one party. A party applies for an *ex parte* proceeding, and if granted, the adversary may not be notified that it will occur. At an *ex parte* hearing, only one side to a dispute is heard. An *ex parte* order may be issued from such a proceeding. Temporary restraining orders, for example, may be granted *ex parte*. In such cases, the plaintiff must persuade a court that the defendant's actions are so harmful that the restraining order should be issued absent arguments from the defendant. An *ex parte* order may also be issued following a proceeding where one party, despite notification, fails or chooses not to appear. *See also* INJUNCTION, 226.

Significance   An *ex parte* proceeding is uncontested. It allows an individual to pursue legal support from a court on his or her own behalf. In addition to restraining orders, *ex parte* proceedings are often used in uncontested civil actions, such as divorces or *habeas corpus* prisoner petitions. *Ex parte* cases are easily identified in reports of judicial proceedings because the words *"ex parte"* will appear first, followed by the name of the party seeking a remedy from the court.

Expert Witness (225)

A person who has special knowledge of a subject matter about which he or she is to testify in a legal proceeding. An expert witness is a person who has knowledge or expertise not usually found in the average person. Educational degrees may provide the basis for a person being an expert witness, but special skill or knowledge based on experience may also qualify a person as an expert witness. Whether a person possesses the necessary qualifications to serve as an expert witness is a determination of the trial court. The testimony of an expert witness is based directly on his or her status as an expert. A lay witness, on the other hand, provides testimony based on personal knowledge of facts at issue in the case. *See also* WITNESS, 198.

Significance Expert witnesses are crucial in particular kinds of cases. A psychiatrist, for example, is key in attempting to establish an insanity or diminished capacity defense to criminal charges. Similarly, geologists or chemists with particular expertise in water quality may be pivotal witnesses in a case where plaintiffs are seeking damages from a defendant who allegedly contaminated a water supply with discharged industrial waste. Unlike the lay witness, whose testimony is confined to what he or she knows directly about the fact situation, the expert witness can offer expert testimony. This allows the expert to offer opinions and conclusions drawn from their expertise.

Injunction (226)

A writ or order from a court prohibiting a party from acting in a particular way or requiring a specific action by a party. A writ of injunction allows a court to minimize injury to a person or a group until the matter can be otherwise resolved. Injunctions are sometimes called *court orders*, a term too broad to refer exclusively to injunctions. *Restraining order* more effectively conveys the function of an injunction. An injunction was issued in the *Pentagon Papers* cases to keep the *New York Times* and the *Washington Post* from publishing sensitive Defense Department documents. The Supreme Court ruled against use of this injunction in *New York Times v. United States* (403 U.S. 713: 1971), seeing it as an unconstitutional prior restraint on the press. Failure to comply with an injunction constitutes contempt of court.

Once issued, an injunction may be annulled or quashed. *See also* EQUITY JURISDICTION, 49.

Significance   An injunction is an example of a court exercising its equity jurisdiction as distinct from its legal jurisdiction. An injunction is primarily designed to prevent injury that has not yet occurred and is not used as a means to remedy past injury. An injunction may be temporary or permanent. Temporary injunctions, known as interlocutory injunctions or temporary restraining orders, are used to preserve a situation until the issue is resolved through normal processes of litigation. A permanent injunction may be issued upon completion of full legal proceedings. School segregation cases, such as *Brown v. Board of Education I* (347 U.S. 483: 1954), characteristically were cases in which injunctions were sought.

Injury   (227)

Damage done to any legally protected interest of someone else. Injury may take a variety of forms, but generally involves damage to one's person, rights, property, or reputation. Injuries may be private or public. Private injury is infringement of individual interests while public injury violates community interests. Injuries are generally either reparable or irreparable. A reparable injury is damage that can be fully repaired by monetary compensation. Irreparable injury, on the other hand, is not easily redressed in courts because the injury is so large (or small), occurs so frequently, or because monetary standards do not readily measure the damage. Bodily or physical injury typically refers to physical damage to a person although it may include invasion of personal rights as well. It is legally distinct from damage to property or reputation. *See also* CASE OR CONTROVERSY, 6; STANDING, 246.

Significance   The presence of injury is essential to initiating and sustaining legal action. Injury is a critical ingredient in establishing standing to sue. In order for a suit to be heard by a court, the plaintiff in an action must have suffered both legal and direct injury. That is, the injury must be one that is protected by law, and the injury must be suffered by the party bringing the legal action. A third party who has not been injured directly is not permitted to bring suit.

Interrogatories   (228)

A form of pretrial discovery. Interrogatories are a series of written questions sent to an opposing party in a civil action. Interrogatories may also be directed toward witnesses for the opposing party or anyone else having relevant information. Interrogatories require a written response. The person responding to the question typically must sign a statement swearing to the truthfulness of the answers. As a result, responses can be considered to be provided under oath. *See also* DEPOSITION, 217; DISCOVERY, 219.

Significance Interrogatories are an efficient method of obtaining information from the opposing side in a civil case. Interrogatories differ from depositions, where questions and answers are asked and answered orally. Unlike depositions, interrogatories do not permit cross-examination. While interrogatories are not as flexible as depositions and do not produce as extensive a body of information, they are less difficult and expensive to use. The information generated through interrogatories better allows attorneys to prepare for trial or negotiate settlements.

Irreparable Injury (229)

A damage or wrong that has no sufficient remedy. An irreparable injury is the kind of injury for which monetary compensation is not adequate, or it is an injury that cannot be corrected or repaired. The possibility of an irreparable injury is one of the conditions that precedes the granting of an injunction. Such claims assert to a court that the type of injury the claimant has suffered, or will suffer if the court does not intervene, is or will be irreparable. *See also* DAMAGES, 211; EQUITY JURISDICTION, 49; INJUNCTION, 226.

Significance Irreparable injury must be demonstrated before many courts will grant injunctive relief. A potential irreparable injury might be media disclosure of military secrets or an unauthorized disposal of chemical waste into the environment. A case can be made in either instance to enjoin such activity because recovery from the harm caused might be impossible.

Judgment (230)

The decision of a court on the issues raised in a legal action. A judgment is the final determination of a court on matters placed before it. The judgment may be based on the court's own conclusions on the facts or on a jury verdict. The judgment often includes an order that requires some action necessary to give effect to the judgment. The term *judgment* is sometimes used to refer to the rationale upon which a court decision is based. A court's reasoning is more appropriately termed its *opinion*. *See also* DECREE, 213; DEFAULT JUDGMENT, 214; ORDER, 236; SUMMARY JUDGMENT, 248.

Significance   The judgment in a case comes after one of several kinds of proceeding. A case may, for example, require full adjudication of the facts. A judgment based on adjudication of the basic facts is said to be a judgment on the merits. Different from this would be a judgment based entirely on a procedural or technical ground. A summary judgment would be of this kind. It is also possible for a court to render judgment in the absence of one party's participation. A dispute in which one party fails to assert a defense could lead to a default judgment.

Justiciable Issue (231)

A question that is appropriate for resolution by judicial action. A justiciable issue is one that may properly come before a court for decision. Justiciability differs from jurisdiction in that the latter focuses on whether a court possesses the power to act. Justiciability presumes that the power to act exists, but it focuses on whether it is proper or reasonable to exercise that power. A court may have jurisdiction over a case, but it may find the question involved to be nonjusticiable. *See also* CASE OR CONTROVERSY, 6; JURISDICTION, 56; STANDING, 246.

Significance   Considerations of whether an issue is justiciable come in the form of real or bona fide cases as opposed to controversies raising abstract or hypothetical issues. A justiciable issue satisfies all requirements of standing, and it is not more appropriately resolved by the legislative or executive branches. Justiciability allows the courts to limit or expand the extent to which judicial power is exercised. It directly affects the functional relationships of the courts to the legislative and executive branches. To be justiciable, an issue must involve an actual controversy in which one party can show harm or injury. The justiciability requirements are used to define the boundaries of the judicial function. Justiciability is an outgrowth of the separation-of-powers concept. Courts possess substantial discretion in determining whether an issue is justiciable, but will generally proceed with caution before taking action. Such an approach serves to heighten the impact of judicial actions in those cases where justiciability clearly exists.

Liability (232)

Legal responsibility for an action or inaction that causes injury or loss.

Liability extends to a broad range of situations where a plaintiff suffers injury at the hands of a defendant. Liability may be civil or criminal. In a civil context, liability may flow from, among other things, failure to honor provisions of a contract, personal injury, or some other injury covered by tort law. A plaintiff must establish the liability of a defendant in order to obtain relief through a court. Liability is a term that has broad legal application. In addition to the condition of being responsible, liability also refers generally to monies owed (the opposite of an asset) or to an obligation to perform in a particular manner. *See also* DAMAGES, 211; PERSONAL INJURY, 237; TORT, 38.

Significance   Liability is established if it can be shown that a defendant caused injury to a plaintiff. One way of establishing liability is to demonstrate negligence on the part of the defendant. Negligence is conduct that fails to sufficiently protect others from an unreasonable risk of harm. Negligence does not encompass intent as such, only an insufficient degree of care. Occasionally, a defendant is able to establish an affirmative defense that the plaintiff's own conduct failed to provide sufficient self-protection. In such cases, it is asserted that the defendant's and the plaintiff's behaviors combined in a way to produce the injury. A situation where the plaintiff's own conduct is a partial cause of the injury is called contributory negligence. Some kinds of liability do not require a showing of negligence, however. Consider, for example, the area of product liability. Product liability suits are designed to hold manufacturers accountable for the items they produce. Suits of this kind include such things as automobiles, food, pharmaceuticals, or appliances. Services rendered are also subject to product liability actions. The legal standard used in product liability cases is strict liability. This standard allows a plaintiff to recover, even if the manufacturer acted with reasonable care, if it can be shown that the product, used properly by the plaintiff, was the cause of injury.

Mandamus (233)

An extraordinary writ issued by a court under its equity jurisdiction to require anyone, but most often a public official, to perform a specified official act. *Mandamus* is an affirmative command calling for an action to occur. When a *mandamus* is issued against a public official, it cannot compel a discretionary act. Rather, *mandamus* can only be directed toward an act the official has a clear legal obligation to perform. A command preventing an action from occurring comes in the form of an injunction. *See also* EQUITY JURISDICTION, 49; INJUNCTION, 226.

Significance   A *mandamus* may be directed by a higher court to a lower court to require an action that a party has a legal right to expect. Failure to comply with a command issued through a writ of *mandamus* constitutes judicial contempt. *Mandamus* is regarded as a remedy of last resort, and is pursued only under extraordinary circumstances.

Mootness (234)

A case in which the courts can no longer provide a party any relief because the dispute has been resolved or has ceased to exist. A moot case is no longer a real controversy, and Article III of the U.S. Constitution requires that cases that come before courts be bona fide controversies. An action becomes moot when circumstances remove the underlying controversy or issue in the case. Without a justiciable issue, the case raises only a hypothetical question. *See also* ADVISORY OPINION, 200; JUSTICIABLE ISSUE, 231; STANDING, 246.

Significance   Mootness is the absence of an active question. The matter is therefore nonjusticiable. When the Supreme Court refused to address the reverse discrimination issue in *DeFunis v. Odegaard* (416 U.S. 312: 1974) on grounds of mootness, for example, it said the controversy was no longer definite and concrete. The Court found the controversy moot because while DeFunis challenged the affirmative action admissions practices of a public law school, he had been allowed to attend class and otherwise function as though he had been admitted throughout the litigation. The Court refused to rule on the merits of the case because it no longer touched "the legal relations of parties having adverse interests." Exceptions to the mootness threshold involve situations where time is too limited to litigate an issue fully and where a likelihood exists that the question will reoccur. Abortion cases qualify for an exception to the mootness rule, for example, because no appellate court can ever hear an abortion issue prior to a pregnancy running to full term. The Court observed in *Roe v. Wade* (410 U.S. 113: 1973) that appellate review would forever be foreclosed by mootness because a pregnancy would not last beyond the trial stage. Saying the law should not be that rigid, the Court acknowledged the need for the exception for issues that are "capable of repetition, yet evading review." If the courts responded routinely to cases that had become moot, they would constantly be engaging in rendering advisory opinions.

Motion (235)

An application that requests an action by a court in favor of the applicant. A motion can be sought at virtually any stage of either a criminal or civil proceeding. Certain motions are more likely at particular points in the process, however. A motion may focus on any matter within the authority of the court, but it most commonly addresses some point of law. Motions may be made in writing or orally. In the event of a written motion, the opposing party is usually notified that a motion has been filed, although some motions may be made *ex parte*. *See also* DIRECTED VERDICT, 218; DISMISS, 220; PRETRIAL MOTION, 173.

Significance There are many different kinds of motions. Motions are often the medium through which issues are clarified or actions are hastened to conclusion. A civil litigant may ask a court, for example, to examine the legal adequacy of the opponent's complaint with a motion to dismiss. If such a motion is granted, the case is resolved without going through any adjudicatory steps. A directed verdict is also sought by motion. In a similar manner, a criminal defendant may wish to challenge some evidence as the product of an unreasonable search. The court would rule on this challenge in response to a pretrial motion to suppress the evidence. A motion may also be used to ask a court to reconsider the outcome of a case. A motion to set aside a judgment is used for this purpose.

Order (236)

A written directive, issued by a judge, that can require a wide range of actions. An order may stand alone or be issued in support of a judgment or decision. An order is obtained from a court by motion. Orders are either final or temporary. A final order resolves the substantive question(s) contained in the case and concludes the legal action. Appeal may be sought from a final order. A temporary order, on the other hand, focuses only a component or intervening issue and does not finally resolve a dispute. Such an order is called an interlocutory order. *See also* DECREE, 213; INJUNCTION, 226; JUDGMENT, 230.

Significance An order can be used to address either the central or an incidental issue in a case. An order can be issued to conclude an action at some preliminary point. An order is commonly used at the conclusion of civil actions as a means of executing a judgment. If a jury decides a plaintiff is entitled to damages, that judgment is often supported by an order to pay if the defendant fails to comply voluntarily. An example of an interlocutory order is the temporary restraining order. A restraining order prohibits a defendant from performing a particular act (or acts) until a hearing is held.

Personal Injury (237)

Civil law disputes that stem from an accident of some kind. Personal or bodily injury cases account for a substantial number of actions under tort law. Tort law covers noncriminal wrong done by one person to another. Although tort law also includes damage done to property, personal injury cases are confined to injury to one's person. A majority of these cases derive from motor vehicle accidents. Personal injury cases require that the plaintiff establish the defendant's responsibility for the injury. If liability can be established, it is then necessary to consider the relief to which the plaintiff is entitled. Relief may be confined to actual damages, the costs incurred from the injury. In other situations, there may be some consideration of damages to compensate in some way for the injury. Such compensation includes, but goes beyond, mere recovery of costs. While the vehicle accident case is the single largest category of personal injury dispute, there are other types. A rapidly increasing category is medical malpractice. *See also* DAMAGES, 211; LIABILITY, 232; TORT, 38.

Significance Many people suffer personal injuries, but relatively few actually pursue formal litigation. Indeed, what is noteworthy about personal injuries is that less than five percent of these situations produce lawsuits. Rather, claims are usually settled out of court prior to the initiation of a lawsuit. Many potential plaintiffs are interested in quick settlements, and insurance companies who represent most personal injury defendants prefer settlements prior to the injured party securing legal counsel. Thus, while personal injuries do produce considerable litigation, the number of cases actually filed represents only a small proportion of those cases that might have been litigated. If a settlement cannot be reached between the parties directly, those with personal injury claims usually seek assistance from an attorney. Securing counsel may or may not result in litigation. Settlement is still the probable outcome, even after a lawyer is brought into the situation. Lawsuits are eventually commenced in a small proportion of cases. The lawsuit reflects the inability of the parties to arrive at a settlement, but commencing the suit does not foreclose out-of-court settlement. On the contrary, the discovery process might facilitate settlement. So, too, might judicial intervention, as pretrial conferences conducted by judges often enhance settlement prospects.

Judges may also require some alternative method of dispute resolution, such as mediation, which might, in turn, produce a settlement. Settlement remains the probability throughout because both plaintiff and defendant want to avoid the cost, risk, and delay associated with a trial. Adjudication of personal injury claims at trial is the final step, but it takes place in less than one percent of all cases filed.

Plaintiff (238)

The person who commences or initiates a civil legal action. A plaintiff is also called a complainant because it is the plaintiff who complains about some kind of legal injury and seeks relief through a lawsuit. The counterpart to the plaintiff in a criminal case is the prosecution who brings charges on behalf of the victim and the state in the name of the "people." The party who responds to the initiative of the plaintiff is called the defendant. *See also* PETITIONER, 280; STANDING, 246.

Significance The plaintiff is the point of origin of a civil action. In order to commence the lawsuit, the plaintiff must have standing to sue. That is, the plaintiff must have directly suffered legal injury, allegedly at the hands of the defendant. The plaintiff basically directs the flow of a civil case. The case commences at the initiative of the plaintiff and remains active only so long as the plaintiff wishes. At any point in the civil process, an action may be terminated by the plaintiff. Thus a plaintiff possesses far greater control over a civil action than a victim has in a criminal case.

Pleadings (239)

Formal statements of claims and responses by parties to a legal action. The pleadings become the basis of the questions taken to trial. The civil process commences with the filing of a complaint by the plaintiff. The complaint is answered by the defendant. Additional submissions, governed by the rules of civil procedure, may follow. The pleadings are the total of these submissions filed by the parties. *See also* ANSWER, 203; DISCOVERY, 219.

Significance Under common law, pleadings were an involved process. Through a series of successive statements, legal issues were narrowed or focused for adjudication. Contemporary federal and state rules of civil procedure have generally confined pleadings to the initial complaint, an answer, responses to counter or cross claims, and arguments pertaining to third parties. The focusing function performed by pleadings under common law is now largely handled through processes of discovery.

Preponderance of Evidence (240)

Standard of proof used in civil cases. The preponderance of evidence standard requires that one party to the legal action offer proof that is more persuasive or convincing than the other. The standard demands evidence that convinces the fact-finder—whether judge or jury—that one party's case is more probable or has superior weight than the case of the other party. A party possesses a preponderance of evidence when he or she provides sufficient proof to overcome doubt or mere speculation. *See also* REASONABLE DOUBT, 179; STANDARDS OF PROOF, 188.

Significance Preponderance of evidence is not a quantitative standard. Evidence is not measured by numbers of witnesses appearing for one side, for example. Rather, it is a qualitative standard that reflects the believability and persuasive weight of evidence. Use of the preponderance of evidence standard is one of the major differences between civil and criminal cases. In the latter, the more stringent "beyond a reasonable doubt" standard of proof is used. This standard requires proof so conclusive that it eliminates all reasonable uncertainty.

Pretrial Conference (241)

Meeting called by a judge to prepare a case for trial. A pretrial conference occurs just prior to trial and is called at the discretion of the court. The conference participants include the judge and attorneys for the parties. Conferences are designed to eliminate or narrow the questions that need to be tried. The idea is to produce some agreement on at least some of the fact questions. Agreement on such a question of fact is called a stipulation. If several issues can be stipulated, the trial need examine only the remaining contested questions. The point(s) of agreement and disagreement that emerge from a pretrial conference are embraced in an order that governs the remaining proceedings in the case. The conference thus serves to aid in the disposition of a case by focusing the trial on the fewest and narrowest items. *See also* STIPULATION, 247.

Significance Pretrial conferences used to be devices through which a trial judge could try to facilitate settlement of a case. Such an objective is no longer realistic. As a result of discovery, most cases that might settle do so before the time pretrial conferences are normally convened. This makes the removal of extraneous issues a primary objective of the conference. The conference also serves to reduce the element of surprise. To that end, witness lists and other documents not produced in discovery are exchanged. The conference, thus, is a device by which complete disclosure can occur. This minimizes the number of issues still needing court attention and may bring to light information that prompts settlement. Either of these consequences is of value to the court and probably the parties.

Pro Bono Publico   (242)

Latin for the "public good" or "welfare." The term *pro bono publico* refers to attorneys donating their time to represent indigent parties in civil matters. Lawyers represent indigent clients *pro bono* as a way of meeting a perceived obligation of the profession to make legal services available to those who could not otherwise afford counsel. *See also* LEGAL SERVICES CORPORATION, 100; PUBLIC DEFENDER, 111.

Significance   While the legal profession has acknowledged a public interest dimension to the practice of law, *pro bono* representation grew most substantially as a by-product of court rulings requiring appointment of counsel in criminal cases with indigent defendants. The amount of time made available *pro bono* is insufficient to meet the demand. This has been especially true since funding for the Legal Services Corporation has diminished. Beyond actual representation of indigent clients, the term *pro bono* includes legal work aimed at advancing public interest positions or causes.

Ripeness   (243)

Readiness of a case for judicial response. Ripeness involves whether a case has matured sufficiently to require the exercise of judicial power. Courts only exercise power in cases where there are *bona fide* legal controversies. Cases that are not ripe may not have fully developed as controversies worthy of judicial attention. If, for example, a person wishes to challenge a decision of an administrative agency, the person must have exhausted all appeals options within the agency before turning to the courts. If those other options are not pursued first, the case is not yet "ripe" for judicial resolution; it has come to the courts too early. *See also* JUSTICIABLE ISSUE, 231; STANDING, 246.

Significance   Ripeness is one of the critical conditions required by courts for establishing standing to sue. If a plaintiff's claim is not ripe, the case lacks standing and courts do not consider it to be a justiciable controversy. The ripeness doctrine also applies to appellate courts. The doctrine is a manifestation of judicial self-restraint and directs that cases not be decided before it is absolutely necessary to do so. In the case of appellate courts, this means that all administrative and lower court remedies must be exhausted.

Settlement (244)

Resolution of a dispute by mutual agreement. A settlement is reached after negotiation on the merits and brings about a final disposition of the controversy. A settlement is achieved by the parties before a court actually adjudicates the facts in a case. Indeed, a settlement obviates the need for a trial. Settlements do not fully eliminate expenditure of court resources, however. Settlements become more likely after some form of court intervention, such as the holding of a pretrial conference. *See also* DELAY, 215; PLEA BARGAINING, 168.

Significance Parties pursue settlements in cases because they wish to reduce the risk that comes with a trial. Settlements typically reflect a compromise on at least one of the key issues. Such compromises are attempts by both sides to hedge against losing completely at trial. Settlements produce certainty of outcome for both sides. The likelihood of resolving a case by settlement increases substantially as the case comes closer to the trial date and the parties develop greater apprehension about success in the trial. A settlement is also the final disposition of a dispute. Appeals are virtually never taken from settlements. The settlement reduces anxiety and eliminates the costs associated with a trial. The courts are supportive of parties settling disputes because settlements free trial time for other cases. Since there is always a substantial backlog of civil cases, courts have a strong interest in having cases resolved without trial. It is for this same reason that alternative dispute resolution has become so widely used. The criminal counterpart to settlement is the plea bargain or plea agreement. While the processes may vary somewhat, criminal defendants and prosecutors negotiate plea agreements for the same reasons civil litigants negotiate—greater control of the outcome.

Show Cause Order (245)

A court order requiring a party to appear and demonstrate why a particular action should not occur. A show cause order is a method of accelerating the beginning of legal action. A plaintiff files a complaint and asks a court by motion to issue a show cause order. The order compels the defendant to appear and answer the complaint. The burden rests with the defendant to show cause why the court should not do what the plaintiff is asking. If the defendant does not carry this burden or fails to appear at all, the court will take the action sought by the plaintiff. *See also* ANSWER, 203; MOTION, 235.

Significance   A show cause order is designed to bring prompt response. In most cases, response must be made within several days. The show cause order may contain certain conditions or temporary restraints. When a court issues a show cause order, it has been asked to take an action based on a claim by the plaintiff. The defendant must persuade the court of one of two things in order to prevent it from acting on the plaintiff's request. The first is that the fact situation giving rise to the claim is such that a full trial is needed. Such a finding could remove the time urgency and place the case into the regular processing period. Second, a defendant might establish that even if the plaintiff's claim is true, it is not sufficient to justify whatever action the plaintiff is requesting.

Standing   (246)
The requirement that a real dispute exist between the prospective parties to a lawsuit. Standing must be established in order to proceed in either federal or state courts, although the requirements differ somewhat. The concept of standing has several important components. Federal judicial power extends to cases or controversies through Article III of the U.S. Constitution. This has been interpreted to mean that bona fide disputes must exist if judicial resolution is to be sought. The federal courts are thus unable to respond to hypothetical or friendly suits, and they cannot render advisory opinions. This is generally true at the state level as well, but some state courts may issue advisory opinions. Standing means that the plaintiff bringing suit must have suffered direct injury, and the injury must be protected by constitutional or statutory provisions. This means suits cannot be brought by a third party or someone indirectly related to the legal injury. Further, each suit must specify the remedy being sought from the court. The burden rests with the plaintiff to define what relief the court might order. Standing also relates to the timing of a suit. A court must find a suit ripe, which means that all other avenues of possible relief must have been exhausted. Similarly, a case will not be entertained by a court if events have made pursuit of the original remedy inappropriate. A case that is too late is considered moot because there is no longer an adversarial situation. Exceptions will be made when the limited duration of a situation or condition interferes

with the litigation of issues. Abortion cases demonstrate the need for such an exception. *See also* CASE OR CONTROVERSY, 6; JUSTICIABLE ISSUE, 231; MOOTNESS, 234; RIPENESS, 243; TAXPAYER SUIT, 251.

Significance   Standing is discussed in several important Supreme Court decisions. The matter was first raised in *Frothingham vs. Mellon* (262 U.S. 447: 1923). Frothingham attempted to enjoin the implementation of a federal program by claiming injury by virtue of paying federal taxes. The Supreme Court denied standing and suggested that Frothingham's injury was shared by millions of others. The injury was therefore "comparatively minute and indeterminate." A plaintiff seeking review of a federal statute must be able to show "direct injury as the result of its enforcement, and not merely that he suffers in some indefinite way in common with people generally." Inability to establish such injury will prevent consideration of the constitutional issue regardless of how real and pressing the issue may be. The *Frothingham* precedent lasted as an absolute barrier to judicial review of congressional spending legislation by taxpayers until *Flast v. Cohen* (392 U.S. 83: 1968). The Court held in *Flast* that a taxpayer could achieve standing by showing a "nexus" between the taxpayer and the challenged program. *Flast* involved a challenge to federal aid to private as well as public elementary schools. The Warren Court found the relationship among the federal taxing power, the payment of federal taxes, and First Amendment protections against establishment of religion adequate to produce standing. *Flast* immediately raised questions about judicial review of congressional spending initiatives. It distinguished between the *Frothingham* direct injury requirement and the litigant who might be acting on behalf of broader public rights. The Supreme Court has shown since *Flast* that access is still difficult. In *United States v. Richardson* (418 U.S. 166: 1974), the Court refused to allow a taxpayer to inquire into Central Intelligence Agency appropriations. The Court said that allowing "unrestricted taxpayer standing would significantly alter the allocation of power at the national level." Another case, *Schlesinger v. Reservists' Committee to Stop the War* (418 U.S. 208: 1974), challenged the military reserve status of more than a hundred members of Congress. The Court denied standing, saying that to allow such a challenge by someone who has no concrete injury would require the Court to respond to issues in the abstract. The Court said this would create the potential abuse of the judicial process and distortion of the role of the judiciary. Standing too easily granted would open the courts to an arguable charge of government by the judiciary. Taxpayers can establish standing more easily in state courts.

Stipulation (247)

An agreement between parties to a legal action on some matter related to that action. A stipulation may be to a point of fact or procedure. The parties may stipulate or agree, for example, that the incident on which the suit is based occurred on a particular day at a particular time. Given the agreement, there is no need to call witnesses to establish that fact. A stipulation may also be procedural. The parties might, for example, agree to extend the deadlines for various submissions. Stipulations are committed to writing and signed by attorneys for both parties. *See also* PRETRIAL CONFERENCE, 241.

Significance   Stipulations are valuable in focusing the issues that require adjudication. The stipulation isolates uncontested fact and eliminates the need to resolve fact on that question. By reducing the number of questions that need to be resolved, trials are shortened. Trial judges actively attempt to dispose of questions by stipulation during pretrial conferences.

Summary Judgment (248)

Decision rendered by a court on a matter before it goes to a jury. A summary judgment is a decision on the merits of a case. A summary judgment is requested on motion by either party to a suit. The motion asserts that there is no substantial fact dispute, but rather only a dispute in law. The law questions are then placed before the court for decision instead of taking the matter to a jury. *See also* SUMMARY PROCEEDING, 249.

Significance   A summary judgment is a technique intended to obtain prompt resolution in a legal action. If the pleadings and other supporting materials reveal no bona fide fact question, the court may enter a summary judgment, which will finalize the case. For example, a summary judgment might be used in a suit involving an insurance claim. Both parties may agree as to what happened, but differ on whether the policy covers the situation. The case rests entirely on the scope of the insurance contract, a purely legal question. A judge can review the contract and decide whether the contract covers the fact situation. Use of motions for summary judgments are confined to civil matters.

Summary Proceeding (249)

An abbreviated process wherein certain legal questions may be expeditiously resolved. A summary proceeding takes the general form of a trial, but it is brief and conducted under simplified procedural rules. For example, discovery is usually limited and no fact questions go to a jury. A summary judgment may be issued from a summary proceeding. *See also* SUMMARY JUDGMENT, 248; SMALL CLAIMS COURT, 64.

Significance A summary proceeding attempts to settle a legal issue promptly and simply. A summary proceeding does not have a single form. The process is summary when it does not contain the same procedural steps as a regular civil trial. Small claims proceedings are generally summary. Often tenant-landlord relations and bankruptcies are handled in summary proceedings as well. The tenant-landlord situation provides a good example. The failure of a tenant to pay rent may automatically terminate a lease. A summary proceeding may yield an eviction order.

Summons (250)

An instrument used to notify people of a legal cause against them and direct their appearance at a court. A summons is used to notify a person that a criminal complaint has been filed. Summons notification in criminal cases is usually reserved for nonserious charges. A summons is also used to give notice in civil matters. Whether the case is civil or criminal, the person named in the summons must answer the complaint, either by personal appearance or through the filing of an answer. A copy of the complaint is normally attached to the summons. *See also* DEFAULT JUDGMENT, 214; SUBPOENA, 193.

Significance The summons is a means by which jurisdiction over a party is obtained. A summons is served by a public agent, such as a deputy sheriff, or by a private agency. Failure to comply with a summons has one of two consequences, depending on whether the case is civil or criminal. Failure to appear to answer a criminal complaint can lead to the issuing of an arrest warrant. Failure to offer response within a specified period in a civil case can subject the defendant to a default judgment, a judgment for the plaintiff entered against the defendant because of his or her absence or default. A summons notifies a defendant that he or she has been sued and orders response. A subpoena is distinguished in that it seeks to compel appearance of a person for the purpose of providing testimony.

Taxpayer Suit (251)

Legal action brought by a citizen to challenge a particular governmental expenditure. A taxpayer suit attempts to establish standing to sue through the injury suffered by the citizen as a taxpayer. Taxpayer status is generally sufficient in state courts to establish standing to sue. While the taxpayer suit is possible in federal court, it is much more difficult to satisfy standing requirements. *See also* CHALLENGE, 204; STANDING, 246; TEST CASE, 252.

Significance   Standing to sue requires that the plaintiff to a legal action has suffered direct and legal injury. The taxpayer suit is based upon the idea that such injury comes from the payment of money to the public treasury. If taxpayer status easily satisfied the standing requirement, then virtually anyone could challenge any expenditure of public money. It is for this reason that the Supreme Court restricted taxpayer suits in *Frothingham v. Mellon* (262 U.S. 447: 1923), ruling that no taxpayer suffered sufficiently individualized injury to establish standing. For several decades, *Frothingham* categorically precluded federal taxpayer suits. An important modification was made in 1968 in the Court's decision in *Flast v. Cohen* (392 U.S. 83: 1968). *Flast* established the so-called "nexus" rule, which allows taxpayer challenges so long as a nexus or connection exists between taxpayer status, the particular program under challenge, and a specific constitutional limit on such government spending. In the *Flast* case, the taxpayer challenged a particular congressional spending action on First Amendment establishment of religion grounds, a circumstance sufficient to create the nexus needed to qualify for an exception to the *Frothingham* doctrine.

Test Case   (252)

A legal action begun to challenge the constitutionality of a government action. A test case is undertaken to obtain a judicial ruling on the challenged action. Since courts will not consider hypothetical or abstract issues, test cases require a plaintiff who has been directly injured by the action. Often this requires that a person deliberately violate a suspect law or regulation in order to establish an adversarial situation appropriate for judicial consideration. *See also* CHALLENGE, 204; INTEREST GROUPS IN COURT, 272; STANDING, 246; TAXPAYER SUIT, 251.

Significance   A test case is undertaken to establish a particular right or principle of law. Through the device of the test case, many issues of social policy are placed before the courts for their examination. Legal challenges to a wide range of discriminatory practices, for example, have been brought to the courts in test cases. The test case is a particularly effective strategic device for interest groups. While the groups themselves may not be able to meet standing requirements, groups are usually able to locate individuals who can. These individuals are usually group members. The groups can then assume management of the case, including underwriting the costs.

Third Party (253)

A person (or entity) unnamed in a legal action who may be affected by or connected to it. Third-party situations are numerous and diverse. A defendant to a civil action, for example, may become a third-party plaintiff by bringing a complaint against yet another party. The third-party complaint alleges that the third party is liable for at least part of the initial plaintiff's claim. Similarly, contract provisions may be enforced by and yield benefits to third parties. A person who is not a formal party to an insurance contract may possess legally enforceable interests under the contract. It is also possible to establish standing to sue as a third party. In *Singleton v. Wulff* (428 U.S. 106: 1976), for example, the Supreme Court ruled that a group of physicians had standing to challenge a state policy excluding reimbursement of abortion costs under Medicaid. The physicians were a third party to the dispute between the state and those seeking Medicaid reimbursement. A key issue in this case was whether the physicians could establish standing by asserting the rights of their patients. The Court ruled that the abortion decision is one in which the physician is "intimately involved." Thus, the physician is "uniquely qualified to litigate the State's interference with . . . that decision." *See also* AMICUS CURIAE, 257; STANDING, 246.

Significance   Legal situations typically do not have a third-party dimension. The existence of a third party, however, complicates a case because it takes the case outside the more common "one-on-one" confrontation of plaintiff and defendant. In some instances, the third party may be the key. In *United States v. Matlock* (415 U.S. 164: 1974), for example, the Supreme Court upheld a consent search of a residence. The consent had been voluntarily obtained, but it had not been given by the person ultimately charged with a crime. Instead, it had been given by the person who shared the residence with him. Third-party involvement in a legal action may also take the form of *amicus curiae* participation. *Amicus* participants typically file briefs that attempt to demonstrate the broader implications of a case.

Verdict (254)

A finding by a jury on a fact question formally submitted to it for deliberation. The verdict is reported to the court and announced. Either party is entitled to request that the jury be polled. This requires that each juror disclose in open court his or her vote. Verdicts in criminal cases must be unanimous in most jurisdictions, although the Supreme Court has ruled that verdicts reached on the basis of ten-to-two and nine-to-three votes do not violate the jury trial requirements of the Sixth Amendment. A verdict to convict in a criminal case requires evidence that demonstrates guilt beyond a reasonable doubt. Civil verdicts are arrived at by using the preponderance of evidence standard. *See also* ACQUITTAL, 121; CONVICTION, 134; JURY, 155.

Significance   The verdict is the conclusion of a jury in a fact dispute. The verdict gives effect to the belief that an impartial group of citizens ought to play a decisive role in the adversary process. Most often, juries are expected to render general verdicts. Such a verdict simply decides for one party or the other. A special verdict, on the other hand, is a response to particular fact issues. A judgment based on the responses to such issues is subsequently made by the court. Assignment of proportionate fault in a personal injury case, for example, is a special verdict upon which a court bases its judgment. Finally, there are verdicts called directed verdicts, which may be ordered by the court. These occur if a judge rules as a matter of law that the party carrying the burden of proof has failed to establish a *prima facie* case. Given the requirement that the prosecution establish at least a *prima facie* case before trial, the directed verdict is not used in criminal cases.

6. The Appellate Judicial Process

The appeals courts differ from trial courts in several ways, but the principal difference is functional. Trial courts are designed to deal with questions of fact. A trial jury may determine, for example, that an accused has been factually proven guilty of a crime. Appeals courts almost always defer to the trial court's fact decision and focus instead on the way the trial court reached its decision. The appeal is intended to make sure that no legal errors occurred at the trial. The case is literally transformed as it moves to the appellate level. It becomes singularly a question of law or procedure rather than one of fact. A criminal case that focused on whether the accused committed the crime at the trial level may focus on, for example, the adequacy of a police search or warnings given prior to eliciting an incriminating statement from the defendant.

Correcting errors that occur at trial is one of the primary functions of appellate courts. As important as that function is, its impact is muted somewhat by the relatively small number of cases that pursue appeals and the even smaller number that are successful. Greater significance attaches to the function of establishing or clarifying principles of law or policy, which then apply to all similar situations. The only issue before an appeals court is the legal question (or questions) raised by the case, which will be resolved exclusively by the judges of the appeals court. The court hears no new evidence and operates without such crucial fact-finding elements as juries or witnesses.

The jurisdiction of appeals courts tends to parallel the jurisdiction of the trial courts in the system, although the match is not exact. Federal appellate courts generally hear cases from federal trial courts, although review of certain agency and regulatory commission decisions takes place as well. The federal court system and many state systems contain two levels of appeals courts. The first level—known as the intermediate level—is typically required to review cases pursuing appeal; their jurisdiction is mandatory. Second-level courts are usually the courts of last resort or supreme courts. They generally have discretionary jurisdiction. Where an appellate court has mandatory jurisdiction, the appeals process commences when the losing party in a lower court case decides to seek review. The party initiating the appeal (the appellant) then furnishes the court with a record of the lower court proceeding, including a transcript of the trial, and a written brief arguing the appellant's case. The other party (the appellee) is entitled to submit arguments in response.

If review is sought from a court with discretionary jurisdiction, the process is somewhat more involved. The party wishing review of a lower court decision (the petitioner) is required to convince the appellate court to hear the case. The petitioner submits a record of the case and a brief supporting the request for review. The court then rules on the petition for review. If review is not granted, the decision of the lower court becomes final. If the case is accepted, it is treated from that point in the same manner as a case before a court with mandatory jurisdiction.

The written materials addressing the merits of the case are considered by the judges involved in the review. Appellate courts typically function with more than one judge per case; most intermediate courts use three-judge panels, while second-level courts generally use their full memberships. As a result, group processes such as the conference become key locations of decision making. The opposing parties are then permitted to make oral presentations, which supplement their written submissions. Following oral argument, the court meets in conference and reaches a preliminary decision. Its choices are to affirm (uphold), reverse (change completely), or modify (change in part) the lower court decision. One of the judges from the majority side is assigned the task of explaining the decision. This opinion of the court discusses the legal principles found to govern the case, and the court's rationale for their use. Drafts of the majority opinion are circulated and modifications made on the basis of the responses of the other judges. Other judges hearing the case have the option of offering individual and alternative opinions. Before each judge takes a final position on a case, extensive negotiations may occur in an effort to reach consensus. When the decision is finally announced, an opinion of the court is issued on behalf of the majority. This opinion and its representation of the key rules of law is the precedent established by the decision. A judge arriving at the same decision as the majority but for different reasons may issue a concurring opinion. Any judge in the minority in a case may write a dissenting opinion.

Both first- and second-level appeals courts feel sufficient pressure from their case backlog to screen cases or use summary procedures to expedite review. Second-level courts typically have discretionary jurisdiction, and they can refuse to hear certain cases. These courts have screening procedures in place to enable docket decisions to be efficiently reached. The most important screening criteria in the selection of cases appear to be the policy preferences of the judges, lack of clarity on a legal issue as reflected in conflicting decisions of lower courts, and the significance of the legal issues present in a case. Courts with mandatory jurisdiction do not have the option of denying review. They can, however, separate cases into categories and dispose of many cases summarily, thus preserving the bulk of their time for more compelling questions.

The output of the appellate process consists of decisions, which establish legal principles for cases that follow and have policy impacts reaching outside the court system. The decisions reached by appellate courts are influenced by several things. First, of course, are the policy preferences of the judges. These preferences are clearly ideologically driven. Second, appellate decisions are influenced by the collective decision making processes used by appeals courts. Finally, appellate court decisions are subject to the influences of factors external to the courts. Especially significant are influences emanating from the legal community, public opinion, and the political system.

Abbreviated Procedures (255)

Methods used to expedite disposition of cases at the appellate level. Abbreviated or shortened procedures are designed to move some cases through the steps more quickly or eliminate some of the steps altogether. Giving certain cases less than the "full treatment" requires the screening of incoming cases. Courts that use abbreviated procedures depend on support staff to do this preliminary screening and review. Once it has been determined that a case does not require full review, a court may limit or dispense with oral arguments, for example, and decide cases on the basis of the initial petition and supporting briefs. Similarly, an appellate court may be able to decide certain cases immediately after oral argument and without group discussion in conference. In some cases, a court may choose to adopt the recommendation from the staff as to disposition. Courts may also expedite the process by announcing outcomes unaccompanied by written opinions. Indeed, many appeals courts issue full opinions in less than half of their cases. *See also* MANDATORY JURISDICTION, 275.

Significance   Abbreviated procedures are largely used by appellate courts having mandatory jurisdiction. These are the courts, commonly at the first level of a two-level appellate structure, that must decide all cases that are filed. As a result, they are more vulnerable to the pressures of high case volume. Abbreviated procedures allow these courts to process some cases more quickly. The technique clearly heightens efficiency. Courts that employ abbreviated procedures increase productivity as measured by cases disposed. There is a possible qualitative downside, however. Cases categorized as those not needing full review remain with staff for a least a preliminary decision in the form of a recommendation. This makes it probable that a case will be treated as "unimportant;" that the appellant's case is "weak." If this occurs, the integrity of the appellate process is diminished. Finally, the same case volume pressure that prompts use of abbreviated procedures also creates pressures on appellate judges to defer to staff judgments. In the face of burdensome caseloads, judges may not wish to closely scrutinize staff screening because to disagree with the staff judgment is to increase the number of cases needing full review. Questions about judicial control and independence are raised in such situations.

Affirm (256)

Decision by an appellate court that the judgment of a court below is correct. When an appeals court affirms a lower court, it declares that the lower court handled the case properly, that its judgment was reasonable, and that its decision will stand. Affirming a lower court judgment is the opposite of reversing it. A reversal sets aside the lower court judgment as improperly decided. *See also* REVERSAL, 285.

Significance A court that affirms a lower court ratifies the judgment and confirms its correctness. An appeals court may affirm a lower court decision after full argument. In such cases, a formal opinion on the substantive question(s) in the case is usually issued. An appellate court with discretionary jurisdiction may, however, refuse to review particular cases. Indeed, failure to get a full review on the merits is the norm. Refusing to grant review also affirms the judgment of the lower court. In both these instances, the party seeking review has failed to obtain a reversal of the lower court decision. In another context, the term *affirm* is used to refer to the truthfulness of a statement. An affirmation of the accuracy of an assertion is often substituted for making such statements under oath.

Amicus Curiae (257)

A third party submitting a brief to a court expressing views on a legal question before the court. An *amicus curiae,* literally meaning "friend of the court," is not an actual party to an action. He, she, or it is an interested third party who attempts to provide the court with information or arguments that may not have been offered by the actual parties. So long as the parties to a controversy agree, *amicus* briefs can be filed at virtually any stage of the legal process. Such submissions, however, are typically submitted with cases under review by appellate courts. Indeed, most cases heard by the U.S. Supreme Court are accompanied by at least one *amicus* brief. The *amicus* participant is typically representing an interest group. It is not unusual to have an *amicus* brief from the NAACP or ACLU in civil rights or civil liberties cases. Similarly, many economic interest groups and professional associations present *amicus* arguments in various cases having commercial content. Government entities may also act as *amicus* participants. In fact, the federal government, represented by the solicitor general, frequently appears as an *amicus* participant on questions that relate directly to federal policy, such as environmental protection or affirmative action. *See also* BRIEF, 259; INTEREST GROUPS IN COURT, 272.

Significance   *Amicus curiae* participation is a common court-related interest group activity. It typically occurs in cases with substantial public policy ramifications. As the U.S. Supreme Court considered whether a woman has a constitutional right to an abortion in *Roe v. Wade* (410 U.S. 113: 1973), *amicus* briefs were submitted by 36 pro-abortion and eleven anti-abortion organizations. Some of the groups filed jointly. *Amicus* arguments tend to focus on the broader implications of a particular case. Submission of an *amicus* brief is not a matter of right, however. With the exception of *amicus* participation by an agency of the federal government, an *amicus* brief may be filed only with the consent of both parties in an action, on motion to the court, or by invitation of the court.

Appeal (258)

A request to an appellate or superior court to review a final judgment made in a lower court. Appellate jurisdiction is the power conferred upon appeals courts to conduct such a review. It empowers the court to set aside or modify the lower court decision. An appeals court has several options in reviewing a lower court decision. It may affirm, which means the lower court result is correct and must stand. The appeals court may, on the other hand, reverse or vacate, which means that it sets aside the lower court ruling. Vacated judgments are often remanded to the lower court from which they came for further consideration under terms of the appeals court ruling. If an appellate decision overrules a precedent, it supersedes the earlier decision and the authority of that decision as a precedent. A party seeking appeal is typically referred to as the appellant or petitioner, while the party against whom an appeal has been filed is the appellee or respondent. Appellate jurisdiction is distinguished from original jurisdiction. In the former, some other court or agency must render a judgment in a case before an appeal can be sought. *See also* CERTIORARI, 261; DISCRETIONARY JURISDICTION, 266; JUDICIAL REVIEW, 18; MANDATORY JURISDICTION, 275; ORIGINAL JURISDICTION, 62.

Significance   Appeals courts are generally structured on two levels. One is an intermediate court that handles cases first, and the other is a supreme court or court of last resort. Appellate jurisdiction is conveyed through constitutional or statutory mandate. Federal appellate jurisdiction is granted by Article III of the U.S. Constitution, which says that the Supreme Court possesses such jurisdiction "both as to law and fact, with such exceptions and under such regulations as the Congress shall make." Appeals may be undertaken as a matter of right. The appellate court that hears first round appeals typically has mandatory jurisdiction. That is, it must review the case. Appeals that follow from that occur at the discretion of higher level appellate courts. The writ of *certiorari* is a discretionary means of access to the U.S. Supreme Court. Even review as a matter of right is subject to some discretion by the Supreme Court through the writ of appeal. The party seeking appeal has a right to review, but the Court may reject the appeal for, among other reasons, lack of a substantial federal question.

Brief   **(259)**
A written document presented to a court in support of a party's position on a legal question. A brief contains a statement of the facts, applicable law, and arguments drawn from the facts and the law as well as from related, pertinent material. A brief urges a judgment compatible with the interests of the party submitting it. In a law school context, a brief is a short outline of a case prepared for recitation and review. *See also* AMICUS CURIAE, 257.

Significance   A brief is a medium through which arguments are placed before courts. While briefs generally present only legal arguments, they may advance arguments with other bases. For example, when Louis D. Brandeis sought to defend a state hours-of-work law for women, he presented various sociological as well as legal arguments. Brandeis was successful with this approach as the Court upheld

the law in *Muller v. Oregon* (208 U.S. 412: 1908). His technique of supplementing legal arguments with other than legal data became known
as the "Brandeis brief." In a similar fashion, the briefs submitted on
behalf of the plaintiffs in *Brown v. Board of Education I* (347 U.S. 483:
1954) sought to establish the damaging consequences of racial segregation in public schools by offering evidence from the field of social
psychology. Briefs are generally submitted by the parties themselves,
although *amicus curiae* briefs may also be received by the courts.

Certification (260)

A request to a higher court by a lower court for guidance on a legal
question relating to a pending case. Request for certification in the
federal courts can come from either the U.S. court of appeals or the
U.S. district court. The U.S. court of claims may also initiate such a
request. This process allows lower courts to obtain clarification of key
legal questions. Provisions of state law typically allow certification of
questions within state courts. When the U.S. Supreme Court receives
a certified question, it may offer specific instructions to the lower
court. These instructions are binding. Otherwise, the Court may request forwarding of the entire record and make final judgment on the
matter itself. *See also* APPEAL, 258; CERTIORARI, 261.

Significance   Certification is a method by which the U.S. Supreme
Court or state courts of last resort may review legal questions. This
method of review differs from appeal or *certiorari* in that it is not initiated by the parties to a dispute but by the court having jurisdiction
over the case. Because certification is a departure from usual procedures, it is seldom used.

Certiorari (261)

A writ or order to a lower court, whose decision is being challenged,
to send up the records of the case so a higher court can review the
lower court's decision. *Certiorari* means "to be informed," and may
be granted to the losing party by the Supreme Court. Until 1891 the
Court was formally obliged to take all appeals that came through the
federal court system or that concerned a federal question and were
appealed from the highest state court. In 1890 the Court had to deal
with more than 18,000 cases, a nearly impossible task. The problem
of an overcrowded docket was addressed in the Everts Act of 1891
when Congress created three-judge circuit courts of appeal to function as intermediate courts between the federal district courts and the
Supreme Court. The act restricted the means of appeal to the Su-

preme Court by introducing discretionary *certiorari* power. Through *certiorari* the Court could decline to hear certain cases if a given number of justices felt they were not sufficiently important. Denial of a *certiorari* petition meant the decision of the federal circuit court or state supreme court was upheld. Despite the Everts Act, the Court's workload continued to expand, however. This was occasioned by major population increases, a more extensive governmental administrative apparatus, and the widespread use of the writ of error by which cases came to the Court by the losing party's assertion of legal error committed by a court below. The Judiciary Act of 1925 largely did away with the writ of error and gave the Court even wider discretion in broad classes of cases by reaffirming the writ of *certiorari*. The writ is granted when at least four of the nine members of the U.S. Supreme Court agree that a particular case should be reviewed. In the years following the Judiciary Act, the proportion of *certiorari* petitions granted by the Court has never exceeded 22 percent. More often, the Court grants *certiorari* in fewer than ten percent of the cases seeking it. *Certiorari* is one of four ways by which cases may be reviewed by the Supreme Court. The others are appeal, the extraordinary writ, and certification. Certification is a process through which a lower court requests a higher court to resolve certain issues in a case while the case is still pending in the lower court. *See also* CERTIFICATION, 260; DISCRETIONARY JURISDICTION, 266; SCREENING CRITERIA, 286.

Significance   The *certiorari* power is the Supreme Court's principal means of keeping current with its docket. It can also be an effective administrative tool. When Charles Evans Hughes became chief justice in 1930, he read and summarized all *certiorari* petitions coming to the Court. He weeded out some of the easily disposable cases and put them on a separate list before conferences. In conference Chief Justice Hughes attempted to average only about three and one-half minutes for discussion of each *certiorari* petition. Since his preparation far exceeded that of the other justices, his views on whether to grant petitions were seldom challenged. Thus a chief justice, as the chief administrative officer of the Court, can restrict access to the Court by his manipulation of *certiorari* petitions. He can also direct the Court's attention to policy areas he thinks are important, as when Hughes expanded the Court's scrutiny of *in forma pauperis* petitions to the point where *habeas corpus* arguments by prisoners became an important part of the Court's docket. Chief justices continue to prepare lists of cases that may summarily be denied *certiorari*. The writ of *certiorari* extends to any civil or criminal case in the federal courts of appeal regardless of the parties, the status of the case, or the amount of money in controversy. Any state court decision that involves the construction and application of the federal Constitution, treaties, or laws, or the determination of a federal title, right, privilege, or immunity, falls within the Court's *certiorari* jurisdiction. *Certiorari* allows the Supreme Court to enter the policy making process at virtually any point it chooses to do so. Refusal to grant *certiorari* leaves a case as it stands. Denial of *certiorari* means that the issue contained in the case is insufficiently compelling for review. It may also reflect the Court's view that the decision of the lower court is satisfactory on the merits.

Collateral Attack (262)

A challenge to a court decision in a special proceeding. Collateral attack is like an appeal, but it occurs in an auxiliary or secondary proceeding. The most common challenge to a judgment occurs directly. An appeal or a petition for a new trial is a direct attack. It takes place in the court from which the original judgment was obtained or follows directly from it. Collateral attack, on the other hand, is an action in a separate proceeding and typically in another court. *See also* APPEAL, 258; *HABEAS CORPUS*, 270.

Significance Pursuit of a *habeas corpus* petition is a remedy sought by collateral attack. What occurs in these cases is that federal courts are requested to examine the adequacy of state criminal convictions. The *habeas corpus* petition thus essentially creates a second avenue of appellate review for state prisoners. The *habeas corpus* remedy in such cases was created by statute in 1867, but produced very few petitions until after World War II. In the 1980s, nearly 10,000 petitions were filed annually, making this kind of collateral review a matter of substantial consequence. Critics of this practice argue that it extends *habeas corpus* beyond its historic purpose, is unnecessarily duplicative, and creates federal-state tensions. Accordingly, the U.S. Supreme Court has attempted to limit collateral review to cases where state courts did not provide a full opportunity to raise certain constitutional issues.

Concurring Opinion (263)

Statement from a member of an appellate court that reflects agreement on the outcome, but differences in rationale for that outcome. Concurring opinions may vary quite widely in the extent to which they depart from the majority opinion. In some instances, it may be only a narrow difference. A justice may wish to mention, for example, one additional reason for arriving at the outcome, or place emphasis a little differently across several supporting points. On the other hand, a justice may disagree on virtually all the reasons upon which the rest of the majority bases its decision. In such a case, the justice may be among the majority "in result only," and the concurring opinion would depart extensively from the reasons featured in the majority opinion. *See also* DISSENTING OPINION, 267; MAJORITY OPINION, 274; PRECEDENT, 28.

Significance   A concurring opinion is optional. It is issued by judges on an individual basis when they wish to express different reasons for arriving at the same decision as the rest of the majority (or plurality). The role of the concurring opinion can be seen in the case of *Furman v. Georgia* (408 U.S. 238: 1972). The majority of the Court decided that Georgia's practice of assigning total discretion to juries in death penalty cases was unconstitutional. The outcome was represented in a brief *per curiam* opinion. Justice Stewart concurred in this result and emphasized the arbitrariness of unstructured sentencer discretion. Justice White also found the practice defective, but because it was so infrequently imposed by juries. Justice Douglas found particular fault with the racially discriminatory impact of its application. Finally, the concurring opinion of Justices Brennan and Marshall asserted that capital punishment is unconstitutional under any circumstance. It is evident from this case that concurring opinions may represent a broad array of viewpoints. The only common ground is agreement by those justices writing the concurring opinions on which of the parties should win.

Conference   (264)

A group meeting of all nine justices of the U.S. Supreme Court. The conference is the place where important Court business is conducted and is used at a number of stages in the decision process. The conference is used to consider appeals, writs of *certiorari*, and indigent prisoner (*in forma pauperis*) petitions. These are essentially jurisdictional or screening decisions through which the court determines which cases it will review. Only a small proportion of cases seeking review by the Court are actually considered on the merits. Once a case is accepted for review, the Court will examine the briefs that have been filed and hear oral arguments. Following oral argument, the justices discuss the case in conference. A nonbinding vote is taken and the task of writing the majority opinion is assigned. Votes taken on cases become final only when a justice actually agrees to the language of the opinion offered on behalf of the majority position. The discussion begun in conference continues even after opinion assignments have been made and draft opinions are circulated. *See also* CERTIORARI, 261; GROUP PROCESSES, 269; SCREENING CRITERIA, 286.

Significance The conference is considered by many to be the core of the Court's decisional process. It is in the conference that the justices engage in rather intensive discussion with one another. The process yields decisions on cases to review and basic "on the merits" decisions on cases reviewed. The conference discussion not only shapes voting alignments, but also the substance of the majority opinion. The conference sessions occupy the better part of two work days per week during the period the Court hears oral arguments. The conference is closed to everyone but the justices. When the conference is entertaining docket issues especially, the chief justice facilitates the process by fashioning an agenda and by pre-screening the petitions. In this way, many petitions regarded as "frivolous" may be summarily denied. Use of the conference is not confined to the U.S. Supreme Court. Rather, it is a technique employed by most state courts of last resort.

Declaratory Judgment (265)

A form of relief invoked when a plaintiff seeks a declaration of his or her rights. A declaratory judgment does not involve monetary damages, but rather is an assessment of a party's rights prior to a damage occurring. It differs from a conventional legal action in that no specific order is issued by the court. It differs from an advisory opinion in that parties have a bona fide controversy in a declaratory judgment proceeding, although actual injury has not yet occurred. The federal courts are empowered to render declaratory judgments by the Federal Declaratory Judgment Act of 1934. In a declaratory judgment proceeding there must be a real controversy, but the plaintiff is uncertain of his or her rights and seeks adjudication of them. As in injunctive relief, a declaratory judgment request is a petition for a court to exercise its powers of equity. No jury is permitted. The judge is asked to declare what the law is regarding the controversy. The Supreme Court upheld, for example, the Voting Rights Act of 1965 in *South Carolina v. Katzenbach* (383 U.S. 301: 1966). This case began with South Carolina seeking a declaratory judgment against the federal law. *See also* ADVISORY OPINION, 200; EQUITY JURISDICTION, 49.

Significance Declaratory judgment actions are a comparatively recent development in American jurisprudence. For many years they were considered the equivalent of advisory opinions, and the traditional concept was that courts could only act when a plaintiff was entitled to judicial remedy. A plaintiff may find it necessary, however, to determine if he or she is bound by contractual language that the plaintiff believes to be void or unenforceable. If the plaintiff should fail to comply, he or she is risking suit for breach of contract and for damages that flow from that breach. The declaratory judgment procedure is helpful to all parties because it circumvents the necessity of an actual breach and the lengthy litigation that such action invites. Contract disputes frequently form the basis of declaratory judgments. Courts are generally reluctant to issue them on broad public policy issues.

Discretionary Jurisdiction (266)

Power of appellate courts that permits them to decide which cases they will review. Discretionary jurisdiction is the opposite of mandatory jurisdiction. Appellate courts beyond the first level, most commonly courts of last resort, typically have discretionary jurisdiction. The procedures used by appellate courts with discretionary jurisdiction to screen cases varies by law and by volume of cases. The U.S. Supreme Court, for example, experiences heavy demand to review and has developed a screening process that operates at two levels. Cases viewed as not warranting close scrutiny are rejected without group discussion. For most cases, *certiorari* is denied in this manner. Somewhere between a quarter and a third of the cases receive closer scrutiny, which takes place in conference. If four justices agree to review a particular case, *certiorari* is granted. In this manner the Supreme Court reduces to about 300 (out of an original 4,000 to 5,000) the number of cases reviewed in a year. Some variation of this technique will be used by state appellate courts with discretionary jurisdiction. No state court rejects as many cases for review as the U.S. Supreme Court, so their screening approaches are seldom as stringent. *See also* APPEAL, 258; *CERTIORARI*, 261; MANDATORY JURISDICTION, 275; SCREENING CRITERIA, 286.

Significance Appellate courts with discretionary jurisdiction control their own dockets. Exercise of such authority requires establishment of at least two levels of appeals courts. If a court system has but a single appellate court, its jurisdiction must be mandatory since litigants have a right to one round of review. The key judgment for appeals with discretionary jurisdiction is often which cases to accept for review. The selected cases tend to have certain characteristics. They generally raise, for example, broad policy questions rather than narrow ones. The questions also tend to be complex and reflect uncertainties in the lower courts. An issue selected for review is often one decided differently by different intermediate level courts. Thus a court with discretionary jurisdiction will take a case in order to establish uniformity. Cases may also be selected if lower courts fail to properly adhere to higher court rulings. Discretionary jurisdiction gives an appeals court substantial power. Not only can it render authoritative decisions, but it can also establish its own priorities through case selection. Refusal to review a case by a court with discretionary jurisdiction leaves the decision of the court with mandatory jurisdiction intact.

Dissenting Opinion (267)

Statement from a member of a court disagreeing with the disposition of the case by the majority. A dissenting opinion is essentially a judicial minority report. A dissent may represent the views of a single judge or may be joined by additional judges. A dissenting opinion does not have precedent value as such in that it cannot authoritatively define a point of law. As a result, judges who write dissents have greater freedom with the arguments they advance. Since dissenters need not attend to finely focused legal points as majority opinions must, they are often sweeping in scope and contain powerful and abstract phrasing. It is possible to dissent "in part." If a court reviews a case containing multiple issues, a judge may agree with the majority's disposition of some, but not all, points. In such a case, a judge disagrees only on one or two points or only partially disagrees with the court. *See also* CONCURRING OPINION, 263; MAJORITY OPINION, 274; PRECEDENT, 28.

Significance A dissenting opinion allows a member of a court to convey his or her disagreement with a case outcome. The dissent expresses the reasons for that disagreement. Dissents also have two other purposes. First, a dissenter disagrees with the decision and may try to limit its impact. A dissent may invite Congress or a state legislature to modify the ruling if it is based on the interpretation of statute. The dissent may otherwise indicate ways to interpret the ruling narrowly. This can affect the way a lower court applies the ruling. Second, the dissent can encourage future appeals on the same question. Occasionally, a dissenting position in one case becomes the majority position when the issue is subsequently reviewed. For example, Justice Black's dissent in *Betts v. Brady* (316 U.S. 455: 1942) argued that states must provide legal counsel to indigent felony defendants. A majority of the Court eventually moved to that position and established the right to appointed counsel in *Gideon v. Wainwright* (372 U.S. 335: 1963).

En Banc (268)

A decision or proceeding made or heard by the entire membership of a court. *En banc* distinguishes cases having full participation from the typical use of only a fraction of a court's membership to hear a particular case. The term *en banc* is used most often when referring to state and federal intermediate appellate courts, which usually assign only three members of the court to hear the appeals. On these courts, the full membership of the court seldom hears a case. The *en banc* procedure is requested by either the judges of the court or the litigants. Use of the procedure is subject to rules established by that court itself. *See also* INTERMEDIATE APPELLATE COURT, 53; PANEL, 278.

Significance The U.S. Supreme Court and each state's court of last resort always sit *en banc*. An *en banc* court in U.S. Court of Appeals cases is usually reserved for highly controversial or public interest cases or for cases where one or more of the court's panels have disagreed on a major point of law. Except for courts that always sit *en banc*, the practice is infrequently used. Rather, resolution of appeals cases by three-judge panels is standard. *En banc* proceedings occur in less than one percent of U.S. court of appeals cases, for example.

Group Processes (269)

Methods of decision making used by multi-judge appellate courts. Unlike trial courts, appeals courts act in groups. This influences not only the decision, but the way in which those decisions are made. Intermediate appeals courts typically act in groups or panels of three, while courts of last resort usually sit *en banc*. That means the entire membership of a particular court participates, commonly seven or nine. The principal device of group decision making is the conference. It is here that a court seeks consensus in an effort to enhance the prospects of full compliance. The judges discuss the cases and the arguments submitted on behalf of both parties. In appeals courts with discretionary jurisdiction, the conference is also the place where decisions about which cases to review are made. The judges also hear oral arguments as a group and interact with one another on a regular basis with respect to the content of the opinions that accompany decisions. It is through these various interactions that judges attempt to convince their colleagues to join them, especially in cases where major policy issues are under review, such as abortion regulation or the exclusionary rule. *See also* CONFERENCE, 264.

Significance Group processes are one of the key influences on appellate court decision making. While these processes are not as determining as personal value orientations, the group processes create opportunities for judicial interaction. Judges have a dual interest in pursuing policy priorities and achieving consensus, and group processes facilitate the negotiation and compromise needed to reach those ends. Between the time a case is accepted for review and the time a decision is announced, several months will pass and a number of interactions will occur. Several will occur at formal conferences, where each judge or justice will offer his or her views and ultimately cast a vote. Draft opinions representing both the tentative majority statement and individual views will be circulated and memos exchanged. Over the course of these interactions, positions may alter the initial voting alignment. The impact of group processes varies by court, but these processes always tend to create issue dynamics that impact on appellate court decision making.

Habeas Corpus (270)

A court order requiring the state to show cause for a person's detention. *Habeas corpus* is a Latin term meaning "you have the body." *Habeas corpus* was originally a procedure in English law designed to prevent governmental misconduct, especially the improper detention of prisoners before any kind of trial. Its primary purpose was to force jailers to bring a detained person before a judge who would examine the adequacy of the detention. If the judge found the person to be in custody improperly, he or she could order the prisoner's release through a writ of *habeas corpus*. A writ is an order from a court requiring the recipient of the order to do what the order commands. In American law, the preliminary hearing functions as the point of examination into the propriety of pretrial detention, as well as into the charges brought against an accused person. Article I, Section 9, of the U.S. Constitution provides that the "privilege of the Writ of Habeas Corpus shall not be suspended, unless when in cases of rebellion or invasion the public safety may require it." President Lincoln attempted to suspend the writ early in the Civil War, but it was determined in *Ex parte Merryman* (17 Fed. Cas. No. 9487: 1861) that suspension was entirely a congressional prerogative. Congress subsequently authorized Lincoln to suspend the writ of *habeas corpus* at his discretion. This action was challenged and eventually decided by the Supreme Court in *Ex parte Milligan* (4 Wallace 2: 1866). A unanimous Court said the president could not suspend *habeas corpus* under any circumstances. A five-member majority held that Congress did not have the power either. There has been no subsequent attempt to suspend *habeas corpus* in the United States. *See also* COLLATERAL ATTACK, 262; WRIT, 39.

Significance   *Habeas corpus* seldom involves pretrial detentions now. The early steps in the criminal process attend to the problems against which *habeas corpus* was originally directed. The *habeas corpus* review has come to have a different function in contemporary law. *Habeas corpus* today involves, among other things, federal court review of state criminal convictions. After the Fourteenth Amendment was ratified, Congress enlarged *habeas corpus* to include persons already convicted and in custody in the states. These prisoners could apply for a writ of *habeas corpus* if they believed a violation of the U.S. Constitution or federal statutes had occurred in their cases. The allegations of violations were limited to jurisdictional issues at the time, but this apparently insignificant change began a transformation of the traditional concept of *habeas corpus.* It eventually turned *habeas corpus* into an avenue for collateral attack of state judgments. The Supreme Court has expanded the *habeas corpus* remedy several times. *Frank v. Magnum* (237 U.S. 309: 1915) held that *habeas corpus* review existed when a state failed to provide an effective means for convicted prisoners to pursue alleged violations of their federal constitutional rights. *Brown v. Allen* (344 U.S. 443: 1953) said that federal courts could reexamine a prisoner's constitutional allegations even if the state had provided corrective processes. The defendant had only to exhaust those processes. In *Fay v. Noia* (372 U.S. 391: 1963), the Warren Court determined that even if all state processes are not utilized, a defendant can access the federal courts through the *habeas corpus* application. The number of state prisoners seeking *habeas corpus* relief in the early 1940s was slightly over 100 annually. By the early 1970s, however, there were over 8,000 applications per year. The Burger Court was critical of this trend. It frequently expressed disapproval of the contemporary use of *habeas corpus* as a means of collateral review. In *Schneckloth v. Bustamonte* (412 U.S. 218: 1973), the Court said *habeas corpus* was being taken "far beyond its historical bounds and in disregard of the writ's central purpose." In one of its most recent decisions on the issue, the Court held in *Stone v. Powell* (428 U.S. 465: 1976) that the *habeas corpus* remedy is not available to a state prisoner pursuing a Fourth Amendment search violation when the defendant had been afforded a "full and fair" opportunity to press the allegations in a state court. While *habeas corpus* still provides substantial access for state as well as federal prisoners, the scope of the remedy in state proceedings has been reduced since the early 1970s.

In Forma Pauperis   (271)
Latin for "in the manner of a pauper." If a person is determined to

be indigent, a court will allow him or her to proceed *in forma pauperis.* This status relieves the person of the burden of court costs and fees. It also frees the person from some of the requirements associated with the presentation of a case, such as submission of multiple copies of all materials. People who request pauper status must support their claim by affidavit. Indigent criminal defendants who had counsel appointed at the trial level are categorically entitled to proceed *in forma pauperis.* *See also* PUBLIC DEFENDER, 111.

Significance   Proceeding *in forma pauperis* is intended to address the disadvantages of indigence. By permitting people to proceed *in forma pauperis,* an indigent person's right to sue and appeal is better protected. Approximately half of the cases reviewed annually by the U.S. Supreme Court are filed by indigents. While paupers' cases are generally handled in the same manner as cases from parties who pay their own costs, they do have separate docket status. Matters filed *in forma pauperis* appear on the Miscellaneous Docket while "paid" cases are found on the Appellate Docket. Most of the paupers' cases, upwards of 80 percent, are brought by federal and state prisoners. Only one to two percent of these indigent prisoners' petitions are accepted for review, but it is from this group of cases that the U.S. Supreme Court frequently finds important questions affecting the rights of criminal defendants.

Interest Groups in Court   (272)
Interest groups often involve themselves in litigation. An interest group becomes involved with courts because certain cases contain policy issues about which the groups have strong views. There are several ways interest groups attempt to influence judicial decision making. One avenue exists outside the form of the case when groups represent their interests in the judicial selection process. This is especially true with the selection of appellate judges. Participation also takes place in the actual litigation process. An effective way of advancing group interests may be to challenge a particular public policy. A favorable ruling may be obtained if the group can get the proper case to the courts. Indeed, groups often initiate (or have initiated) "test cases." The test case usually contains group members as named parties. A group may also facilitate the filing of class actions, a single lawsuit raising claims for a group of similarly injured persons. If a case has already been commenced, groups may assume sponsorship of the action by underwriting some or all of the costs. Groups may also supply legal counsel. Finally, groups frequently submit arguments on pending cases through the device of *amicus curiae* or "friend of the

court" briefs. Interest group use of litigation has increased substantially since World War II. The Supreme Court's decision in *NAACP v. Alabama* (375 U.S. 449: 1958) was a particularly important factor. The Court's ruling in this case was based on the associational rights that derive from the First Amendment. The Court acknowledged that "effective advocacy of both public and private points of view, particularly controversial ones, is undeniably enhanced by group association." Further, the Court suggested that association for litigation may be the "most effective form" of political association. *See also* AMICUS CURIAE, 257; CLASS ACTION, 205; TEST CASE, 252.

Significance   Interest groups find that litigation provides an effective avenue for participating in the public policy making process. This is especially true for organizations unable to participate effectively before other branches or agencies of government. The Jehovah's Witnesses, for example, have historically been unsuccessful in preventing the adoption of legislative and administrative policies that impinge on their religious practices, especially proselytizing. Court challenges to some of these regulations, however, have produced favorable outcomes for the Witnesses. The influence of interest groups is largely exerted in two ways. First, groups generate cases. In particular situations, groups perceive the opportunities to legally challenge certain policies. Groups often offer to sponsor cases under these circumstances. Some of this litigation would not occur otherwise. Second, after the cases are in the courts, groups are able to affect decisions through the presentation of arguments, especially at the appellate level. Indeed, group involvement with a case frequently enhances the prospect of it being reviewed by those appellate courts having discretionary jurisdiction. Groups that appear in the process on a regular basis, such as the American Civil Liberties Union or the NAACP (through their Legal Defense Fund), have been particularly effective at protecting or advancing the interests of their memberships.

Interpretive Approaches   (273)
The ways in which appellate courts go about determining the meaning of constitutional or statutory provisions. A number of factors influence the actual decision, but in each case the courts tend to apply one or more interpretative approaches. One approach is to follow previous decisions. Indeed, adherence to legal precedent may be a critical factor in a decision, yet other considerations are required as well. For example, a court must consider the language of the constitutional or statutory provision. One way to interpret this language is to take a literal approach. Those who advocate strict construction would

generally subscribe to such an approach. A similar approach is to adopt the simplest or "plain meaning" of the language. The plain meaning of words may not be clear, however, in which case courts might take a more creative or adaptive approach. Such an approach tends to regard language as offering broad directives that require interpretative adaptation when applied to particular situations. This approach generally suits judicial activists because it allows courts to leave their mark on public policy. Another approach is to interpret law from the standpoint of the objectives of those who wrote the provision under review. In the instance of constitutional provisions, one first needs to determine what the constitutional framers intended. Such a determination is often quite difficult. Legislative intent, on the other hand, may be more readily determined through the records of the legislative debates or the legislative history of a statute. *See also* JUDICIAL ACTIVISM, 309; JUDICIAL REVIEW, 18; JUDICIAL SELF-RESTRAINT, 311; STATUTORY CONSTRUCTION, 36; STRICT CONSTRUCTION, 287.

Significance A number of factors, including interpretive approaches, influence an appellate court decision on a constitutional or statutory question. These factors overlap, with the result that some combination of factors is required to understand a court's reasoning. Legal precedent is clearly one relevant factor. There are a number of prior decisions that might apply to a particular case, however, and new situations may arise that do not quite fit existing precedent. In such situations, other interpretive approaches are used. Also influencing decisions are the value orientations of the individual judges on the court. Justification of a policy direction can be facilitated by selection of a particular interpretive approach. Finally, judicial decisions are influenced by the political environment in which they are made. Thus, one interpretive approach may be appropriate at one time, but unwise at another.

Majority Opinion (274)

A statement of the reasons an appellate court reached a particular decision. The opinion is the rationale for a finding or conclusion, and a majority opinion represents the thinking of at least a majority of the judges hearing the case. A court's opinion is distinct from its decision, which is the judgment itself. A majority opinion is written by one member of the court rendering the decision and reflects the principle(s) of law that a majority of the court views as governing a particular decision. An opinion from a clear majority of an appellate court has greater value as a legal precedent than an opinion representing less than a majority. *See also* CONCURRING OPINION, 263; DISSENTING OPINION, 267; *PER CURIAM* OPINION, 279; PRECEDENT, 28.

Significance   The presence of a majority opinion produces the most valuable statement of a legal principle under *stare decisis*, or adherence to previous decisions. In some cases, a court may not be able to fashion consensus around one opinion, in which case a plurality opinion is issued. Its language is agreed to by less than a majority, but the case can be resolved as members of the court concur or agree to the result if not the supporting rationale. Apart from the majority opinion are the separate or individual opinions, such as the concurring and dissenting opinions. A concurrence is an opinion that agrees in result with the majority, but disagrees with the majority reasoning. A dissent disagrees with both result and rationale. Assignment of majority opinion writing responsibility occurs in conference. On the U.S. Supreme Court, the chief justice assigns the task to one of the justices among the majority. If the chief justice is in the minority, assignment is handled by the most senior associate justice on the majority side. The assigned justice drafts an initial version of the opinion trying to integrate the views of those among the majority. The draft is then circulated and discussed. The discussion is aimed at both retaining the original voting majority and persuading those previously in the minority to join the majority position. When the majority position cannot accommodate all views, individual opinions will be written. When no opinion will be supported by a majority, the designated opinion of the court is a plurality opinion. A case that does not have a majority opinion lacks any authoritative statement on the legal issue(s) considered in the case.

Mandatory Jurisdiction   **(275)**
Appellate authority that must be exercised in every case. Mandatory jurisdiction at the appellate level is typically located in those courts that handle the first round of appeals. Intermediate appellate courts such as the United States court of appeals have mandatory jurisdiction. Litigants are entitled to one appeal as a matter of right; thus, an appeals court in a system with only a single level or tier of appellate courts must have mandatory jurisdiction. Mandatory jurisdiction is the opposite of discretionary jurisdiction, where appellate courts may choose which cases to review. Courts with mandatory jurisdiction first receive an appeal and supporting brief from the losing party in a lower court. A response is then received from the opposing side, after which a date is set for oral argument. The court (or a smaller panel drawn from its membership) then meets in conference and arrives at

a preliminary decision. A draft opinion is then prepared and circulated among the members of the court (or panel). If continued discussion does not alter either the outcome or the contents of the opinion, the decision and the accompanying opinion are announced. Individual opinions expressing agreement or disagreement, called concurring and dissenting opinions, respectively, may be issued by one or more of the judges. The conference and opinion drafting processes used by courts with mandatory jurisdiction closely resemble those of the discretionary jurisdiction appellate courts. *See also* ABBREVIATED PROCEDURES, 255; APPEAL, 258; DISCRETIONARY JURISDICTION, 266.

Significance Courts with mandatory jurisdiction must decide all cases that seek review. Because these courts cannot control their dockets, they are vulnerable to the pressure of case volume. One of the things courts with mandatory jurisdiction have done is develop processes to expedite disposition of cases. These alternative processing methods generally require substantial support staff. The staff can review each of the cases that has been filed and tentatively determine whether it requires full consideration or can be resolved with a more limited or abbreviated review. Limited treatment might include eliminating oral arguments, reaching a decision without conference discussion, or issuing only a very brief opinion. Courts with mandatory jurisdiction face the largest number of appealed cases, and the use of some or all of these abbreviated procedures is a technique that can relieve some of the pressure created by case volume.

Obiter Dictum (276)

A statement contained in a court's opinion that goes beyond what is necessary to dispose of the question. *Obiter dictum* (singular) or *obiter dicta* (plural), sometimes simply called *dictum* or *dicta*, are normally directed at issues upon which no formal arguments have been heard. The positions represented in *obiter dicta* are therefore not binding on later cases. *Dicta* are not considered precedent-setting and should be distinguished from *ratio decidendi*, which provides the legal basis of the court's ruling. *See also* PRECEDENT, 28; *RATIO DECIDENDI*, 282.

Significance *Obiter dicta* can be found in many appellate court opinions. If *dicta* are not recognized as such, they can blur the principles contained in a ruling. In *Myers v. United States* (272 U.S. 52: 1926), for example, the Supreme Court held that Congress could not require Senate consent for presidential removal of postmasters. Postmasters are executive branch subordinates serving at the pleasure of the president. If the opinion had been confined to postmasters, it would not have been particularly important. Chief Justice Taft, a former president, wrote the majority opinion and asserted that the removal power is incident to the power of appointment, as distinguished from the power of advice and consent. The principle that emerged from this view was that presidents could remove anyone nominated by them to any position, including members of quasi-judicial agencies such as regulatory commissions. *Myers* did not require disposition of that broader question to settle the postmastership issue. Thus the remarks of the chief justice went beyond those necessary to decide the case and were therefore *dicta*.

Overrule (277)

To set aside or replace a holding from a previous decision. A decision can be overruled by the same court or a higher court in a case that raises the same question of law as the prior decision. When a court overrules a previous decision, it negates the value of that decision as a legal precedent. The overruled decision is replaced as legal precedent by the new ruling. For example, the Supreme Court established the doctrine of "separate-but-equal" in the decision of *Plessy v. Ferguson* (163 U.S. 537: 1896). The doctrine remained intact for several decades before it underwent serious reconsideration in the late 1940s and early 1950s. The Warren Court eventually overruled the doctrine in *Brown v. Board of Education I* (347 U.S. 483: 1954). Overruling a decision is different from reversing a decision. In the latter instance, a higher court sets aside a lower court's judgment in the same case. The term *overrule* has a second application. A court that denies a motion or a point raised in court overrules that motion or point. If a lawyer objects to a certain question posed by opposing counsel at trial, for example, the court can either sustain or overrule the objection. The effect of overruling the objection is to allow the question to be asked. *See also* PRECEDENT, 28; REVERSAL, 285.

Significance A previous decision is overruled when a basic legal question is decided in an opposite way in a subsequent case. The doctrine of *stare decisis* directs that once a matter is decided, the holding should be adhered to. Thus, decisions are infrequently overruled. More often, a court chooses to distinguish a case from an incompatible precedent. This approach avoids the need to overrule a decision by placing the current case under a new or different line of precedents. On other occasions, courts overrule previous decisions without explicitly acknowledging that result. Overruling a prior decision in this way is doing so "under silence," or *sub silentio*. If a court does choose to overrule a decision, it may do so in a direct and explicit manner. Consider the Supreme Court decision in *United States v. Darby Lumber Company* (312 U.S. 100: 1941). Among other things, the Court considered in *Darby* whether congressional power over interstate commerce extended to the regulation of child labor. The controlling precedent was *Hammer v. Dagenhart* (247 U.S. 251: 1918), in which the Court struck down congressional efforts to regulate child labor through use of the commerce power on the grounds that production preceded commerce, and that child labor was production-based. The Court explicitly overruled this thinking in *Darby*, saying that *Hammer* was based on a premise which had "long since been abandoned." Since the value of *Hammer* had been "exhausted," the Court concluded that "it should be and now is overruled."

Panel (278)

A group of judges who decide a case. Panels of judges are usually found on intermediate appeals courts such as the U.S. court of appeals. Cases at this level are normally heard by panels of three judges rather than by all the judges of the court. U.S. court of appeals panels occasionally include district judges from the circuit or retired federal judges. Membership of a panel varies from case to case. A number of possible combinations can occur when composing three-judge panels from a pool of twelve or fifteen judges. Panels may be assigned by the chief judge of the court, but such a procedure may lead to charges that assignments are designed to influence outcomes. To avoid such criticism, many of the courts that use panels select them randomly. The term *panel* is also used to refer to a list of people summoned for jury service. *See also* EN BANC, 268; GROUP PROCESSES, 269; INTERMEDIATE APPELLATE COURT, 53; UNITED STATES COURT OF APPEALS, 71.

Significance   The use of three-judge panels conserves judicial resources. It allows cases to be reviewed simultaneously and yet receive full consideration on the merits. Intermediate appellate courts that utilize the panel approach may choose to have the court's full membership hear a case, or sit *en banc*. This is unusual. Courts of last resort, on the other hand, typically hear cases *en banc* rather than by panels. Even with three judges, however, the panel approach opens the appellate process to the dynamics of group decision making. Which party wins and what is to be said in the opinion will almost invariably be affected by this shared decision-making responsibility. One other consequence of using panels is that outcomes in cases are products of the composition of the specific panel. A particular panel may not necessarily reflect the thinking of a majority of judges of the full court. This is especially true of the U.S. court of appeals where, as with all federal judges, the judges enjoy life tenure, which enhances the probability of ideological diversity.

Per Curiam Opinion (279)

An unsigned opinion of a court. *Per curiam* opinions are used to briefly summarize a ruling without extensively developing the court's reasoning. The term is Latin and translates "by the court." *See also* CONCURRING OPINION, 263; DISSENTING OPINION, 267; MAJORITY OPINION, 274.

Significance   *Per curiam* opinions are generally used with cases that are reviewed on the merits but without oral argument. In such cases, the issue may be less involved or complicated than the issue in cases given a fuller treatment by the reviewing court. Thus a brief opinion summarily representing the decision is sufficient. Occasionally, *per curiam* opinions are found in very important cases. For example, in *Furman v. Georgia* (408 U.S. 238: 1972) the Supreme Court struck down the capital sentencing method used in Georgia. A brief *per curiam* opinion summarily described the decision. Individual members of the Court then entered lengthy concurring or dissenting opinions. While a majority agreed that the Georgia process was constitutionally defective, no majority existed on a rationale. Thus, the *per curiam* opinion was used to represent the outcome of the case, the only point on which the justices in the majority could agree. A similarly functioning *per curiam* opinion can be found in the Pentagon Papers case, *New York Times v. United States* (403 U.S. 713: 1971).

Petitioner (280)

One who asks or petitions a court to commence a proceeding. At the trial level, it is the petitioner who seeks some remedy from a court. His or her role is the functional equivalent to that of a plaintiff. One who opposes the petitioner is called the respondent. A petitioner may also seek review of a judgment at the appellate level. In this instance, the petitioner seeks to reverse an adverse judgment by a lower court. *Appellant* is another name for a party initiating appellate review. *See also* PLAINTIFF, 238; RESPONDENT, 284.

Significance   It is the petitioner who initiates some kind of legal action. In doing so, the petitioner defines the legal issue(s) to be considered by a court. Not only must the respondent focus on the petitioner's issues, but the court before which the matter is heard is seldom able to enlarge or otherwise alter the issues. In other words, some degree of control or influence is linked to taking the initiative. At the same time, the petitioner is commonly trying to recover from a loss or adverse judgment. This is certainly true in the appellate context. Despite the capacity to frame the questions, statistical probabilities of success do not reside with the petitioner. Appeals courts do not commonly find reversible error in cases they review. If a petitioner is successful, however, the losing party may be able to appeal further. When this occurs, the original petitioner becomes the respondent.

Political Question (281)

An issue that is not justiciable or not appropriate for judicial determination. A political question is one in which the substance of an issue is primarily political or involves a matter directed toward either the legislative or executive branch by constitutional language. The doctrine the Supreme Court has fashioned for political questions emanates from the concept of judicial self-restraint. When a political question exists, the doctrine requires judicial deference to the prerogatives of the other branches. While the scope of the political question category has varied over time, examples of those issues generally accorded political question status include certain foreign policy decisions, determination of whether the form of government in a state is "republican," governance matters internal to legislative bodies such as determining committee assignments, and proceedings of national party nominating conventions. Until 1962, the Supreme Court justified its refusal to intervene in legislative apportionment issues on political question grounds. *See also* JUDICIAL SELF-RESTRAINT, 311; JUSTICIABLE ISSUE, 231.

Significance The political question doctrine is sometimes invoked by the Supreme Court not because the Court is without power or jurisdiction but because the Court adjudges the question inappropriate for judicial response. In the Court's view, to intervene or respond would be to encroach upon the functions and prerogatives of one of the other two branches of government. Moreover, such encroachment would constitute a breach of the principle of separation of powers. In *Luther v. Borden* (7 Howard 1: 1849), the Court was asked to rule on the status of Dorr's Rebellion in Rhode Island. The Court refused to do so, holding that the guarantee clause of Article IV had committed the issue to Congress rather than the Supreme Court. Chief Justice Taney said it is the duty of the Court "not to pass beyond its appropriate sphere of action, and to take care not to involve itself in discussions which properly belong to other forums."

Justice Brennan was more precise in characterizing a political question in *Baker v. Carr* (369 U.S. 186: 1962), the first case in which the Court held legislative apportionment to be a justiciable issue. Justice Brennan described a political question as one with a "textually demonstrable constitutional commitment of the issue to a coordinate political department; or a lack of judicial discoverable and manageable standards for resolving it." He added that such questions typically require a "policy determination of a kind clearly for nonjudicial discretion." On such matters the court cannot undertake "independent resolution without expressing lack of respect due coordinate branches of the government."

Ratio Decidendi (282)

The essential legal basis upon which a judicial decision rests. The *ratio decidendi* constitutes the principle of law established by the decision. It is this essential core of the decision that becomes a precedent upon which subsequent decisions are to be based. The *ratio decidendi* is distinguished from *obiter dicta,* which are statements in a court opinion on matters not essential to the resolution of questions of law. The principle of *stare decisis* rests on the idea that courts will embrace the *ratio decidendi* of a particular decision when a subsequent case involving the same issue comes before it. *See also* MAJORITY OPINION, 274; OBITER DICTUM, 276; PRECEDENT, 28.

Significance The *ratio decidendi* is the central proposition that resolves a question of law. It is the irreducible core of a decision. The *ratio decidendi* produces *res judicata,* a matter resolved by judgment. There are many cases that contain both *ratio decidendi* and *dicta.* One is *Watkins v. United States* (354 U.S. 178: 1957), in which the Warren Court considered the investigatory power of Congress. The House Un-American Activities Committee (HUAC) had found Watkins in contempt for his refusal to disclose certain information. The core of the decision was the pertinency issue. In the Court's view, HUAC had not properly indicated to Watkins how the questions on which he withheld response were "pertinent" to the Committee's inquiry. This defect was in itself enough to reverse Watkins's contempt conviction on vagueness grounds. Chief Justice Warren proceeded further, however. He responded to dimensions of the case that were more directly argued by Watkins and spoke to the matter of witness rights vis-á-vis congressional power to investigate. Warren concluded this discussion with the *dictum* that Congress did not possess the power to "expose for the sake of exposure."

Remand (283)

The sending of a case back to the original trial court after an appeal. The case is remanded when there are matters that require reconsideration under the terms of the appellate court decision. The term *remand* also applies to a prisoner who is sent back to detention following a court proceeding. *See also* DOUBLE JEOPARDY, 142; REVERSAL, 285; VACATE, 288.

Significance   A case is typically remanded when the judgment of a trial court is vacated. The effect of either reversing or vacating is to set aside the outcome of the basic fact dispute because of legal error in the initial trial. When a court vacates or reverses, it does not address the fact issues after it sets aside the judgment. Rather, it sends the dispute back to the court that heard the case originally. The court may then hear the case in a manner that eliminates or otherwise remedies the error found in the original trial. The plaintiff in a civil dispute will likely bring the case again, although he or she is under no legal obligation to do so. Criminal cases are a little different because of the presence of the double jeopardy protection. Reprosecution after successful appeal has never, however, been barred by the double jeopardy prohibition. Thus, prosecutors may recharge in remanded criminal cases. The prosecutorial decision rests on what the appeals court found wrong with the first trial and whether a strong enough case remains after taking the appellate ruling into account. If, for example, the error found in the first trial focuses on a vague jury instruction, the prosecutor's case remains intact; the prosecutor may use all the evidence presented in the first case. In this situation, the prosecutor will file charges. If, on the other hand, the original case was reversed because the defendant was improperly advised prior to interrogation, the prosecutor cannot use any statements from the defendant produced by the interrogation. It is possible that those statements constituted the bulk of the prosecution's case. Given that the statements are inadmissible in a second trial, the prosecutor may conclude that reprosecution is pointless because conviction is not possible.

Respondent (284)

The party against whom a motion is filed. The respondent responds to or answers the motion. The term *respondent* may be used to refer to defendants at the trial level or the party against whom an appeal is commenced. At the appellate level, the respondent may also be called the appellee or defendant in error. The respondent is the party who won at the lower level and defends against an appeal. The role of the respondent is wholly independent of whether the respondent had been the plaintiff (or prosecution) or defendant at trial. *See also* PETITIONER, 280.

Significance The objective of the respondent in an appellate proceeding is to preserve the outcome from a lower court. In a criminal case, this means the respondent in the first appellate review will be the prosecution, which will attempt to preserve the conviction. If the respondent is unable to keep the outcome from being reversed, the respondent has the option of changing roles and appealing to a higher court (if possible). In such a situation, the sides switch roles; the respondent becomes the petitioner and the party who had been the petitioner becomes the respondent.

Reversal (285)

The setting aside of a lower court judgment by an appellate court. A reversal changes the outcome of a case because of some error made in processing the case at a lower level. For example, a criminal conviction may be reversed because the jury became aware of some improperly obtained evidence. Since the appeals court cannot determine the extent to which such an error contributed to the conviction, the outcome must be reversed altogether. Another term with essentially the same meaning as reverse is *vacate*. If a lower court judgment is vacated, the effect is to leave it or set it aside. *See also* OVERRULE, 277; REMAND, 283; VACATE, 288.

Significance A reversal occurs when a losing party successfully challenges a lower court ruling at the appellate level. In order to have a lower court reversed, an appealing party must show one of two things: a procedural error occurred that might have influenced the outcome, or the law or regulation applied in the case is unconstitutional. An unreasonable search is an example of a procedural error. This kind of error typically occurs in criminal, as opposed to civil, cases. If a trial judge erred in allowing certain search evidence to be placed before a jury, a conviction based at least in part on that search evidence would require reversal. The claimed defect in the lower court proceeding may not be procedural, however. Rather, the problem may by substantive. A conviction for disturbing the peace, for example, may be challenged on First Amendment grounds if the disturbance was caused by political expression. Reversals on either procedural or substantive grounds are rare. Most laws do not lend themselves to attack because of unreasonable regulation of conduct.

Neither do trial courts frequently make reversible errors. In any event, a case will not be reversed simply because the losing party is displeased with the outcome. A specific point of law, procedural or substantive, is a necessary ingredient of an appeal that might produce a reversal.

Screening Criteria (286)

The bases upon which appeals courts decide which cases to review. Screening criteria are most critical for those appellate courts with discretionary jurisdiction, but screening is important for courts having mandatory review as well. In the latter instance, screening is necessary to determine whether abbreviated procedures should be used. These judgments are based on considerations similar to those used by courts not required to grant review. The most important criterion is the importance of the policy issue(s) or law question(s) raised by the case. If the case will have consequences for many people, or raises a new question, or represents a constitutional challenge to a major legislative enactment, the chances of a court's deciding to review the case are increased. Some cases are selected because they advance the policy preferences of individual judges. This element is often key to the assessment of case importance. Second, courts consider the extent to which there is conflict of interpretation between or among lower courts. Courts with discretionary jurisdiction often seek to further the cause of consistency by rendering a decision that will resolve conflicting lower court rulings. Third, courts consider the parties involved, particularly the party pursuing review. Certain interest groups are themselves selective about cases they choose to sponsor or join. Group attachment to a question may signal the importance of that issue to a court. Similarly, if the federal government is party to a suit, the case is more likely to be accepted for review. Finally, appellate courts will be more likely to review cases where they suspect a lower court has erred in its judgment. *See also* CERTIORARI, 261; DISCRETIONARY JURISDICTION, 266.

Significance The screening of cases for appellate review serves several purposes, and the criteria used are tailored to further those ends. Some criteria are used to service technical needs. Jurisdictional and standing requirements, for example, are examined. No case will be accepted if it fails to establish those threshold conditions. In addition to policy priorities, screening criteria allow the court to implement particular role orientations or interpretive approaches. An appellate judge who subscribes to the self-restraint view will screen cases accordingly. It may also be possible to screen in such a way as to avoid, at least for the short term, handling highly controversial issues. The delay may produce a legislative response to the problem, a preferred outcome for the advocate of self-restraint.

Strict Construction (287)

An approach to constitutional or statutory interpretation that calls for a literal adherence to the law. The basic concept of strict construction is that courts should not engage in lawmaking through interpretation. Neither should they recognize governmental powers that go beyond the scope of those specifically set forth in law. The opposite of strict construction is loose or adaptive construction. In many respects, the idea of strict construction is similar to the concept of judicial self-restraint. *See also* INTERPRETIVE APPROACHES, 273; JUDICIAL REVIEW, 18; JUDICIAL SELF-RESTRAINT, 311.

Significance The concept of strict construction has greater political meaning than it has legal meaning. The term is frequently used by those critical of a judicial decision. The term embraces neither liberal or conservative values as such, but rather is occasionally asserted by persons or groups who object to the particular rulings of courts. The criticisms generally assert that rulings are wrong because courts have departed from the plain or literal meaning of the Constitution or of statute. Richard Nixon, for example, was highly critical of the Warren Court's decisions, especially as they pertained to criminal defendants. He pledged to remedy the situation by appointing only strict constructionists to the Supreme Court, people who would presumably render decisions more supportive of law enforcement. The real focus of strict construction is the role of the courts relative to the other branches in making policy decisions.

Vacate (288)

The setting aside of a court judgment. If a court judgment is vacated, it is rendered void. A judgment is often vacated on appeal. When this occurs, it is the functional equivalent of a reversal. A trial judge may also vacate a judgment, however, while a reversal is exclusively an appellate action. *See also* REMAND, 283; REVERSAL, 285.

Significance When a judgment is vacated, it is completely wiped away. Vacating a judgment does not necessarily end a case, however. The basic fact situation that produced the case still remains. Generally, when a judgment is vacated the controversy is remanded back to the trial court from which it started. The fact issue may then be reconsidered, but in a manner consistent with the ruling that vacated the original judgment. For example, if a judgment was vacated because a judge erroneously instructed a jury on a point of law, the case can be retried and resolved so long as the jury instruction problem is not repeated at retrial. The objective in vacating a judgment is to set aside a flawed decision and create the opportunity to resolve the conflict without error. When a case is remanded, it may be retried, but the parties are not legally obligated to seek retrial.

7. Judicial Policies and Impact

The decisions of courts, especially at the appellate level, often establish policy. Judicial policy making involves more than just resolution of discrete disputes. Rather, judicial decisions have impact on the broader political and social problems confronting the governmental process. The role defined for courts in the American legal system includes a policy making dimension, but a great deal of debate has taken place over the scope of this role and the capacity of courts to address broad social problems. The public, however, continues to bring disputes to courts in ever-increasing numbers. Many of these disputes raise fundamental policy issues, and the response of courts will continue to have policy implications whether desired or not. The objective of this chapter is to examine the characteristics of judicial policy making.

The nature of the policy making activity of any particular court is governed by its location in the organizational structure. Appeals courts generally have a different kind of policy making role from trial courts. Appellate court policy making has several distinctive features. First, decisions of appeals courts are intended to establish rules and principles to be followed by lower courts when similar issues arise in the future. The importance of this function is seen, for example, in the activities of interest groups. They involve themselves in litigation hoping the courts will embrace their positions on a particular policy question. Second, appellate policy making is conveyed through written explanations of the decisions. The opinions become the substance of the precedent a case sets. Third, appellate courts are better able than trial courts to enlarge the scope of a case beyond the parties and their fact dispute. While this is not always done, it may allow an appellate court to more fully consider the broader policy implications of a case. Finally, judicial policy set by appellate courts has heightened significance because it often involves review of already existing government policy, usually policy initiated by the legislative or executive branches.

The policy making significance of the trial courts is more limited. Cases at this level are bound by the narrow parameters of the fact dispute. As a result, many see the role of trial courts as enforcing policies established elsewhere, rather than engaging in policy making of their own. An alternative perspective would suggest that policy is made at the trial level through patterned responses to particular categories of disputes. Patterned responses to such matters as pretrial release, criminal sentencing, child custody, or zoning ordinance issues are examples of cases where consistently applied judicial values essentially set policy.

Considerations of judicial policy making almost always prompt the normative question of the extent to which courts should pursue policy opportunities—the degree to which judges ought to be judicial activists. Judicial activism would have judges pursue a course that would maximize their impact on policy. While American courts have engaged in activism since the time of John Marshall, contemporary courts seem to be activist to an unprecedented degree. One possible explanation is that courts are presented with more questions about the legality of governmental policies and practices. As government regulation becomes more pervasive at all levels, more legal challenges follow. Large numbers of interest groups have compounded the situation by actively seeking to generate policy challenges.

There are, however, limits that apply to judicial policy making. Some limits are self-imposed in that a large number of judges reject judicial activism and subscribe instead to the judicial self-restraint. Beyond that, substantial limits exist because of the principle of separation of power. While courts have the power to decide cases, they do not possess the authority to enforce them. Rather, such power resides with the legislative and executive branches. In addition, such matters as judicial selection, jurisdiction, and numbers of judges on a court are legislative issues. Courts that engage in policy making of a kind unacceptable to the legislature may eventually find themselves subject to legislative "court curbing." Other limiting factors exist as well. Courts tend to make policy of a narrower scope than do legislatures. The focused character of the case format acts to limit the span of a court's considerations. Neither can courts create the cases that require judicial decisions. Rather, they must wait for parties external to the courts to bring the policy "vehicles" to them in the form of cases.

Abstention (289)

A doctrine designed to reduce conflict between federal and state courts. Abstention allows a federal court to withhold exercise of its jurisdiction on a federal constitutional issue until a state court has rendered judgment on state law that may have a bearing on the federal question. The abstention doctrine also directs a federal court to refuse to decide some question if the matter can be resolved wholly on the basis of state law applied by a state court. Abstention is regarded as essential to the operation of a dual court system where both federal and state judges have an obligation to uphold the federal Constitution. The case of *Younger v. Harris* (401 U.S. 37: 1971) is illustrative. Harris had sought an injunction from a federal court to prevent his prosecution at the state level. The Supreme Court refused to permit federal intervention even in the presence of First Amendment issues without a clear showing that the state's actions produced irreparable injury for Harris. *See also* COMITY, 297; DOCTRINE, 302; DUAL SYSTEM, 48.

Significance Abstention addresses the question of proper forum for judicial involvement in a controversy. The doctrine maintains that a federal court should not assume jurisdiction in a case until the uncertainties of state law are addressed by the appropriate state courts. Abstention by the federal court may prevent or minimize conflict by limiting federal court interference in matters pertaining primarily to state law. Abstention also permits a federal court to relinquish its jurisdiction if the federal court determines that the central issue in a case has been appropriately resolved at the state level. A particular form of abstention is known as *comity*. Comity is a courtesy by which one court extends deference to another in the exercise of authority. Comity is offered out of respect and goodwill rather than obligation. Like abstention, it is aimed at preventing friction between two courts, both of which may have legitimate jurisdictional claims in a case.

Affirmative Action (290)

A program designed to remedy the effects of past discrimination. Affirmative action programs are typically used in employment or educational situations and tend to offer advantage or preference to a particular group that has suffered previous discrimination. Racial minorities and women are most commonly targeted, although some programs focus on such groups as veterans or the handicapped. The affirmative action approach is advocated by those who wish to eliminate long-standing patterns of discrimination, particularly in the workplace. Affirmative actions thus becomes remedial in that it is part of a process aimed at relieving members of particular groups from the effects of discrimination. Affirmative action is compensatory. The principal justification advanced in its support is to remediate or compensate for past practices. Those critical of affirmative action, on the other hand, see it as race or gender preference that itself impinges on equality of opportunity. They see affirmative action as reverse discrimination—the relief of one wrong through the commission of another. Certainly the constitutional question raised by affirmative action is whether benevolent discrimination is permissible because of its compensatory or remedial character. Affirmative action may be required by law for governmental agencies or established as a matter of operating policy by private entities. Affirmative action is an approach that differs from equal opportunity laws in that the former attempts to require particular remedial measures while the latter prohibit discriminatory conduct. *See also* CIVIL RIGHTS, 295; EQUAL PROTECTION, 303.

Significance   The issue of affirmative action has appeared before the U.S. Supreme Court on a number of occasions. The first important decision came in the case of *Regents of the University of California v. Bakke* (438 U.S. 265: 1978). In *Bakke,* the Court upheld the use of race-conscious admissions policies for a state university graduate program, although it disallowed the allocation of seats on a quota basis. The Court found that recruitment of a diverse or heterogenous student body was a substantial enough interest to allow race-conscious admissions. A more extensive program was permitted in *United Steelworkers of America v. Weber* (443 U.S. 1979), in which the Court allowed a private employer to give preference to unskilled black employees over white employees for training programs designed to elevate the unskilled workers to craft levels. The Court permitted the preferential treatment because racial discrimination had demonstrably disadvantaged black workers in the past. The use of "set-asides" was upheld by the Court as a remedial solution in *Fullilove v. Klutznick* (448 U.S. 448: 1980). A set-aside reserves a certain percentage of federal funds for minority businesses. The Court determined that Congress may allow narrowly tailored corrective actions to redress historical disadvantages. In 1989, however, the Court struck down a local "set-aside" plan in *City of Richmond v. J.A. Crosan, Inc.* (102 L. Ed. 2d 854: 1989) on the grounds that it was not limited or "narrowly tailored" enough. The Court was also dissatisfied with the supporting data Richmond used in attempting to establish that such a remedial initiative was necessary. As a rule, the Court has been receptive to affirmative action efforts undertaken by parties as a result of settling a challenge to employment practices. Often such agreements are embraced in court orders called consent decrees. In *Local #28, Sheetmetal Workers v. Equal Employment Opportunity Commission* (478 U.S. 421: 1986), the Court upheld an affirmative action plan contained in a consent decree that produced benefits to individuals who were not themselves victims of discrimination. Similar support of programs designed to produce promotions for minorities and women already on the job was revealed in *United States v. Paradise* (480 U.S. 149: 1987) and *Johnson v. Transportation Agency* (480 U.S. 616: 1987). Greater uncertainty about Court-approved plans, however, was prompted by the decision of *Martin v. Wilks* (104 L. Ed. 2d 835: 1989). Here the Court permitted people who were not parties to original agreements contained in consent decrees to challenge them at a later date. All that is clear is that the issue of affirmative action will remain before the courts for some time to come.

Balancing Doctrine (291)
An approach used by courts to weigh the adverse interests contained in a case. The balancing doctrine is most often used in those cases that involve a governmental action on the one hand and an asserted constitutional right on the other. The balancing doctrine presumes that constitutionally protected rights are not absolute and that governmental initiatives are probably acceptable. In this outlook, the balancing approach differs substantially from the "preferred position" view, which presumes that laws affecting protected rights are unconstitutional. The balancing approach is used to determine the extent to which governmental authority may be exercised to prevent society from substantial harm. The "clear and present danger test" is an example of a test used under the balancing doctrine. *See also* CLEAR AND PRESENT DANGER TEST, 296; PREFERRED POSITION DOCTRINE, 317.

Significance   Use of a balancing test in certain individual rights situations reflects the view that individual rights are not absolutely protected. Rather, there are occasions when a public interest outweighs an individual's liberty. The balancing approach is somewhat open-ended and leaves room for judges to make determinations on the basis of their own preferences. Balancing, however, is not often undertaken on an *ad hoc* basis, but is instead governed by certain guidelines depending on the nature of the case. Consider, for example, time, place, and manner restrictions. These are regulations imposed on the how, what, or where aspects of expression. The balancing question facing the courts is whether the public interest outweighs the expression interest of those subject to the regulation. The balancing done by the courts in time, place, and manner regulation cases is not wholly unguided, however. Time, place, and manner restrictions are evaluated by the courts using three principal criteria. First, any such restriction must be content neutral. That is, it cannot regulate expression on the basis of the expression itself, but only on the associated how, when, or where elements. Second, the state must be able to demonstrate a substantial interest for imposing the control. Restricting demonstrations from areas adjacent to hospitals or in-session schools would be such an interest. Finally, time, place, and manner restrictions must be sufficiently narrow in scope to allow alternative ways to communicate particular information. Restrictions that are so broad as to forestall all opportunities for expression will likely be invalidated by the courts.

Bill of Rights (292)

The enumeration of rights of individuals legally protected against violation by government. The Bill of Rights for the United States is found in the federal Constitution and its amendments, especially the first ten. The Bill of Rights is broader than just the first ten amendments, however. The protection of a number of rights was included in the body of the original Constitution of 1787. For example, Article I, Section 9, prohibits bills of attainder and *ex post facto* laws, and Article VI bans religious tests for public officials. In addition, there are personal rights protected by the amendments added subsequent to the Civil War. The Thirteenth and Fifteenth Amendments prohibit slavery and racially discriminatory voting practices, respectively. The Twenty-fourth Amendment outlaws the poll tax while the Twenty-sixth Amendment establishes 18 as the minimum voting age throughout the country. Although it does not enumerate any new personal rights, the Fourteenth Amendment, added in 1868, has played a crucial role in broadening the enforcement of all rights by extending the basic protection of most rights to the states. The first ten amendments guarantee: (1) the freedom of religion, speech, press, assembly, and peaceful protest; (2) the right to bear arms in order to maintain a well-regulated militia; (3) freedom from having soldiers quartered in one's home; (4) freedom from search and seizure without probable cause; (5) the requirement of grand jury indictment for all but military crimes, freedom from double jeopardy and judicial self-incrimination, and the guarantee of legal due process, as well as just compensation for publicly appropriated private property; (6) the right to a speedy, public, and impartial trial, with the right to know the charge, the right to compel witnesses for the defense, and the right to have legal counsel; (7) the right to jury trial for civil matters concerning $20 or more, and the prohibition of judicial review of such trials except in accordance with civil law; and (8) prohibition of excessive bails or fines and of cruel and unusual punishment. The last two of the original ten amendments declared that of those rights not enumerated in the Constitution or its amendments, individuals enjoy all other rights except those delegated to the central government, reserved to individual states, or forbidden by the states. When the federal Constitution was drafted in 1787, it contained various guarantees in the body of the text but lacked a specific bill. The omission received more public criticism from opponents of ratification than did any other aspect of the Constitution. Among the proponents for ratification without a bill of rights, Alexander Hamilton considered a separate bill unnecessary because he said the states already had the power to protect individual rights. He believed an enumeration of rights to be dangerous because any listing might be considered exhaustive. Hamilton argued that social diversity and watchfulness were the ultimate guarantees of personal rights. Although James Madison originally agreed with Hamilton, he eventually came to support the drafting of a separate bill of rights. Madison was persuaded by his friend, Thomas Jefferson, and perhaps convinced by political necessity as well. Two months after the Congress convened in 1789, Madison proposed a federal bill of rights. He became the document's prime author, relying heavily on the Virginia Declaration of Rights and Jefferson's Virginia Statute for Establishing Religious Freedom. On September 25, 1789, Congress approved the Bill of Rights, which was subsequently ratified by the state legislatures. *See also* CIVIL LIBERTIES, 294; JUDICIAL REVIEW, 18.

Significance   Enforcement of a bill of rights serves the ultimate purpose of constitutionalism or limited government. The key structural elements of a bill of rights are an enumeration of personal rights, a statement of the government's obligation to protect them, and effective provisions for their enforcement. Whether and how federal governments guarantee these elements determines the authenticity of their bills of rights. Great Britain, for example, has no single document containing a bill of rights, just as Great Britain has no written constitution. It does, however, have a long tradition of protecting the rights of individual citizens, a tradition contained in centuries of common and statutory law such as the Bill of Rights Act of 1689. On the other hand, the Soviet Union's single-document constitutions of 1936 and 1977 contained a highly developed bill of rights. But given the Communist Party's unlimited power, at least until the regime of Mikhail Gorbachev, the document does not have the enforcement provisions that would qualify it as an authentic bill of rights. For different reasons the United Nations Universal Declaration of Human Rights of 1948 also lacks the enforcement provisions of a genuine bill of rights. The U.S. Supreme Court has established itself as the ultimate guarantor of individual rights in the United States. While the institution of judicial review has generally worked well as a vehicle for the Court to monitor compliance with the Bill of Rights, there are examples of the Court's willingness to balance individual rights against the public interest or to the will of the other two branches of government. In *Dred Scott v. Sandford* (19 Howard 393: 1857), for example, the Court actually quoted the Fifth Amendment to oppose abolition of slavery. In World War I, the Court upheld federal convictions of persons who were critical of the draft. In *Korematsu v. United States* (323 U.S. 214: 1944), the Court justified the federal government's indiscriminate internment of Japanese Americans during World War II. When the Supreme Court overturned state abortion laws in *Roe v. Wade* (410 U.S. 113: 1973), critics accused it of simply yielding to the social prejudices of the times. Nonetheless, the Bill of Rights enforced through judicial review remains an irreplaceable protection for individual freedom in the United States.

Citator (293)

Reference source that indicates the current status of court decisions or laws. A citator is used to determine which cases or laws apply to a particular issue and whether these cases or laws remain authoritative on the question. The most commonly used citator is *Sheppard's Citations.* It contains virtually every printed case and law in the United States. *Sheppard's* is so widely used that the term "Sheppardize" has come to mean searching for cases with a citator. More than one set of citators exists. For example, *Sheppard's United States Citations* contains U.S. Supreme Court decisions and federal laws. *Sheppard's Federal Citations,* itself broken into two series, contains decisions from lower federal courts. One series contains cases from the *Federal Supplement* (district court cases) while the other has citations from cases in the *Federal Reporter* (court of appeals cases). *See also* FEDERAL SUPPLEMENT, 304; NATIONAL REPORTER SYSTEM, 312; PRECEDENT, 28; UNITED STATES REPORTS, 322.

Significance A citator will indicate whether a case is still followed as a legal precedent or if the case has been overruled or distinguished on a particular point. Citators are comprehensive and relatively easy to use. As a result, they are invaluable to the conduct of legal research.

Civil Liberties (294)

Protections from arbitrary actions by government. Civil liberties are those rights enumerated in constitutions or bills of rights. The American Bill of Rights, for example, creates an insulating barrier between the individual and government, and it sets certain behaviors by government out of bounds. The government cannot, for example, censor political expression because the First Amendment protects freedom of speech. This kind of restriction is substantive—it specifies what government can and cannot do. Other civil liberties restraints on government focus on process or procedure. Government has the power to prosecute someone for alleged criminal conduct, but it may not deny the accused the procedural protection of having his or her guilt adjudicated by an impartial jury in a public trial. It is the substantive and procedural restrictions on government taken together that define civil liberties. Civil rights are different from civil liberties in that they refer to affirmative acts of government designed to protect a person from other individuals or the government itself. *See also* BILL OF RIGHTS, 292; CIVIL RIGHTS, 295; INCORPORATION, 308.

Significance Civil liberties protect citizens from actions of the government. Civil liberties may be spelled out in a single constitution, but that is not a necessary pre-condition. The British experience is illustrative of a political system where safeguards are not so set forth, but statutory and common law limits are effective nonetheless. The U.S. Bill of Rights was formally added to the Constitution in the first ten amendments. The American tradition of protecting civil liberties is drawn from a variety of sources, principally British. Documents like the Magna Carta (1215), the Petition of Rights (1628), and the Bill of Rights (1689) firmly established such concepts as limiting the power of governmental institutions and equality. Similarly, the works of such political thinkers as John Locke were well known to those who framed the U.S. Constitution and its Bill of Rights. Civil liberties provisions in the Bill of Rights direct government not to interfere in certain areas of individual activity, but such interference is generally not categorically or absolutely prohibited. Rather, government may only interfere where the public interest in doing so is compelling. Even then, the government may only proceed in limited ways. The task of the courts is to weigh the often competing public welfare and individual liberty interests. A variety of tests or devices have been created to facilitate in making these judgments. Through a process known as selective incorporation, virtually all of the provisions of the federal Bill of Rights have come to apply also to the state level of government.

Civil Rights (295)

An affirmative act of government intended to protect citizens from unlawful conduct by government agencies or private parties. Civil rights are different from civil liberties. Civil liberties are prohibitions on certain government conduct. They define areas where government cannot interfere with individual activity. Civil rights, on the other hand, are initiatives of government designed to implement its social contract obligations to protect citizens' basic rights to "life, liberty and property." People are entitled, among other things, to vote and to own property. Government can protect these interests by adopting laws and regulations that prohibit arbitrary or discriminatory interference with these rights. For example, people cannot be "singled out" for arbitrary treatment because of certain characteristics such as race or gender. Thus, government may enact civil rights laws that prohibit discrimination in the conveyance of property or participation in the electoral process. *See also* AFFIRMATIVE ACTION, 290; CIVIL LIBERTIES, 294; EQUAL PROTECTION, 303.

Significance   Civil rights initiatives in the United States date back to the aftermath of the Civil War. Following the war, three amendments were added to the Constitution. The Thirteenth Amendment forbid involuntary servitude, but also enabled Congress to act to eliminate "vestiges" of slavery. The Fifteenth Amendment was aimed at discriminatory interference with voting rights. The Fourteenth Amendment was more broadly scoped and prohibited denial of "due process" and "equal protection." These three amendments provide the constitutional basis for most contemporary federal civil rights laws. Indeed, by 1875 Congress had enacted several civil rights statutes based on these amendments. Some provisions of these early enactments remain in effect. For example, civil damage suits may be brought against government officials whose actions violate the rights of individual citizens. It was under the terms of one of these statutes that criminal prosecutions were undertaken in the 1960s against those who deprived others of their rights by means of criminal violence. Since the end of World War II, a number of federal, state, and local legislative initiatives have been made in efforts to secure civil rights for blacks, other minorities, and women. These initiatives have focused primarily on such fields as education, housing, employment, and access to public services and facilities. The Civil Rights Act of 1964, based on congressional power to regulate interstate commerce, was a broadly scoped enactment that prohibited discrimination in public accommodations, employment, and education. The act also authorized withholding federal funds from recipients acting in a discriminatory manner. The Voting Rights Act of 1965, adopted the following year, has through numerous renewals continued to direct substantial federal authority toward the elimination of discriminatory voting practices.

Clear and Present Danger Test (296)

One of the standards used to determine if a particular expression is protected by the First Amendment. The clear and present danger test was first articulated in *Schenck v. United States* (249 U.S. 47: 1919), a case involving an Espionage Act prosecution for obstruction of military recruitment. The Supreme Court upheld Schenck's conviction, saying that expression is a conditional freedom that must be evaluated in a situational context. It was in *Schenck* that Justice Oliver W. Holmes said in explaining this test that the freedom of speech could not be interpreted in such a way as to allow a person to shout "Fire!" in a crowded theater. Rather, each situation must be reviewed to determine whether expression occurs in such a way and is of "such nature as to create a clear and present danger that it will bring about the substantive evil that legislatures are empowered to prevent." If speech is linked closely enough to illegal acts, the speech may be restricted. The Court said it was a matter of "proximity and degree." *See also* BALANCING DOCTRINE, 291; PREFERRED POSITION DOCTRINE, 317.

Significance   The clear and present danger test presumes that free speech is not an absolute right. The test is designed to justify interference with speech only when the government can show that the speech creates a danger both substantial and immediate. In this respect clear and present danger is a more demanding test for restrictive enactment than the "bad tendency" test. The bad tendency test allows restriction of expression if the expression could lead to unlawful ends. It and the clear and present danger test differ from the preferred position doctrine, which holds that any restrictive enactments are unconstitutional. The purpose of devices like the clear and present danger test is to aid the courts in balancing society's interest in protecting itself and the individual's interest in unrestricted expression.

Comity (297)

A courtesy by which one court defers to another in the exercise of judicial power. Comity is not a rule of law, but rather a practice of convenience. The principle prevents interference by courts in matters appearing before other courts. Comity is based on the proposition that the court that first asserts jurisdiction will be able to take a legal matter to conclusion. Comity is especially important in preserving the autonomy of federal and state courts in the American dual system. *See also* ABSTENTION, 289; DUAL SYSTEM, 48; FEDERALISM, 51.

Significance The principle of comity provides that the courts of one jurisdiction will give effect to the laws and court judgments of another jurisdiction. This occurs not as a function of legal obligation but rather of general deference and respect. Comity is a form of abstention. The abstention doctrine provides that a federal court should not take jurisdiction in a case until appropriate state courts address all questions of state law. The doctrines of comity and abstention are both directed at preventing friction between courts that may have legitimate jurisdictional claims to a case.

Compliance (298)

Obedience to the requirements of a court decision. Compliance is normally obtained voluntarily. This means that the party who needs to take an action or stop an action as a result of a court decision usually does so on his or her own. Compliance is obviously not obtained from a losing party because of agreement with the decision. Rather, the party complies because the decision is "the law," and the court has the authority to make such a judgment. Compliance may also occur because sanctions will be imposed without it. Conversely, noncompliance with judicial decisions may result if no sanction is forthcoming in the absence of compliance. The likelihood of noncompliance also increases if the court is not perceived as the appropriate or authoritative source of a decision. Failure to comply with court decisions on school prayer, for example, is often attributed to school board member perceptions that secular courts were not the final or legitimate authority on matters of religion and prayer. In addition, compliance often depends on the clarity of a court's decision. The courts must effectively communicate what needs to be done in order to comply. Finally, compliance depends on how lower courts apply the decision to particular cases. Lower courts can demand full compliance or can avoid it by making limiting interpretations of what is required. This is a distinct possibility because appellate decisions are normally returned or remanded to lower courts for implementation. *See also* IMPACT, 306; IMPLEMENTATION, 307.

Significance Judicial decisions are legally binding, and compliance usually follows. While compliance is the norm, full compliance is sometimes not achieved. In extreme cases, there may be noncompliance. Compliance is a function of the losing party's willingness to abide by the decision. Threat of sanctions creates great incentive to comply. In some cases, effective sanction possibilities do not exist. Under such circumstances, attempts to deliberately evade or avoid compliance can result. Resistance to the school desegregation decisions of the 1950s was extensive, especially in the South. Assistance in implementing the decisions was not immediately forthcoming from the other branches. Indeed, noncompliance was furthered by such actions as the signing of the "Southern Manifesto" by a large number of congressional members. The "Manifesto" was highly critical of the Supreme Court's decision in *Brown v. Board of Education I* (347 U.S. 483: 1954). The resistance to *Brown* was based on the policy content. In other situations, full compliance may not occur because the Court fails to effectively set forth what the decision requires. Ambiguity in opinions creates opportunities for lower courts or others who may be key to implementation to determine what compliance requires. Compliance problems seldom arise at the trial level. The nature of the issues and the enforcement mechanisms are such that full compliance is hard to avoid. Appellate decisions, on the other hand, are of a different order. Compliance with appellate decisions, especially those involving highly controversial public policy issues, is not automatic.

Constitutional Amendment (299)

A change in the content of the Constitution by adding an additional provision. A constitutional amendment can be pursued for many reasons, one of which is to reverse the effect of a Supreme Court decision. The process for amending the Constitution is set forth in Article V. It may be utilized in two ways. When two-thirds of both houses of Congress "shall deem it necessary," they may propose amendments. All twenty-six amendments to the U.S. Constitution have been initiated this way. Article V also permits the calling of a constitutional convention "on the application of the legislatures of two-thirds of the several states." For a proposed amendment to take effect, regardless of how it was initiated, it must secure the approval of the legislatures or specially called conventions of three-fourths of the states. Congress may determine which of these two modes of ratification is required and set any other rules for the ratification process. While all proposed changes to the Constitution have occurred by congressional resolution, it is possible that Congress may call a national constitutional convention to consider a balanced budget amendment if two-thirds of the states pass resolutions asking that such a convention be convened. A number of issues attend the convention approach, such as how delegates are to be selected and the scope of the convention's authority once convened. Each of the fifty state constitutions contain provisions for amendment. Most of them require approval by the electorate in a referendum. *See also* COURT "CURBING", 300; STATUTORY REVERSAL, 320.

Significance   When a constitutional amendment is used to reverse Supreme Court decisions, it may be used not only to achieve a different policy result, but to direct a political message to the Court as well. In this sense, the amendment process becomes a device of restraining, or "curbing," the Supreme Court's authority. To date, four amendments have been formally adopted to nullify decisions, although a number of others have been proposed. Section 1 of the Fourteenth Amendment, for example, reverses the portion of *Dred Scott v. Sandford* (19 Howard 393: 1857) that held that blacks were not citizens. The Twenty-sixth Amendment overturned *Oregon v. Mitchell* (400 U.S. 112: 1970) that had invalidated a congressional effort to lower the voting age to eighteen in state as well as federal elections. Similarly, the Eleventh Amendment prohibited suits by plaintiffs from one state against other states in federal courts. This directed reversal of *Chisholm v. Georgia* (2 Dallas 419: 1793). Finally, the Sixteenth Amendment restored federal power to enact an income tax previously denied in *Pollock v. Farmers' Loan & Trust Company* (157 U.S. 429: 1895). The amendment process is exceedingly difficult, which may account for the infrequency of success. Nonetheless, amendments are often introduced in controversial policy areas such as legislative apportionment, school prayer, and abortion. Amendments can also be aimed at the Court's procedures or the tenure of the justices. Amendments have been introduced, for example, that call for mandatory retirement at a certain age, such as 70 or 75, or that require extraordinary majorities when the Court strikes down a federal law. No such amendment has been adopted, but the efforts have directed political messages toward the Court nonetheless.

Court "Curbing"   (300)
Efforts directed at constraining the influence of courts. Court "curbing" occurs because the courts make decisions that disturb other public officials or the public. If court decisions are sufficiently disturbing, one or another "curbing" initiatives may result. The courts, particularly the U.S. Supreme Court, are vulnerable to these initiatives because they are linked in a variety of ways to the other branches. The initiatives have two objectives. One is to apply enough political pressure to bring about a change in decisional behavior. The other, more extreme objective is to make structural adjustments to judicial institutions. These adjustments may keep the courts from

being able to render certain kinds of decisions at all. Policy directions of the courts can generally be kept in check through the normal processes of judicial selection. Beyond that, the Congress determines the jurisdiction and size of federal courts. This is true even for the Supreme Court, where Congress has the authority to regulate or otherwise make exceptions to the Court's appellate jurisdiction. These are potentially very effective court "curbing" methods. Moreover, the executive and legislative branches are often critical in securing compliance with court rulings. Finally, courts can be constrained by actions taken to directly nullify particular decisions. This often takes the form of statutory reversal, but the constitutional amendment process may be accessed for this purpose as well. *See also* CONSTITUTIONAL AMENDMENT, 299; COURT "PACKING", 301; STATUTORY REVERSAL, 320.

Significance   Court "curbing" is not a permanent condition. Indeed, the courts are normally headed in the same policy directions as the other branches, thus there is no need to "curb" them. Efforts to constrain the courts are usually prompted by substantial and rapid shifts in direction by the electorate, by the lack of turnover in incumbents, or a combination of the two. The court "packing" initiative of President Franklin D. Roosevelt is illustrative. Economic conditions during the Depression produced extensive political realignment. The priorities of the Hoover Administration were replaced by those of Roosevelt's New Deal. A majority of justices on the Supreme Court did not reflect these same priorities. Conflict between the Court and other branches resulted. The problem was aggravated because none of the sitting justices left the Court during Roosevelt's first term. Following his reelection, Roosevelt sought to "curb" the intransigent Court by adding justices. He wanted to "pack" the Court with justices who would support New Deal legislation. Congress declined to adopt the plan to enlarge the Court. Although the initiative was not formally successful, subsequent decisions of the Court were more supportive of the New Deal, even without a change in Court personnel. Congressional control over jurisdiction can also be used as a means of court "curbing." Because Congress has the authority to create all lower federal courts, it has complete control over the definition of the jurisdiction of any court it creates. If so inclined, Congress could keep lower federal courts from ruling on one or more issues, possibly the more controversial social issues such as the busing of school students. The Congress can also regulate the appellate jurisdiction of the Supreme Court. This approach has a downside because it might remove from the Supreme Court the ability to fashion doctrine that applies uniformly across the nation. Nonetheless, the Supreme Court's appellate jurisdiction has been regulated. After the Civil War, for example, the Congress wished to keep the Court from considering the constitutionality of the Reconstruction Acts. It did so by withholding the Court's jurisdiction over all *habeas corpus* actions. The Court itself upheld this congressional action in *Ex parte McCardle* (7 Wallace 506: 1869). Similar exceptions to the Court's appellate jurisdiction have been proposed, but have not been formally adopted. Like other court "curbing" techniques, however, threatening jurisdictional changes conveys a political message. Occasionally, the Court's response to these messages is to modify its own decisional behavior.

Court "Packing" (301)

Changing the orientation of an appellate court by increasing its size. Court "packing" is legally possible because Congress and most state legislatures have the power to change the size of federal and state appellate courts, respectively. If a particular appellate court, the U.S. Supreme Court for example, renders a series of decisions that are incompatible with the policy priorities of Congress or the president, the Congress could increase the size of the Court. New justices could be added, and the larger Court would then presumably render more acceptable decisions. Six justices were authorized for the first Supreme Court. The number was temporarily reduced to five in 1801, but returned to six in 1804. The number of justices was then elevated one at a time as new judicial circuits were created with the addition of new states. The number stabilized at nine in 1869. *See also* COURT "CURBING", 300.

Significance The most blatant attempt to influence Supreme Court decisions by changing its size was the "packing" plan proposed by President Franklin D. Roosevelt in 1937. He had just been reelected by overwhelming majority and had introduced a number of proposals designed to facilitate economic recovery. Most of his proposals were adopted by Congress as part of the New Deal, but many were subsequently struck down by the Supreme Court. Frustrated by the Court's decisions, and having had no opportunity to nominate a justice during his first term, Roosevelt decided to enlarge the Court. The proposal he sent to Congress called for the nomination of an additional justice to the Court any time one of the sitting justices reached the age of 70 and did not retire. Had the Congress adopted Roosevelt's proposal, he would have been able to add six justices to the Court. Roosevelt attempted to sell the plan as one to aid the Court in handling its caseload, although his motives were otherwise quite clear. Roosevelt's plan to "pack" the Court was designed to "curb" its decisional behavior. Congress rejected the plan, but the Court almost immediately altered its course in the wake of the political pressure.

Doctrine (302)

A principle or rule of law. Doctrine is normally defined or set by a court decision and used in subsequent cases raising the same legal questions. The term doctrine is used in reference to legal precedents. The subject matter of the rule is often captured in a doctrinal title, e.g., the judicial immunity doctrine. While narrowly scoped principles may be called doctrine, the term is usually reserved for broader principles of substantial policy importance. The exclusionary rule is such a doctrine. That doctrine requires that improperly obtained evidence is inadmissible in criminal trials. Similarly, the preferred position doctrine holds that legislative enactments that affect First Amendment rights be scrutinized very closely by courts. *See also* EXCLUSIONARY RULE, 145; PRECEDENT, 28; PREFERRED POSITION DOCTRINE, 317.

Significance Doctrine is established through the convergence of several elements or influences. Once established, doctrine remains intact, expands over time, or eventually contracts and is replaced. One doctrine often spins off from another doctrine. A question before a court is distinguished from the question already addressed by a line of legal precedents, and a separate doctrine is established. The factors that most heavily influence the development of doctrine are the political setting and the policy priorities of the individual judges hearing a case. An example is the separate-but-equal doctrine developed by the Court in *Plessy v. Ferguson* (163 U.S. 537: 1896). The doctrine held that racial segregation does not necessarily violate the Equal Protection Clause. So long as separate facilities were equivalent for both races, state-mandated segregation was constitutional. This doctrine survived into the 1950s when a Supreme Court, composed of different justices with very different value orientations and operating in a different political environment, reexamined the issue. The doctrine was formally abandoned by the Court in *Brown v. Board of Education I* (347 U.S. 483: 1954).

Equal Protection (303)

Prohibition of discrimination and the use of unreasonable classifications. The protection is drawn from the Equal Protection Clause of the Fourteenth Amendment. This clause was added to the Constitution after the Civil War. At the time of ratification, the protection was intended to guarantee former slaves equal treatment under the law as well as certain basic civil rights. The Supreme Court made an effort to confine the language of the clause to blacks in the *Slaughterhouse Cases* (16 Wallace 36: 1873). *Slaughterhouse* held that the clause was to be used when state laws "discriminated with gross injustice and hardship" against "newly emancipated negroes." The Court said federal authority could be used only when racial discrimination resulted from the actions of a state because the coverage of the clause was aimed only at "that race and that emergency." After confining the clause to racial classifications, the Court set out in subsequent years to define the nature of the protections afforded blacks under the clause. In 1883, the Court struck down the Civil Rights Act of 1875, ruling that the Equal Protection Clause applied only to state actions. The holding in the *Civil Rights Cases* (103 U.S. 3: 1883) was consistent with the Court's position in *Slaughterhouse.* It placed private acts of discrimination outside the reach of the clause and the courts. The Court categorically rejected the argument that the clause authorized Congress to "create a code of municipal law for the regulation of private rights." The Fourteenth Amendment authorized only corrective, rather than general, legislation that "may be necessary and proper for counteracting such laws as the State may adopt." Regulation of private discrimination, if it were to occur at all, was left to state discretion and initiative. Soon thereafter a comprehensive network of state segregation statutes or Jim Crow laws was enacted. The Court found the segregative approach to be constitutional in *Plessy v. Ferguson* (163 U.S. 537: 1896), using the separate but equal doctrine. The Court said Jim Crow statutes only made a legal distinction between races and had "no tendency to destroy the legal equality of the two races." No constitutional provision could go further and "abolish distinction based upon color, or to enforce social, as distinguished from political, equality, or a commingling of the two races upon terms unsatisfactory to either." Little attention was paid to the equivalent-treatment-under-separate-circumstances idea until certain professional education cases came to the Court in the 1950s. Then the equality of the separate but equal doctrine was carefully examined. The doctrine was struck down in the landmark decision of *Brown v. Board of Education I* (347 U.S. 483: 1954). The Court found that racial segregation imposed by law materially interfered with equal educational opportunity. Subsequently the Court used the Equal Protection Clause to require that affirmative steps be taken to desegregate where constitutional violations could be shown. The authority of the federal courts to mandate relief in such situations was utilized extensively. The Supreme Court went on to hold that race can be a permissible consideration in university admission procedures and in establishing policies extending preferential treatment to those subjected to past discrimination. The state action requirement still provides some insulation for private discrimination, however, even though the Court has become more receptive to claims that private discriminators are acting closely enough to state authority to be reached. While softening the line of demarcation between public and private acts, the Court has kept purely private discrimination outside the scope of the equal Protection Clause and has modified the nature of state action criteria by holding that prohibited behavior turns on discriminatory intent rather than discriminatory impact. *See also* AFFIRMATIVE ACTION, 290; STATE ACTION, 319.

Significance　　Addition of the Equal Protection Clause to the Constitution had only a limited impact on public policy for many years. It was reserved exclusively for racial discrimination and was not always aggressively applied even in that context. The Due Process Clause of the Fourteenth Amendment proved to be of far greater importance as a means of examining the reasonableness of state legislation. The character of equal protection began to change in the post–New Deal period, however, as the Court became more extensively involved with civil liberties questions. The Warren Court, in particular, began to consider application of the Equal Protection Clause to classifications other than race. The expanding scope of the clause is sometimes called the "new" equal protection. Because much legislation engages in some form of classification, the clause became an attractive vehicle for challenges. The clause does not preclude the use of classifications. It merely requires that a classification be reasonable. The main problem of the "new" equal protection is that of distinguishing reasonable and permissible classifications from arbitrary and impermissible ones. Legislatures are generally afforded wide discretion in making classifications. Legislative classifications are typically evaluated by the rationality test, which is a standard reflecting the Court's understanding that the drawing of lines that create distinctions is peculiarly a legislative task as well as an unavoidable one. Classifications are presumed to be valid under this approach and need not achieve perfection. If the legislative objective is legitimate, a classification may be used as long as it rationally relates to its objective. This doctrine places the burden of proof on the party claiming that the legislation has no rational or reasonable basis. Under certain circumstances, a classification may be subjected to the strict scrutiny standard, a closer examination requiring a state to show more than reasonableness for a classification scheme. The state must demonstrate a serious need or a compelling interest that can be addressed only by use of the challenged classification. Thus the burden of proof shifts to the state in cases where strict or close scrutiny is used. The strict scrutiny standard applies when the classification impinges on a fundamental right, understood as a right expressly protected, such as freedom of speech, religious exercise, or the right to vote. Or a fundamental right may be a right fashioned by implication, such as the right to cross state lines or the right to have an abortion. In *Shapiro v. Thompson* (394 U.S. 618: 1969), the Court struck down a residency requirement for public assistance benefits because the classification inhibited movement of persons from state to state. The Court said a classification that touches on the fundamental right of interstate movement is "patently unconstitutional." Similarly, interference with the fundamental right of an unimpaired and undiluted vote prompted the Court to develop the one person–one vote principle in legislative apportionment cases. The close scrutiny standard also applies if the classification is "suspect." A suspect class is one that is saddled with such disabilities, is the recipient of such purposeful unequal treatment over time, or occupies such a politically powerless position as to require extraordinary protection within the political process. Classifications based on race and alienage are considered to be inherently suspect. The racially conscious affirmative action policies upheld by the Court have demonstrated a compelling interest served by classification. If a classification is to be used in such situations, it must also be precisely drawn or carefully tailored, and it must employ the least drastic means possible to achieve its particular legislative objectives. The Court has stricken a number of gender-based classifications, but to date has not found gender to be a suspect class. Some members of the Court have suggested that gender receive heightened, although not strict, scrutiny. Neither are such classifications as age, illegitimacy, or wealth or poverty considered to be suspect, although the Court has required that indigent criminal defendants be entitled to appointed counsel and free transcripts for appeal. The "new" equal protection has dramatically altered the scope of the Equal Protection Clause, and it is likely that additional changes in this policy area will be forthcoming.

Federal Supplement (304)

Record of opinions issued by the U.S. district court. Citations from the *Federal Supplement* are shown by the abbreviation F. Supp. The volume number precedes the abbreviation, which is followed by the page number. The state in which the district court issuing the opinion is located and the year of the decision are included in parentheses. Decisions of the U.S. court of appeals can be found in the *Federal Reporter*. The abbreviations Fed. and F.2d are used for this set of volumes, now in its second series. The court of appeals circuit number and decision date appear as part of the citation. *See also* CITATOR, 293; NATIONAL REPORTER SYSTEM, 312; UNITED STATES REPORTS, 322.

Significance   The *Federal Supplement* and *Federal Reporter* provide an authoritative record of the decisions of the lower federal courts. These series make decisions of these courts available to the legal and academic communities, and to the general public as well. Citations of decisions rendered on particular issues may be obtained by use of a citator. The citator also indicates whether a specific decision is still applicable. *Sheppard's Federal Citations,* for example, covers decisions reported in the *Federal Supplement* and *Federal Reporter.*

Harmless Error (305)

A mistake made during a criminal trial that is not serious enough to affect the outcome. Harmless error is a defect in proceeding that is regarded as formal or academic in character. The error, however, is regarded as nonprejudicial to the rights of the defendant. Error that is so limited is not a ground for vacating or modifying a judgment. Harmless error is the opposite of reversible error, which does require the reversal or vacating of a conviction. The harmless error concept is an analytic device used by appellate courts as they review actions of lower courts. The "beyond a reasonable doubt" standard applies in making such review. That is, the reviewing court must conclude beyond a reasonable doubt that the mistake was harmless. *See also* APPEAL, 258; REVERSAL, 285; REVERSIBLE ERROR, 318.

Significance   The harmless error doctrine is based on the premise that criminal trials are designed to adjudicate guilt. There will be occasions when that function is fulfilled even though a technical mistake was made. The harmless error approach focuses on the underlying fairness of the trial rather than the presence of minimal or immaterial error. As a rule, if an error occurs in a criminal trial, a conviction will be set aside. The harmless error analysis does not take place when a fundamental search or self-incrimination issue exists. In those situations where it applies, however, it is possible to preserve a conviction even in the presence of error. A helpful illustration can be found in the case of *Rose v. Clark* (478 U.S. 570: 1986). Clark was charged with both first- and second-degree murder. Under Tennessee law, the state had to prove malice but not premeditation to obtain a conviction for second-degree murder. The judge instructed the jury that malice was presumed in all murders in the absence of evidence to the contrary. Clark appealed his conviction arguing that the instruction erroneously shifted burden of proof to him on the malice question. Clark eventually prevailed with this argument. At the same time, the Supreme Court ruled that a jury instruction that so alters the burden of proof basically interferes with a fair trial and could never be considered harmless. Thus, this kind of case is subject to harmless error analysis. Accordingly, if the reviewing court was convinced beyond a reasonable doubt that the erroneous instruction was harmless with respect to the outcome, the conviction could be upheld.

Impact (306)

Direct and indirect effects of appellate court decisions. Impact reflects the extent to which behaviors are changed as a consequence of a court decision. The impact of a decision is dependent on first achieving some degree of compliance. The most direct kind of impact a decision can have is when actual behaviors are modified. For example, utilization of the exclusionary rule discourages unreasonable searches by law enforcement authorities because improperly obtained evidence cannot be used at a criminal trial. At the same time, strict adherence to the exclusionary rule may negatively affect the prospects of successfully prosecuting some defendants because it precludes the use of reliable evidence. Court decisions may also have less direct impacts. Some decisions may influence attitudes and reinforce pressure for social change. Decisions that support challenges to gender-based discrimination have contributed to the decrease of some stereotyping about women, especially in the workplace. *See also* COMPLIANCE, 298; IMPLEMENTATION, 307.

Significance The impact of an appellate decision is produced in part by its policy content. Appellate courts are expected to rule on questions of law. This is an activity that necessarily involves establishment of norms and standards. The impact of such judgments is often substantial. There can be no doubt, for example, that Supreme Court decisions since 1960 have extensively changed the character of the criminal justice process. This has been particularly true in the wake of the extention of most federal constitutional safeguards to state criminal courts. Similarly, the Supreme Court's decision in *Baker v. Carr* (369 U.S. 186: 1962) ultimately led to adoption of the one person–one vote principle for legislative districting. The redistricting prompted by *Baker* and subsequent decisions dramatically altered the composition of state legislative bodies, local legislatures, and the U.S. House of Representatives. The impact of court decisions varies. While the impact of decisions in certain policy areas might be extensive, there are conditions that tend to limit decision impact. Areas of doctrine such as those applying to the rights of the accused are often composed of many decisions, not all of which are entirely compatible. Thus, some decisions tend to impinge on others. Under *Miranda v. Arizona* (384 U.S. 436: 1966), police are obligated to provide certain warnings to persons prior to initiating custodial interrogation. At the same time, statements by a suspect made in the absence of *Miranda* warnings can be used during cross-examination if the person testifies in his or her own defense. Second, policies also come from other branches of government. To the extent policy decisions are not coincidental, the impact of judicial decisions may be reduced. Such muting of decision impact can occur if assistance in implementation is not forthcoming from the other governmental branches or their agencies. Finally, court decisions are only one of a number of influences on social attitudes. While court decisions may not permit employment discrimination, for example, practices by employers may be slow to change.

Implementation (307)

Putting into effect a judicial decision. The nature of the implementation process differs between trial and appellate levels. Decisions of trial courts are generally implemented through voluntary compliance or executive action. A criminal sentence, for example, is usually implemented by corrections authorities. Judgments in civil actions are generally implemented voluntarily, but threat of judicial contempt may be sufficient to forestall noncompliance. The courts also depend on external support for implementation. Support of this kind typically comes from administrative agencies. The kind of agency support needed for implementation is a function of the content of the decision. If the decision involves classroom practices in public schools, for example, the implementing agency is the local school district and its trustees. Similarly, decisions involving searches and seizures involve police departments. The implementation of appellate decisions contains an additional step. If an appeals court vacates a lower court decision, the case is normally remanded to the lower court for implementation. Additional administrative support may be required thereafter. Because responsibility for implementing decisions is decentralized, substantial variation can occur. This variation is the product of several factors. The first involves the extent to which those responsible for implementation agree with the policy embraced in the appellate court decision. Implementation efforts tend to be limited where policy preferences of the court and the implementors do not coincide. The second factor is the likelihood of penalty if compliance does not take place. If there are no sanctions for failure to comply with a particular decision, it may not be implemented. Finally, implementation is furthered when the authority of the court to render the decision is clear. This involves perceptions of legitimacy. If the Supreme Court is perceived as the legitimate authority on certain policy questions, implementation of its decision, whatever it may be, will likely occur simply because it is "the law." *See also* COMPLIANCE, 298; COURT "CURBING", 300; IMPACT, 306.

Significance   The legislative and executive branches possess powers that directly affect the implementation process. For example, if legislative bodies are dissatisfied with the way courts interpret or apply statutes, judicial decisions can be reversed by enacting a "clarifying" statute. Legislatures and executives can also have an impact on the implementation process by taking sides on controversial questions. This, in turn, can influence the behavior of key implementors at the local level. Resistance may be encouraged by actions that oppose court decisions. Further, the executive and legislative branches may or may not provide necessary support to bring about implementation. For example, Congress made it clear that financial support would not be forthcoming if the Supreme Court allowed President Harry S Truman to retain operating control of privately owned steel mills in 1952. On the other hand, presidential support has often been decisive in securing implementation. For example, President Dwight D. Eisenhower ordered federal troops to Little Rock, Arkansas, to compel compliance with court orders requiring desegregation of the public schools.

Incorporation (308)

The extent to which the federal Bill of Rights acts as a limitation on state governments. Incorporation was originally defined in *Barron v. Baltimore* (7 Peters 243: 1833). Through Chief Justice John Marshall, the Supreme Court held that the Bill of Rights constrained only "the government created by the instrument," the federal government, and not the "distinct governments," the states. *Barron* was controlling until ratification of the Fourteenth Amendment in 1868. The Fourteenth Amendment reopened the question of incorporation because it clearly directed its proscriptions to the states. Several schools of thought have developed about how to resolve the matter. The most sweeping recommendation was to apply all Bill of Rights provisions to the states through the Due Process Clause of the Fourteenth Amendment. This clause prohibits a state from denying liberty without due process. Those advocating total incorporation viewed the term "liberty" as an all-inclusive shorthand for each of the rights enumerated in the Bill of Rights. The approach has been vigorously advocated by the first Justice John Marshall Harlan and by Justice Hugo L. Black, but it is a view that has never been shared by a majority of the Supreme Court. A second opinion rejected any structural linkage of due process to the Bill of Rights and held simply that the Due Process Clause requires states to provide fundamental fairness. Due process is assessed under this standard by criteria of "immutable principles of justice," or, as suggested by Justice Benjamin N. Cardozo in *Palko v. Connecticut* (302 U.S. 319: 1937), elements implicit in the concept of ordered liberty. Application of such standards would occur on a case-by-case basis. The third option is a hybrid of the first two and is known as selective incorporation. The selective approach resembles the fundamental fairness position in that it does not view as identical those rights contained in the Bill of Rights and those rights fundamental to fairness. Unlike the fundamental fairness approach, however, the selective view holds that rights expressly contained in the Bill of Rights, if adjudged fundamental, are incorporated through the Fourteenth Amendment and are applicable at the state level regardless of the circumstances of a particular case. If the self-incrimination provision of the Sixth Amendment were determined to be fundamental, for example, it would apply in full to any state case bringing whatever substantive standards it preferred into federal courts. The selective approach created an "honor roll" of Bill of Rights provisions, some viewed as fundamental and wholly incorporated and others as less important and not worthy of incorporation. *See also* BILL OF RIGHTS, 292; FEDERALISM, 51.

Significance   Incorporation focuses on the degree to which Bill of Rights guarantees apply to the states. The question assumed critically important dimensions soon after ratification of the Fourteenth Amendment. The matter remained unresolved for several decades. Early decisions such as *Hurtado v. California* (110 U.S. 516: 1884) found the Court refusing to extend federal protections to the states. The Supreme Court eventually settled on the selective incorporation approach, starting with its recognition of the Free Speech Clause of the First Amendment in *Gitlow v. New York* (268 U.S. 652: 1925). This ultimately allowed the Supreme Court, especially the Warren Court, to apply most of the safeguards to the states. The Warren Court added many provisions to the list developed under the preceding fundamental fairness approach. The only Bill of Rights provisions that have not been incorporated are the grand jury requirement of the Fifth Amendment, the civil jury trial provision of the Seventh Amendment, and the Excessive Bail and Fine Clause of the Eighth Amendment. The incorporation doctrine is a central element in contemporary American rights policy. The process of incorporation made it possible to extend federal rights through to the states. This was especially important where state law did not provide such protection. Equally important, the doctrine made the U.S. Supreme Court the source of authoritative rulings on rights policy. This had the effect of creating a uniform rights policy across the states, thus providing in effect for the "nationalization" of individual rights.

Judicial Activism (309)

An approach to decision making in the American judicial system. Judicial activists see the appellate courts as playing a substantial and affirmative policy role. Judicial activism prompts judges to entertain new policies, even those that would depart from adherence to established legal rules and precedents. Judicial activism can manifest itself in a number of ways, but most important is a court's adoption of its own policy preferences over those of the legislative or executive branches. That is exactly what occurs when a court invalidates a governmental action as unconstitutional. Judicial activism may also extend legal rules to establish specific requirements for governmental action. The opposite of judicial activism is judicial self-restraint, an approach that discourages judges from pursuing personal political, economic, and social values and that generally defers to the policy initiatives of the legislative and executive branches. While both activists and self-restraintists acknowledge that a certain degree of policy making is an inevitable result of deciding law questions, they differ on how aggressively and how extensively judges pursue policy making opportunities. *See also* JUDICIAL REVIEW, 18; JUDICIAL SELF-RESTRAINT, 311; LEGAL REALISM, 23; POLICY MAKING, 315.

Significance Judicial activism is sometimes described as legislation by judges to achieve policy outcomes compatible with their own priorities. A judicial activist will find more issues appropriate for judicial response than a judge who subscribes to judicial self-restraint. Judicial activism resembles the jurisprudence known as legal realism. Legal realists see law as the product of social forces and view discretion in the interpretation of law as inevitable and useful. American judges have engaged in activism from the outset of our history. The most obvious early example of activism is Chief Justice John Marshall's establishment of the power of judicial review in *Marbury v. Madison* (5 U.S. 137: 1803). A more recent example of activism is the Warren Court's judgment that legislative apportionment is a justiciable issue in *Baker v. Carr* (369 U.S. 186: 1962), and the Court's subsequent formulation of the one person–one vote districting standard. Activism need not coincide with a liberal policy orientation. Classic examples of judicial activism can be found in the 1930s, when the Court struck down numerous pieces of New Deal legislation in the interest of preserving laissez-faire economic doctrine. The judicial activist sees the Court as appropriately and legitimately asserting itself in the policy making process even if its policy objectives differ from those of the legislative and executive branches.

Judicial Contempt (310)

Any act that obstructs the administration of justice by a court or that brings disrespect on a court or its authority. Judicial contempt may be direct in that it occurs in the presence of the court and constitutes a direct affront to the court's authority. While some due process protections apply to contempt, it is generally a summary order through which penalties of fine or imprisonment may be directly imposed by the court. Contempt may be indirect in that the behavior that demonstrates contempt occurs outside the courtroom. It is also necessary to distinguish criminal and civil contempt. Criminal contempt is an act of obstruction or disrespect typically occurring in the courtroom. A party who acts in an abusive manner in a court is in criminal contempt. He or she may receive a fine and/or imprisonment for up to six months. Such punishment may be summarily imposed. Civil contempt, on the other hand, results from failure to comply with an order of a court. Civil contempt is designed to coerce compliance with an order to protect the interests of the party on whose behalf the order was issued. Civil contempt ends when the desired conduct occurs. A legislative contempt power also exists. It may be used if a disturbance is created within a legislative chamber or if people subpoenaed to appear before legislative committees fail to testify. Congressional contempt is not summarily imposed, however. It is handled through the standard criminal process with trial occurring in a federal district court if an indictment has been secured from a grand jury.

Significance The judicial contempt power provides courts with leverage to maintain courtroom decorum appropriate for judicial proceedings. Contempt enables a court to punish disruptive or disrespectful conduct, and it serves as a deterrent to such conduct. The contempt power also permits courts to compel compliance with a court order. This gives courts some capacity to reinforce the authority of any such order.

Judicial Self-Restraint (311)

A philosophy and style of judicial decision making that minimizes the extent to which judges apply their personal views to the legal judgments they render. Judicial self-restraint is particularly useful in analyzing the behavior of appellate courts like the U.S. Supreme Court. The term describes a self-imposed limitation seen by the judges who practice it as the decision making approach most compatible with democratic principles. The judges who subscribe to self-restraint will go to great lengths in deferring to the policy decisions of the elective branches. In other words, self-restraintist judges seek to limit their role to the enforcement of norms established by those accountable to the electorate. Marginal constitutional problems are typically insufficient to prompt judicial intervention. Only where constitutional violations are flagrant should courts nullify actions of the political branches. The opposite view from self-restraint is judicial activism. The judicial activist is comfortable with an expanded policy role for courts. Activist judges are less inclined to defer to the other branches. Unlike the restraintist, the activist will not so readily presume legislation to be constitutional and will restrict legislative initiatives more frequently. It is for this reason that activists are charged with judicial "legislating." *See also* JUDICIAL ACTIVISM, 309; JUDICIAL REVIEW, 18; NORM ENFORCEMENT, 313.

Significance Judicial self-restraint holds that courts should defer to the policy judgments made by those in the elected branches of government. Judges who adhere to the philosophy of self-restraint also impose a more restrictive definition of justiciability and adhere more strictly to judicial precedent. Self-restraint does not necessarily coincide with a conservative policy orientation. Exercise of self-restraint by deferring to legislative establishment of a minimum wage or to an aggressive Equal Employment Opportunity Commission program, for example, might yield a liberal policy result. Judicial self-restraint is a perception of the judicial role as one that limits the exercise of judicial power and views the legislative and executive branches as the appropriate sources of major policy initiatives. Self-restraintists view a more aggressive or active role as inappropriate for several reasons. First, courts are generally not accountable to the public. This is especially true of federal judges who are appointed and enjoy life tenure. Second, courts seldom win confrontations with the other branches. Indeed, the courts tend to be vulnerable to reprisals aimed at limiting their power. Thus judicial independence may be threatened by activist and provocative decisions. Finally, self-restraintists argue that courts are not a well suited forum for decision making on broad and complex social questions. Among the leading advocates of judicial self-restraint in the history of the Supreme Court are Justice Felix Frankfurter and the second Justice John Marshall Harlan.

National Reporter System (312)

Sets of volumes that contain state supreme court decision. The National Reporter System publishes these decisions on a regional basis. For example, decisions from Illinois, Indiana, Massachusetts, New York, and Ohio appear in the *North Eastern Reporter*. Cases can be found in the *North Eastern Reporter*, now in its second series, by citation numbers that identify both volume and page number. The citation abbreviation for the *North Eastern Reporter* is N.E.2d. The other regional reporters are: *Atlantic Reporter* (abbreviated A.2d and including Connecticut, Delaware, District of Columbia, Maine, Maryland, New Hampshire, New Jersey, Pennsylvania, Rhode Island, and Vermont); *North Western Reporter* (N.W.2d.; Iowa, Michigan, Minnesota, Nebraska, North Dakota, South Dakota, and Wisconsin); *Pacific Reporter* (P.2d.; Alaska, Arizona, California, Colorado, Hawaii, Idaho, Kansas, Montana, Nevada, New Mexico, Oklahoma, Oregon, Utah, Washington, and Wyoming); *South Eastern Reporter* (S.E.2d.; Georgia, North Carolina, South Carolina, Virginia, and West Virginia); *Southern Reporter* (So. 2d.; Alabama, Florida, Louisiana, and Mississippi); and the *South Western Reporter* (S.W.2d.; Arkansas, Kentucky, Missouri, Tennessee, and Texas). The National Reporter System also has sets of volumes for federal court decisions and a digest for each of the regions. *See also* CITATOR, 293; UNITED STATES REPORTS, 322.

Significance   The National Reporter System contains the decisions of state appellate courts. While some states publish these decisions, the system has come to be the official reporter for decisions in many states. The system is a comprehensive and authoritative source for those engaged in legal research on state law.

Norm Enforcement (313)

An approach used by judges in the discharge of their basic dispute-resolution function. Norm enforcement is an approach generally used by trial judges but can be seen in the behavior of appellate judges as well. The norms that are enforced or applied in particular cases generally reflect societal values. The values or norms applied by courts often come from sources outside the courts. Norms are typically expressed in the form of legislative enactments, administrative rulings, and community traditions. Prior judicial decisions are also a source of such norms. While some judicial discretion is involved, judges who engage in norm enforcement try to minimize the extent to which they, themselves, establish the norm to be enforced. This distinguishes the norm enforcer from the judge who more actively pursues judicial policy making. Norm enforcement occurs in both criminal and civil cases. Criminal conduct violates societal norms as set forth in legislatively established criminal codes. Courts not only adjudicate guilt using these norms, but impose sanctions for violations. Civil cases tend to focus on relationships between private parties and generally involve redress for some injury. The function of the courts is to assess liability and then pursue those options established by law in attempting to remedy the particular injury. In both kinds of cases, trial courts seek to apply legal norms to specific fact situations. *See also* JUDICIAL REVIEW, 18; JUDICIAL SELF-RESTRAINT, 311; POLICY MAKING, 315.

Significance Judicial norm enforcement is not mechanical but rather requires the exercise of some discretion. Thus, to an extent, judges make policy even when engaged in norm enforcement. Construction of statutes necessarily clarifies norms in that it chooses between or among slightly divergent means or norms. Similarly, application of particular laws or rules to specific facts may extend norms beyond their original scope. The intent of judges engaged in this kind of activity is not to make new policy, but only to apply the norms where intended by those who legitimately set them. In many ways, the judge who approaches the appellate function as a norm enforcer is like the judge who subscribes to the doctrine of judicial self-restraint. As a rule, the norm enforcer defers to legislative initiatives and validates them in the face of various challenges. Norm enforcers usually give maximum effect to a norm based on legislative enactments or community traditions. Judges who wish to enforce legislatively established norms depend heavily on the meaning of the words chosen by legislators. Such judges refer to records of legislative debates and committee proceedings in attempting to understand legislative intent. When engaged in judicial review, the norm enforcer invalidates legislative enactments only when they are clearly unconstitutional.

Overbreadth Doctrine (314)

Requires that enactments proscribing certain activity must completely avoid affecting conduct that is constitutionally protected. Overbreadth typically refers to a statute that may fail to adequately distinguish between activities that may be regulated and those that may not. The overbreadth doctrine prohibits a law that does not sufficiently focus on or target those things a state may legitimately regulate. Instead, it indiscriminately includes forms of expression or activities that are permissible. A recent example involving the overbreadth doctrine is the Los Angeles ordinance that prohibited all expressive activities within the central terminal at Los Angeles International Airport. The U.S. Supreme Court ruled in *Board of Airport Commissioners v. Jews for Jesus* (482 U.S. 589: 1987) that the ordinance was defective in that it went beyond just regulating expressive activity that might create problems, such as congestion or disruption in the airport. Such a regulation might be a permissible time, place, and manner restriction, but instead the ordinance here banned all expression. Under such a sweeping ban, virtually everyone entering the terminal could be found in violation. Even the intent to reach only expressive activity unrelated to airport purposes was viewed as vague in distinguishing affected from unaffected activity. Thus the Court struck down the ordinance on overbreadth grounds. *See also* DOCTRINE, 302; JUDICIAL REVIEW, 18.

Significance   The overbreadth doctrine is illustrated in *Village of Schaumburg v. Citizens for a Better Environment* (444 U.S. 620: 1980), where the Supreme Court struck down a local ordinance that required all organizations soliciting contributions door-to-door to use at least 75 percent of their receipts for charitable purposes. The intent of the ordinance was to prevent fraudulent solicitations. The Court objected to the approach because it imposed a direct and substantial limitation on organizations such as environmental education groups whose principal activities are research, advocacy, and public education. While such organizations obviously do not meet the ordinance definition of charitable, their activities are constitutionally permissible. Schaumburg's ordinance was simply too inclusive or overbroad. A similar ordinance was invalidated in *Coates v. Cincinnati* (402 U.S. 611: 1972) because the ordinance prohibited an assembly of three or more people on public sidewalks. It subjected such assembled people to arrest if their behavior "annoyed" a police officer or passerby. The ordinance made criminal what the Constitution says cannot be a crime. Neither may an enactment suffer from vagueness. Regulation must convey standards of conduct that people of reasonable intelligence can understand. Enactments that do not clearly convey required or prohibited conduct may be invalidated as vague. Restrictions that are either overbroad or vague may have a "chilling effect" on expression or some other protected activity. A chilling effect comes when persons think sanctions will be imposed if they exercise their rights. As a result, people tend to restrict themselves from engaging in activities that fall outside those clearly protected.

Policy Making (315)

An approach used by judges, particularly appeals judges, as they perform their basic case review function. Judges who engage in policy making intentionally fashion new norms as they reach decisions. Such judges believe that the judicial role is not merely to apply the norms established by others, but to supply their own when necessary. The opportunity to make policy will not exist in every case, nor do judicial policy makers avail themselves of every opportunity that does present itself. Policy making by a judge takes place when a norm is challenged by a party to a case under review, and the court rules in the challenger's favor. While policy making can occur in cases where appellate courts are engaged in statutory construction, it is more likely where judicial review is involved. *See also* INTERPRETIVE APPROACHES, 273; JUDICIAL ACTIVISM, 309; JUDICIAL REVIEW, 18; NORM ENFORCEMENT, 313.

Significance   Judicial policy making involves the setting of norms by judges. Such policy making is undertaken consciously. In many ways, policy making is judicial activism. The judge who pursues a policy making course believes that courts are as legitimate a source of norm creation as, for example, administrative agencies and possibly even legislative bodies. Judicial policy making is manifest in a number of ways. One of these ways is to create policy by interpretation of the Constitution. The formal recognition of a right of privacy in *Griswold v. Connecticut* (381 U.S. 479: 1965) is an obvious example. The Constitution contains no explicit right of privacy, and yet the Court declared such a right exists by implication from provisions of other enumerated rights. Second, courts can develop and oversee the administration of new norms. Judicial establishment of the one person–one vote principle, and the administration of this principle in legislative apportionment situations is illustrative. Finally, rather than validate policy set elsewhere, the courts can nullify such policy and substitute their own preferences. The Supreme Court engaged in this kind of policy making during the 1930s when it found many of the New Deal initiatives unconstitutional.

Preemption Doctrine (316)

Principle that federal laws supersede or preempt state laws in certain policy areas. The preemption doctrine is grounded in the Supremacy Clause of Article VI, which provides that all laws made in pursuance of the U.S. Constitution "shall be the supreme Law of the Land." The doctrine holds that federal law must preempt state law if the national policy considerations are sufficiently great. The national policy interest, of course, must be compatible with the legitimate exercise of federal power. As a general practice, the Supreme Court allows states to enact regulations in the policy field where the federal government has also acted. As long as the state law is supplementary to the federal law or does not interfere with the implementation of federal law, state law is generally left undisturbed. The preemption doctrine does allow, however, that even where no conflict between federal and state law exists, state law may be nullified if Congress wholly "occupies" the policy field. *See also* DOCTRINE, 302; FEDERALISM, 51.

Significance   The Supreme Court said in *Pennsylvania v. Nelson* (350 U.S. 497: 1956) that invoking the preemption doctrine requires the existence of at least one of three conditions. First, the federal regulation must be so pervasive as to allow reasonable inference that no room is left for state action. Congress may explicitly state such a preemptive interest, or the courts may interpret the intent of Congress to fully occupy a policy field. Second, federal regulation must involve matters where the federal interest is so dominant as to preclude implementation of state laws in the field. Third, the administration of federal laws must be endangered by potentially conflicting state laws. The policy area involved in *Nelson* was the regulation of seditious activity. Specifically, the question was whether the federal Smith Act prohibited enforcement of the Pennsylvania Sedition Act, which proscribed the same conduct. On the basis of the preemption doctrine and the criteria described, the Supreme Court concluded that Pennsylvania's statute had to give way.

Preferred Position Doctrine   (317)
Holds that legislative enactments that affect fundamental constitutional rights must be scrutinized more carefully than legislation that does not. The preferred position doctrine says that certain legislative activity deserves priority consideration because it affects such rights as free speech or elections. Any enactment that impinges on such rights must serve a compelling state interest. The burden is clearly on the government to demonstrate justification for limiting a preferred position freedom. *See also* BALANCING DOCTRINE, 291; DOCTRINE, 302; INTERPRETIVE APPROACHES, 273.

Significance   The preferred position doctrine is attributed to Justice Harlan Fiske Stone, who said in a footnote to his opinion in *United States v. Carolene Products Company* (304 U.S. 144: 1938) that a lesser presumption of constitutionality exists when legislation "appears on its face to be within a specific prohibition such as those of the first ten amendments." Stone further suggested that if legislation restricts politically corrective action in the political processes, courts must engage in a "more exacting judicial scrutiny" when reviewing such enactments. The preferred position doctrine was embraced by a majority of the Supreme Court following the appearance of Stone's footnote. In such decisions as *Murdock v. Pennsylvania* (319 U.S. 105: 1943) and *Thomas v. Collins* (323 U.S. 516: 1945), for example, the doctrine was strongly asserted. Since the late 1940s, the doctrine has not been invoked explicitly. Rather, the Supreme Court has come to prefer a balancing test that gives high priority to fundamental freedoms but does not necessarily presume invalid those laws affecting such freedoms.

Reversible Error (318)

A mistake that substantially affects a person's rights and requires the setting aside of a lower court judgment on appeal. Reversible error is of such consequence that a miscarriage of justice results from its remaining uncorrected. Reversible error is prejudicial error in that it adversely affects a person's basic rights. A claimed error in a trial becomes the focus of an appeal. The appellate court must determine if an error did, indeed, occur, and whether the error was substantial enough to require the reversal of the judgment. Reversible error is the opposite of "harmless error," where a mistake is inconsequential or immaterial to the outcome. *See also* APPEAL, 258; HARMLESS ERROR, 305, REVERSAL, 285.

Significance Reversible error renders a criminal conviction void. The task on appeal is to convince an appellate court that an error was actually made. A judge may rule that an item be admitted into evidence. The item may have been obtained by police in a manner that was suspect. The appellate court will determine whether the search that produced the evidence was reasonable. If the reviewing court concludes that the search was proper, there is no error and the conviction stands. If, on the other hand, the search is determined to be defective, the outcome must be reversed. Errors that affect basic constitutional rights are presumed to influence outcomes and, therefore, are reversible.

State Action (319)

A requirement that limits application of the Equal Protection Clause of the Fourteenth Amendment to situations where discriminatory conduct occurs under state authority. The state action requirement was first established by the Supreme Court in the *Civil Rights Cases* (109 U.S. 3: 1883). It placed private discrimination outside the reach of the Fourteenth Amendment. The Court held that the Amendment was intended to provide relief against state enactments rather than to empower Congress to "legislate upon subjects which are within the domain of state legislation" or "create a code of municipal law for the regulation of private rights." *See also* CIVIL RIGHTS, 295; EQUAL PROTECTION, 303.

Significance   State action requires a judgment about whether certain kinds of conduct occur under color of state law. A court must determine if discriminatory action is situated closely enough to state authority to be treated as though it were an overt act of the state. A sufficient nexus between challenged action and state authority is generally not difficult to demonstrate, although some private discrimination remains insulated from regulation. While softening the distinctions between private and state-authorized discrimination, thus expanding the reach of the Equal Protection Clause, recent cases have required that discriminatory intent must be shown in addition to injurious impact in order to establish a constitutional violation.

Statutory Reversal   (320)
Legislative action to overturn a judicial ruling. Statutory reversal can occur most simply when the decision of a court rests on an interpretation of legislation as to meaning or intent. Congress often cannot simply reverse a decision where a court finds a constitutional defect by re-enacting a "clarified" version of the statute. In most cases, however, appellate courts are engaged in statutory construction as opposed to judicial review. Thus, reversal through the normal legislative process is possible. In situations where Congress disagrees with a judicial interpretation of a statute, it may simply enact a new statute that clarifies its objectives and reverses those sections that produced a court interpretation that is incompatible. Statutory reversal is a means by which the legislative branch cannot only "correct" decisions of courts, but also limit the impact of judicial authority more generally. Frequent statutory reversal can be regarded as a method of court "curbing." *See also* COURT "CURBING", 300; JUDICIAL REVIEW, 18; STATUTORY CONSTRUCTION, 36.

Significance   The legislative branch can generally reverse court decisions based on statutory construction. If courts and legislatures disagree as to what a law is intended to do, statutory reversal allows the legislature to essentially have the last word and determine the proper course for its own enactments. Disagreements of this kind are not frequent, but they are more common than those situations where enactments are nullified in their entirety through the process of judicial review. Reflected in this legislative-judicial tension is the dynamic of checks and balances. A recent example of statutory reversal involved the case of *Grove City College v. Bell* (465 U.S. 555: 1984). This case grew out of Title IX of the Education Amendments of 1972, which covers gender discrimination in educational programs. The question focused on sanctions: whether federal funds were to be withheld only from the specific program where violations occurred or from the institution entirely. The Supreme Court ruled that only the offending program could be sanctioned. The violations were confined to student financial aid; thus, only federal funds going through that program could be withheld. Any other federal support going to other programs at Grove City were to continue. Congress disagreed with this interpretation of Title IX and eventually enacted legislation that called for the institution-wide sanctions. The effect of the new legislation was to reverse the Court's *Grove City* decision.

Supreme Court Reporter   (321)

Record of cases decided by the U.S. Supreme Court. The *Supreme Court Reporter* is a privately produced series published by West Publishing Company of St. Paul, Minnesota. The series provides summaries of case fact situations and the full text of all opinions issued. West also uses a "key" system of reference numbers through which topics and subtopics are classified. This facilitates finding related materials in other sources. The text of decisions is published on a twice-a-month basis. These materials are subsequently released in hardbound volumes at the conclusion of a Court term. Cases may be located by a citation that refers to volume and page. The *Supreme Court Reporter* citation for *Miranda v. Arizona* is 86 S. Ct. 1602 (1966). This means the *Miranda* case was decided in 1966 and can be found on page 1602 of volume 86 of the *Supreme Court Reporter. See also* UNITED STATES REPORTS, 322; UNITED STATES SUPREME COURT REPORTS, 323.

Significance   The *Supreme Court Reporter* is an authoritative record of Supreme Court decisions. Unlike the *United States Reports,* which is published by the federal government, the *Supreme Court Reporter* is produced by a private commercial publisher. This series is linked by the "key" system to the *American Digest System,* which is an extensive collection of case summaries. The material contained in the *Supreme Court Reporter* is valuable in developing an understanding of American legal thought and appellate court decision making. The series makes this material readily available to the legal and academic communities as well as the general public.

United States Reports (322)

Record of cases decided by the U.S. Supreme Court. *United States Reports* is published by the Government Printing Office. Court opinions are first published as "slip opinions," reports of individual decisions put out within a few days of the decision. Groups of slip opinions are then published in paperback form as "preliminary prints." Hardbound volumes of *United States Reports* are released following the completion of each Court term. *United States Reports* includes summaries of the fact situations and what happened to the case in the lower courts. Also included is the full opinion of the Court for each case decided and all concurring and dissenting opinions that might have been issued. The first ninety volumes of the *United States Reports* were issued under the names of the Supreme Court reporters. These include Dallas, Cranch, Wheaton, Peters, Howard, Black, and Wallace. Cases may be located in these volumes by a citation that references volume and page. The citation for an early case like *Marbury v. Madison* is 1 Cranch 137 (1803). This means the case was decided in 1803 and can be found on page 137 of the first of the volumes under Cranch's name. Since 1874, the volumes have been numbered consecutively, beginning with volume 91, as *United States Reports. Roe v. Wade*, 410 U.S. 113 (1973), is an example of a more recent citation. *See also* SUPREME COURT REPORTER, 321; UNITED STATES SUPREME COURT REPORTS, 323.

Significance   *United States Reports* is the official record of Supreme Court decisions. It is published by the federal government. In addition to containing the full text of all opinions, the editors summarize all information pertaining to the case, prepare a syllabus of each decision, and write headnotes that outline the legal issues. Since cases decided by the U.S. Supreme Court focus on many major social and political issues, the information contained in *United States Reports* is valuable to an understanding of legal thought and appellate processes. This series makes such information readily available not only to the legal and academic communities, but to the general public as well. *United States Reports* also lists those cases that are denied review by the Supreme Court.

United States Supreme Court Reports (Lawyers' Edition) (323)

Record of decisions rendered by the United States Supreme Court.

United States Supreme Court Reports, also known as the *Lawyers' Edition,* is published by Lawyers Cooperative Publishing Company of Rochester, New York. The series provides the full text of all opinions issued by the Supreme Court. In addition, the editors summarize the fact situations of each case and how each case was decided prior to obtaining review by the Supreme Court. The *Lawyers' Edition* also summarizes the arguments used by the justices in the opinions that are released. Bound volumes are produced at the end of each Court term, but opinions are released throughout the term in the form of paperbound "Advance Sheets." Cases may be located in these volumes by a citation number that references volume and page. The *Lawyers' Edition* citation for *Brown v. Board of Education I* is 98 L. Ed. 873 (1954). This means that *Brown I* was decided in 1954 and can be found on page 873 of volume 98. The series reached volume 100 in 1956, and the publishers chose to commence a second series starting again at volume 1 rather than continuing with volume 101. The citations thus became L. Ed. 2d preceded by a volume number and followed by a page number, e.g., *Regents of the University of California v. Bakke,* 57 L. Ed. 2d 750 (1978). In 1988, the volumes reached 100 in the second series. This time, the numbering continued beyond 100 rather than starting a third series, e.g., *Webster v. Reproductive Health Services,* 106 L. Ed. 2d 410 (1989). *See also* SUPREME COURT REPORTER, 321; UNITED STATES REPORTS, 322.

Significance　　*United States Supreme Court Reports* is an authoritative record of Supreme Court decisions. Unlike *United States Reports,* which is published by the federal government, *United States Supreme Court Reports,* like the *Supreme Court Reporter,* is distributed by a private commercial publisher. The difference between these two records largely comes from the headnotes in each, which link rulings of the Supreme Court to other materials available from the publisher. The material contained in *United States Supreme Court Reporter* contributes to a better understanding of the appellate court decision-making process as well as the arguments advanced in the particular cases. The series enables dissemination of this material to the public generally, as well as to the legal and academic communities.

INDEX

In this index, a reference in **bold** type indicates the entry number where a particular term is defined within the text. Numbers in roman type refer to entries the reader may wish to consult for further information about a term.

299

INDEX

INDEX